MONOGRAPHS OF
THE MEDIAEVAL ACADEMY
OF AMERICA
No. 3

ACADEMY PUBLICATIONS

No. 1, *A Concordance of Boethius*, by LANE COOPER

No. 2, *A Concordance to the Historia Ecclesiastica of Bede*, by P. F. JONES

No. 3, *A Survey of the Manuscripts of Tours*, by E. K. RAND, two volumes, text and plates

No. 4, *Lupus of Ferrières as Scribe and Text Critic*, by C. H. BEESON, with a facsimile of *MS. Harley 2736*

No. 5, *Genoese Shipping in the Twelfth and Thirteenth Centuries*, by E. H. BYRNE, (*Monograph No. 1*)

No. 6, *Greek and Syrian Miniatures in Jerusalem*, by W. H. P. HATCH, with reproductions

No. 7, *Harūnū'l-Rashīd and Charles the Great*, by F. W. BUCKLER, (*Monograph No. 2*)

No. 8, *Alien Merchants in England, 1350 to 1377*, by ALICE BEARDWOOD (*Monograph No. 3*)

ALIEN MERCHANTS IN ENGLAND
1350 TO 1377
THEIR LEGAL AND ECONOMIC POSITION

ALICE BEARDWOOD

Bryn Mawr College;
B. Litt., D. Phil., Oxon.

THE MEDIAEVAL ACADEMY OF AMERICA

CAMBRIDGE, MASSACHUSETTS

1931

The publication of this book was made pos-
sible by a fund granted the Academy by the
Carnegie Corporation of New York

PREFACE

ALL discussions of English mediaeval commerce emphasize the important economic functions of alien merchants.[1] Among these foreign traders, the Lombards, because of their financial preëminence, have been given special attention. The more exclusively mercantile activities of the Hanse of Almain have also been widely investigated, especially in the publications of the *Verein für Hansische Geschichte*. Yet there are no statistics covering the amount of English trade in alien hands in the middle of the fourteenth century. Moreover, there is no such examination of the customs rolls for that century as Schanz has provided for the reign of Henry VIII,[2] although the enrolled customs accounts are the chief source of information about the regulation of foreign trade, the customs rates, and the volume of trade.

Even less attention has been devoted to the legal position of alien merchants in England in relation to the central government, although that authority obviously possessed the power to admit or exclude them, to encourage them by a liberal policy or to hamper them by restrictions or heavy customs rates, to regulate their legal privileges and to determine the status of those who became permanent residents in England. Apart from general treatment in histories of English law,[3] and even more general treatment in the histories of the naturalization laws,[4] the position of alien merchants has, more or less naturally, been regarded from the local rather than from the

---

[1] See W. Ashley, *An Introduction to English Economic History and Theory*, 2 parts (4th edit., London, 1909); W. Cunningham, *The Growth of English Industry and Commerce* (4th edit., Cambridge, 1905); E. Lipson, *An Introduction to the Economic History of England* (2nd edit., London: A. & C. Black, 1919); G. Schanz, *Englische Handelspolitik gegen Ende des Mittelalters, mit besonderer Berücksichtigung des Zeitalters der beiden ersten Tudors Heinrich VII und Heinrich VIII* (Leipzig, 1881); N. S. B. Gras, *The Early English Customs System* (Cambridge: Harvard University Press, 1918).

[2] *Op. cit.*, vol. II.

[3] F. Pollock and F. W. Maitland, *The History of English Law before the Time of Edward I* (2nd edit., Cambridge University Press, 1911); W. S. Holdsworth, *A History of English Law* (3rd edit., London: Methuen, 1922–26).

[4] G. Hansard, *A Treatise on the Law relating to Aliens and Denization and Naturalization* (London, 1844); H. S. Q. Henriques, *The Law of Aliens and Naturalization* (London, 1906).

national point of view. The cities in which they lived possessed important privileges enjoyed only by a favored few, even among English merchants, and the conflict between these privileges and those granted by king and parliament to aliens forms one of the problems of mediaeval economic history. Moreover, many of the difficulties of foreign merchants were mercantile in origin and were adjustable in local courts administering merchant law. But the connection between aliens and the central courts and departments of the state is equally important and less generally known. Their privileges from the king and their obligations to him determined very largely their economic position and influence. Their legal privileges and their access to the courts of common law and equity determined their status as individuals, and provide us with important information concerning naturalization laws and legal developments during the fourteenth century. It is worth while, therefore, for the sake of understanding the position of alien merchants, and also for the sake of sharpening the outlines of certain legal and economic developments, to focus attention upon the merchants and their relations with the central government during a short but important period.

The period from 1350 to 1377 is useful and interesting for this purpose. The half century preceding the accession of Edward III saw the definition of the position of alien merchants in England in the *Carta Mercatoria* of 1303. The next twenty-five years, which included the first campaigns of the Hundred Years' War, marked the increase of their importance as commercial, diplomatic, and financial agents of the crown, but saw also the beginning of their decline. The latter half of Edward's reign is in some ways an anti-climax; but the absence of experimental innovations in finance and, to a great extent, in trade makes possible a more thorough examination of the normal activities and position of alien merchants than is feasible during the period immediately preceding. The enrolled customs accounts for the period from 1350 to 1377 contain abundant material for determining the commercial functions of aliens and for appraising the value which the government put upon their presence, while the records of suits to which aliens were parties in the common law courts, the council, and the exchequer provide the facts from which their legal status can be defined.

This study was begun at the suggestion of the late Sir Paul Vinogradoff, for whose seminar the chapter on *Aliens Before the Council* was originally prepared. To his kindly advice and interest I am deeply indebted and I am glad of the opportunity to acknowledge that debt here. My thanks are due to Mr E. Lipson for advice during the latter stages of the work; to the Mediaeval Academy, which has made possible its publication; to the editors of the *Economic History Review* for permission to reprint part of an article which appeared in January, 1930; to the Master of the Rolls for permission to reproduce the notarial mark on page 122; and to the dean and chapter of Westminster for granting access to the muniments of the Abbey. Thanks are also due to the officials and to the staff of the Public Record Office and the Guildhall for their unfailing courtesy and helpfulness. To Mr H. L. Gray of Bryn Mawr College and to Miss B. A. Lees I owe a special and long-standing debt of gratitude. Both have read the manuscript and improved it by their criticism. But, apart from that, it is very largely from their encouragement and instruction that any merit this work may possess is derived.

ALICE BEARDWOOD

OXFORD, 1931

CONTENTS

ix

LIST OF ABBREVIATIONS OF MANUSCRIPTS AND PRINTED SOURCES

MANUSCRIPTS

Chanc. Misc.—Miscellanea of the Chancery.

Exch. Plea Roll—Plea Rolls, Exchequer of Pleas.

K.R. Accounts, Various—King's Remembrancer's Accounts Various.

K.R. Mem.—King's Remembrancer's Memoranda Rolls.

K.R. Customs—King's Remembrancer's Customs Accounts.

L.T.R. Customs Roll—Lord Treasurer's Remembrancer's Enrolled Customs Accounts.

L.T.R. Mem.—Lord Treasurer's Remembrancer's Memoranda Rolls.

PRO—Public Record Office, London.

W.A.M.—Westminster Abbey Muniments.

PRINTED SOURCES

C.C.R.—Calendar of Close Rolls.

C.Ch.R.—Calendar of Charter Rolls.

C.F.R.—Calendar of Fine Rolls.

C.P.R.—Calendar of Patent Rolls.

Cal. Ancient Deeds—Calendar of Ancient Deeds.

Cal. Coroner's Rolls, London—Calendar of Coroner's Rolls of the City of London, 1300–1378 (R. R. Sharpe, ed., London, 1913).

Cal. Early Mayor's Court Rolls—Calendar of Early Mayor's Court Rolls, 1298–1307 (A. H. Thomas, ed., Cambridge University Press, 1924).

Cal. Letter Books (D–H)—Calendar of Letter Books preserved among the Archives of the Corporation of the City of London at the Guildhall (R. R. Sharpe, ed., London, 1902–1907).

Cal. Mayor's Letters, London—Calendar of Letters from the Mayor and Corporation of the City of London, circa 1350–70 (R. R. Sharpe, ed., London, 1885).

Cal. Plea and Mem. Rolls, London—Calendar of Plea and Memoranda Rolls preserved among the Archives of the Corporation of the City of London at the Guildhall, 1323–1381, 2 vols. (A. H. Thomas, ed., Cambridge University Press, 1926, 1929).

Cal. Venetian State Papers—Calendar of State Papers and Manuscripts Relating to English Affairs existing in the Archives and Collections of Venice and in other Libraries of Northern Italy, vol. I, 1202–1509 (Rawdon Brown, ed., London, 1864).

Cal. of Wills, London—*Calendar of Wills proved and enrolled in the Court of Husting, London, 1258–1688*, 2 vols. (R. R. Sharpe, ed., London, 1869).

Coke on Littleton—E. Coke, *Commentary on Littleton* (19th edit., London, 1832).

D.N.B.—*Dictionary of National Biography.*

E.H.R.—*English Historical Review.*

Foedera—*Foedera, conventiones, litterae, et cuiuscunque generis acta publica inter reges Angliae et alios quosvis imperatores, reges, pontifices principes, vel communitates, 1069–1383*, 4 vols. in 7 parts (T. Rymer, ed., New edition, Record Commission, 1816–1869).

Gras—N. S. B. Gras, *The Early English Customs System* (Cambridge: Harvard University Press, 1918).

Hale, Concerning the Customs—Sir Matthew Hale, *A Treatise in Three Parts: De Jure Maris et Brachiorum eiusdem, De Portibus Maris, Concerning the Customs of Goods Imported and Exported.* In a *Collection of Tracts Relative to the Law of England* (F. Hargrave, ed., London, 1787).

Hanserecesse—*Hanserecesse 1256–1530*, 22 vols. (Leipzig, 1870–1905).

Hansische Geschichtsblätter—Herausgegeben von dem Verein für hansische Geschichte (Halle, 1872).

Hansisches Urkundenbuch, 975–1463—Herausgegeben von dem Verein für hansische Geschichte, 10 vols. (K. Hohlbaum, K. Kunze, W. Stein, ed., Halle, 1876–1907).

Kunze, Hanseakten aus England—*Hanseakten aus England, 1275–1412. Hansische Geschichtsquellen*, vol. IV (K. Kunze, ed., Halle, 1891).

Memorials of London—*Memorials of London and London Life; a series of extracts, local, social, and political from the early archives of the City of London, 1276–1419* (H. T. Riley, ed., London, 1868).

N.E.D.—*A New English Dictionary on Historical Principles* (J. A. H. Murray, ed., Oxford: Clarendon Press, 1888–1928).

Pollock and Maitland—F. Pollock and F. W. Maitland, *The History of English Law before the Time of Edward I* (2nd. edit., Cambridge, 1911).

Report on the Dignity of a Peer—Report of the lords' committees appointed to search the journals of the house, rolls of parliament, and other records for all matters touching the dignity of a peer. 5 vols. (London, 1820–29).

Rot. Parl.—*Rotuli Parliamentorum ut et petitiones et placita in parliamento, 1278–1503*, 6 vols.

Stat.—*Statutes of the Realm, 1235–1713*, 11 vols. (Record Commission, London, 1810–28).

Stubbs—W. Stubbs, *The Constitutional History of England*, 3 vols. (5th edit., Oxford, 1891).

V.C.H.—*The Victoria History of the Counties of England* (W. Page, ed.)

ALIEN MERCHANTS IN ENGLAND
1350 TO 1377
THEIR LEGAL AND ECONOMIC
POSITION

I

ALIEN MERCHANTS IN ENGLAND

DURING the latter half of the reign of Edward III, between 1350 and 1377, some of the most important merchants in England were aliens whose status, either as transients or as residents, has a special interest for students of law and economics. As merchants their position differed from that of aliens of the military and religious classes who came to England. As aliens they were set apart from English merchants engaged in the same trade. Yet, among themselves, they formed a homogeneous group, perhaps the largest and certainly the most influential body of foreigners then in England. Their privileges and limitations are accurate indications of the value put upon the presence of aliens by the English government, and the clearest exemplification of fourteenth-century laws of nationality.

Throughout the fourteenth century, merchants came from all parts of Europe,[1] as they had come in earlier times, to exchange their wine, timber, fish, fine cloth, spices, and jewels for English wool, woollen cloth, and merchandise, for, as a contemporary English chronicler wrote, 'Flaundres loveth the wolle of this lond, and Normandie the skynnes and the velles, Gasquyn the iren and the leed; Irlond the ore and the salt; Europa loveth and desireth the white metal of this lond.'[2] Among these merchants were certain notable individuals and companies, particularly from German and Lombard towns, whose careers will serve as an introduction to the part played by aliens in English commerce, and as illustrations of their varied functions, which were of financial and diplomatic as well as of mercantile

---

[1] After the middle of the fourteenth century, Scandinavian merchants ceased almost entirely to come to England, and trade with Scandinavia became the source of great rivalry between English and Hanseatic merchants. A. Bugge, 'Die nordeuropäischen Verkehrswege im frühen Mittelalter,' *Vierteljahrschrift für Social- und Wirtschaftsgeschichte*, IV (1906), 263. The intermittent war with France prevented much commercial intercourse with that country, except with the wine-growing region of Gascony, which was under English control.

[2] *Polychronicon Ranulphi Higden Monachi Cestrensis* (Translated by John Trevisa, C. Babington, ed., Rolls Series, 1869), II, 19.

3

service to the crown. For example, Genoese and Venetian merchants were welcomed in England because Edward III, particularly in the earlier part of his reign, hoped to secure the aid of Genoese and Venetian naval power against France. For that reason, commercial treaties were made with Genoa, and privileges and protection repeatedly assured to Genoese merchants.[1] The Venetian Flanders galleys came to England under letters of protection[2] and Venetian merchants were exempt from going to host and to the staples.[3] Merchants from Turin, particularly Peter and Hugh Provan, were among the king's bankers,[4] as were the societies of the Malbaille[5] and the Leopardi of Asti.[6] The outstanding Italian company in the middle of the fourteenth century, however, was the society of the Bardi of Florence, which shared, then as later, its importance and fame with the German Hanse. A third notable, but less well-known company now, was the society of Lucca. All deserve further attention here, partly because they are the best examples of foreign merchants' activity in England, and partly because new information is available which alters somewhat the hitherto accepted conclusions concerning important periods of their English connection.

The Bardi were neither exceptional in their position as the king's financiers nor unique in their failure; but the magnitude and the circumstances of their failure in 1346, at a critical time for English and

[1] *C.P.R. 1350–54*, p. 71; *ibid. 1370–74*, pp. 32, 51; *C.C.R. 1369–74*, p. 209; *Foedera*, iii, 1, p. 205; *ibid.*, iii, 2, pp. 904, 964, 1008.

[2] For a general account of the Venetian Flanders galleys, see H. G. Rawlinson, 'The Flanders Galleys,' *Mariners' Mirror*, xii (1926), pp. 145–168. *Foedera*, iii, 1, pp. 351, 397, 420; *ibid.*, iii, 2, p. 1021; *Cal. Venetian State Papers*, i, 9, 10, 11, 18.

[3] G. Schanz, *Englische Handelspolitik gegen Ende des Mittelalters* (Leipzig, 1881), i, 119 120.

[4] PRO K.R. Mem. 132, Brevia directa Mich; *ibid.* 133, Communia Mich; *C.C.R. 1354–60*, p. 336.

[5] Members of the society were Sir Anthony Malbaille (*C.C.R. 1349–54*, p. 405); Daniel Provan and Lewis Ponzano (*ibid.*, p. 482); Anthony Fool (PRO K.R. Mem. 139, Brevia directa Mich.); Hugh Provan (PRO Exch. Plea Roll 77, m. 65*d*).

[6] Members of the society were Conrad Roirer, Gabriel de Montemayn, Boniface de Gosok, John de Pount, Benet de la Kenie, George de Caloce, Jakemyn Canaceon (*C.C.R. 1343–46*, p. 574); Meinfrinus de Sant (*ibid.*, p. 319); George Canaceon (PRO K.R. Mem. 116, Communia Pasch.); and possibly Tisardus Garat (PRO Pipe Roll 189, Item London.). Matthew Canaceon, of this society, lent money to the farmers of the customs in 1348. PRO Exch. Plea Roll 119, m. 17. Before that time he had farmed the receipts from the seals of both benches. B. Wilkinson, 'The Seals of Both Benches under Edward III,' *E.H.R.* xlii (1927), 399.

Florentine finances at the beginning of the Hundred Years' War, have, from the fourteenth century to the present, concentrated interest and attention on the failure and the events leading up to it. The succeeding period of reorganization and the final settlement under Richard II have suffered from the lack of interest in an anticlimax. The complete account of the settlement which exists among the exchequer records, however, throws new light on the end of an important episode in English mediaeval finance, and gives us some measure of the Bardi's transactions with Edward III.

After the failure in 1346, both the Bardi and the Peruzzi, the other Florentine company which had supplied large sums to Edward III and which had also failed, received annually at Michaelmas letters of protection *cum clausula volumus*. The last one to the Peruzzi was issued in 1351.[1] In August of the following year, they received £100 in part payment of the king's debt, and with that payment they seem to disappear from the records.[2] The Bardi, on the other hand, after ten years of readjustment and diminished activity under the king's protection, reorganized their company in 1357, when an agreement was made between Philip de Bardi and the proctors of Rodolf and Sir Doffo de Bardi on the one side, and Gerard Bonanseigne on the other. Arrangements were made for paying the current expenses of the company, for repaying the creditors,[3] and for the division of any remainder after the debts had been paid, at the rate of 18s. 4d. in every pound to the three parties of the first part, and 20d. to Gerard Bonanseigne.[4] They seem thereafter to have maintained a sure but inconspicuous position as bankers and merchants, first under the leadership of Philip de Bardi, until his death in 1362,[5] and then under that of his son, Walter de Bardi, who was for many years, under both Edward III and Richard II, the king's moneyer.[6]

[1] *C.P.R. 1350–54, p. 150.*

[2] *C.C.R. 1349–54,* p. 505; A. Sapori, *La Crisi delle Compagnie dei Bardi e dei Peruzzi* (Florence: Olschki, 1926), p. 85.

[3] It is not known what the English creditors ultimately received. Yver says that the Bardi in Italy paid 9s. 3d., and later 6s. in the pound. *Le Commerce et les Marchands dans l'Italie meridionale au xiii°. et au xiv°. Siècle* (Paris, 1903), pp. 323, 324.

[4] *C.C.R. 1354–60,* p. 489.

[5] Sapori, *op. cit.,* p. 92, n. 1.

[6] PRO K.R. Mem. 137, Communia Trin. In 1368 Walter de Bardi was sent by the king, with Thomas de la Dale, to Flanders, to receive from Galeazzo, lord of Milan, the dower of his

It has been proved that Peruzzi's indictment of Edward III as the cause of the failure of the Florentine companies was too severe. Although Edward's share in it was very great, the failure was caused by the series of disasters which in rapid succession overtook the royal causes which the Bardi and the Peruzzi had been supporting, more strongly, perhaps, than their credit warranted.[1] It has also been known that a final settlement between Richard II and the Bardi took place in 1391. But from the few printed documents relating to it, this settlement looked like a mutual agreement to end a hopeless situation which had continued for almost fifty years, during which time the Bardi had received almost no payments on the enormous debt which Edward III owed them.[2] The complete account of the settlement of 1391–92, contained in the original documents preserved among the records of the king's remembrancer,[3] and also in the enrolments on the memoranda rolls of the exchequer[4] and now

daughter who was married to the Duke of Clarence. Their expense account is in PRO K.R. Accounts, Various, Nuntii, 315/30. In the preceding year, when the goods of the Bardi were seized for debt, he claimed that he 'is not nor ever was of the society of the Bardi,' and secured the release of his goods. *C.P.R. 1364–67*, p. 416. The obvious untruth of this statement is seen in all his earlier connection with them, and is strengthened by the fact that he, with Angel de Bardi (probably his brother) and Thomas and Bartholomew de Bardi were made attorneys of Peter de Bardi in 1384 to receive the debts of the company, and that in 1391 he was the sole representative. When he was made master of the money in 1363, he was definitely called 'one of the said society.' *C.P.R. 1361–64*, p. 318. He received an annuity of £20 from Edward III. PRO Issue Rolls 543, 546, 548. Three members of the company, Philip de Bardi, Gerard Bonanseigne, and Nicholas Marini, were summoned to consult with the king and the council in 1353. *C.C.R. 1349–54*, p. 605. Nicholas Marini was one of the most conspicuous members of the company in the decade after the reorganization. He appeared frequently before the exchequer: to answer for money transferred to Antwerp in 1339 (PRO K.R. Mem. 138, Communia Trin.); to appoint an attorney to sue for payment to the company (*ibid.*, 136, Communia Mich.); to secure the enrolment of two letters patent (*ibid.*, 141, Communia Mich.). In 1367, he was made an arbitrator, with Walter de Bardi, in a case between Thomas Serland of Lucca and Andrew Pontadour. *Cal. Plea and Mem. Rolls, London*, ii, 76.

[1] S. L. Peruzzi, *Storia del Commercio e dei Banchieri de Firenze* (Florence, 1868); Sapori, *op. cit.*, pp. 95 ff.; Yver, *op. cit.*, pp. 316 ff.

[2] *C.P.R. 1391–96*, p. 15. Cf. Sapori, *op. cit.*, p. 93; also *Finance and Trade under Edward III*, (G. Unwin ed., Manchester: Manchester University Press, 1918), p. 128, where it is stated that 'the only payment they appear to have received towards the acknowledged debt of £50, 493.5s. 2½d. was one of £150 in October, 1347.'

[3] PRO K.R. Accounts, Various, Foreign Merchants, 127/38.

[4] PRO K.R. Mem. 168, Communia Hil. The writ of privy seal ordering the letters of acquittance to the Bardi and the enrolment of the documents surrendered by them at the time of the settlement is among the chancery warrants PRO File 529, no. 7671.

printed here,[1] place Edward III and his successor in a slightly more honorable position. They show that the crown did not repudiate its debt; that between 1346 and 1391 it paid a considerable amount to the Bardi; and that the agreement of 1391 was sealed by a further, but inadequate, grant from Richard II. We learn, moreover, from the letters obligatory surrendered by the Bardi, and from the accounts taken from the exchequer rolls, what was ultimately[2] agreed upon as the amount of indebtedness on both sides.

The final settlement falls within the period during which Richard II was asserting his intention to rule in fact as well as in name, the interval between the attacks of the Lords Appellant and the final outbreak which led to his deposition. Apart from the pious motives expressed by the king, there was no doubt a desire on both sides to settle definitely a debt which would have been settled no more profitably if carried on longer. Walter de Bardi's position as representative of the company, on the one side, and as an important official of the crown, on the other, may have expedited the settlement. Whatever the cause, negotiations were carried on throughout the autumn of 1391 between the king's council and the Bardi, and resulted in the settlement of accounts up to 24 October of that year. On that day, Walter de Bardi, in the name of the company, remitted, quitclaimed and released to Richard II, Edward III, the lords who were Edward's guarantors in 1339, and to their heirs and executors, all debts due the company, and all actions arising from the same. On 8 November the king issued a writ to the treasurer and barons of the exchequer announcing that, in return for this act of the Bardi, he pardoned them all the debts they might owe the crown, freed Walter de Bardi from certain obligations he had incurred as master of the mint, and ordered payment or suitable assignment to be made to the Bardi for the sum of three thousand marks.[3] Two days later, on 10 November, he issued letters patent announcing the release of the Bardi from debts and actions, but making no mention of the money granted them.[4] On 13 November the transaction was ratified in

[1] See Appendix A.
[2] Cf. p. 8, n. 6 below.
[3] PRO K.R. Mem. 168, Communia Hil. See Appendix A.
[4] *C.P.R. 1391–96*, p. 15.

chancery. Walter de Bardi presented to the chancellor, the treasurer, and others present *in multitudine copiosa* the power of attorney granted to him and three other members of the society by Peter de Bardi in 1384, and his own recent quitclaim to the king. He also made verbal confirmation of the latter, surrendered for cancellation four letters obligatory of Edward III and ordered drawn up, as record of the transaction, the *publicum instrumentum*, elaborately written by John Russel, clerk of Lincoln, and signed with his notarial mark.[1]

Two months later, 14 January, 1392, Walter de Bardi came into the exchequer bringing *the publicum instrumentum* and the four letters obligatory. These were the letter of 20 April, 1345 in which the king promised to pay £50,493 5s. 2½d. at the exchequer of account,[2] the letter of 28 June, 1339 granting the Bardi £30,000, as a gift in return for their services;[3] a letter of 4 August, 1339 in which the king took them under his special protection and bound the Black Prince and eight magnates to honor his obligations;[4] and the letter of 7 November, 1348 acknowledging a debt of £13,454 2s. 11½d.[5] The debt of the king to the Bardi was therefore £93,947 8s. 2d. According to the endorsements on the letter of 20 April, 1345, Edward III and Richard II paid £23,225 17s. 9d. of the debt acknowledged in that letter,[6] a payment for which they have never received credit. The records of the exchequer were searched to discover the indebtedness of the Bardi to the crown. This was found in 1391 to be £39,298 19s. 6d., an amount which included sums advanced to them for the payment of expenses, as well as for annuities and loans, for which they had never accounted. This indebtedness plus the amount they had received in payment of the king's debt equals £62,524 17s. 3d., which, when subtracted from the total amount due to the Bardi,

---

[1] See pp. 122, 123 below.

[2] *C.P.R. 1343–45*, pp. 467–69. The £2595 18s. 2d. and the price of the wool for which the Bardi ask allowance, is accounted for by them on the pipe roll for 1345 according to the endorsement of the letter patent.

[3] *C.P.R. 1338–40*, p. 388.

[4] *Ibid.*, p. 391.

[5] *C.P.R. 1348–50*, p. 11.

[6] See Appendix A. In 1346 the Bardi claimed £207,700 and the king acknowledged debts to them of £90,000. Sapori, *La Crisi delle Compagnie dei Bardi e dei Peruzzi*, pp. 74 ff.

reduces the king's debt, according to the final agreement in October, 1391, to £31,422 10s. 11d.

When the obligations on both sides had been recorded and certain debts of Walter de Bardi as master of the mint had been taken into account, he again asserted, *pro maiore securitate*, that he was one of the society and their attorney, and acknowledged the receipt of the payments mentioned in the letter patent. After deliberation, the barons of the exchequer decided that there should be a mutual cancellation of all debts between them from the beginning of the world to 24 October, 1391. The documents—the letter of Peter de Bardi, Walter de Bardi's acquittance, the four letters obligatory, and the *publicum instrumentum*—were then surrendered at the receipt of the exchequer, there to be preserved, and John Innocent, the treasurer's clerk, received them. The seven documents remain in one file among the king's remembrancer's accounts.[1] By the mutual quit-claims, Richard II freed himself and his successors from any obligation to pay the Bardi the sum still due them in 1391. On 8 November, in consideration of the cancellation of the debt, Richard II had granted the Bardi £2000 (3000 marks), but he probably did not pay this sum. On the issue rolls, between 12 July, 1392 and 21 January, 1393, three assignments were recorded for the Bardi, amounting in all to £600.[2] With these assignments, records of the transaction end. Walter de Bardi continued to receive an annuity for some years, and traces of the company appear on the records until the sixteenth century.[3] A complete vindication of Edward III is impossible, but the documents relating to the settlement under Richard II contain conclusive evidence that a considerable effort was made to pay the royal debt to the Bardi, and that ultimately an agreement, apparently satisfactory to both parties, was made concerning the cancellation of the unpaid remainder.

No other companies held quite the same position in England as the Bardi and the Peruzzi, but Italian merchants continued to serve

[1] PRO K.R. Accounts, Various, Foreign Merchants, 127/38 (1–7).

[2] PRO Issue Rolls 538 (Easter, 1392, July 12); 541 (Michaelmas, 1393, January 16 and 21).

[3] PRO K.R. Accounts, Various, Foreign Merchants, 129/8. Indenture between Wolsey and the Bardi.

the king and to play a large part in financial and commercial enterprises. Connections with the papal court and in other centres on the continent made the societies of the Strozzi[1] and the Albertini, or the Alberti,[2] 'factors and servants of the Roman curia'[3] henceforth the chief agents for the transfer of money abroad and for supplying letters of credit. The most conspicuous group of Lombards in England between 1350 and 1377, however, were merchants of Lucca. Like most Italians, they were also financiers. Nicholas Bartholomew of Lucca and his associates had lent large sums to Edward III at the beginning of the Hundred Years' War, and were still, toward the end of his reign, receiving dilatory payments.[4] Merchants of Lucca were agents for transferring money abroad, and they imported and exported all commodities. They are noteworthy at this period for their mercantile rather than for their financial activities, being above all dealers in mercery, jewels, and spices. The principal company of merchants of Lucca was usually called simply 'the society of Lucca' or 'the society of Nicholas Bartholomew,'[5] although two merchants frequently associated with this group were, on one occasion, said to belong to the society of the Manchelanak.[6] Whatever their title, this

[1] See p. 23, n. 5 below. Among the members of the company were Peter Peragle, of the new society, John Credy and Francis Johan, of the old society (*C.C.R. 1374–77*, p. 252); and Nicholas Russell, of the new society, (PRO K.R. Mem. 150, Brevia retorn.), Thomas Mark de Strozzi (*C.C.R. 1374–77*, p. 473); Nicholas Cortesely and John Baldewyne (*Cal. Letter Book G*. p. 166); Silvester Nicholas (*Cal. Plea and Mem. Rolls, London*, II, 80); Michel de Strozzi (W.A.M. 9224) all of the old society.

[2] Members of the company were Nicholas Luke, Matthew Johan (*C.P.R. 1374–77*, p. 196); Peter Mark (*C.C.R. 1374–77*, p. 252).

[3] *Foedera*, iii, 2, p. 1005. The Pope also wrote to the king in 1364 on behalf of the Paczini (?Pazzi) of Florence. *Ibid.*, p. 738. There seems to be no other mention of them.

[4] *C.C.R. 1349–54*, p. 490; *Foedera* ii, 2, p. 1081; PRO K.R. Accounts, Various, Foreign Merchants, 601/10.

[5] PRO K.R. Mem. 119, Recogn. Mich.

[6] *Ibid.*, 116, Communia Mich.; *C.P.R. 1338–40*, p. 171. They were Landus de Ivers and Banduchius Maskerel. The latter was included in a letter of protection granted in 1352 to Francis Bandini, Kellas Donas, Francis Bochel, Simon Bochel, Lewis Possarell, Fredus de Gemysane, Francis Dini, Jarinus Moricon, Bartholomew Mordecastell, John Cristofle, Parentus Robert, Matthew Fortegerre, Bartholomew Cristofle, Peter Incapistre and their fellows. *C.P.R. 1350–54*, p. 344. There is also mentioned at this period a society of the Busdrake of Lucca. Among the members were David Jacoby, Peter Busdrake, Castellus Castellon, *C.P.R. 1340–43*, p. 37; James Busdrake, who is also said to be a merchant of the society of Lucca, *C.P.R. 1338–40*, p. 171; and a certain Bonecours, PRO Pipe Roll 188, Item London.

group of merchants has provided us with some of the notable cases concerning aliens in the fourteenth century.

The decade between 1359 and 1369 was particularly turbulent for the Lombards, by whom were usually meant the merchants of this 'society of Lucca.' Their trade rivalry with the mercers of London resulted in street brawls and murderous attacks which required royal intervention and had important legal consequences. Their smuggling was notorious even in an age when smuggling was far from unusual. In 1359 there occurred in London between the mercers of London and the Lombards, what is always called 'a certain affray' which undoubtedly arose out of trade jealousy, aliens being allowed to sell mercery by retail.[1] Although the case is more important in its legal aspect,[2] it is interesting in this connection to note that the Lombards who were assaulted were Francis Bochel of Lucca and Raymond Flamy. Of the latter nothing seems to be known,[3] but Bochel was a prominent member of the society of Lucca and was later a citizen of London.[4] He had been one of those imprisoned in the Tower in 1345–47 because of the arrest of English merchants in Pisa.[5] He had also been, in the following years, one of the creditors of the farmers of the customs,[6] and was one of the twelve aliens summoned in 1353 to consult with the council.[7] A member of the same family, Simon Bochel,[8] was involved in the next event which brought the company and other Italian merchants to public notice. Smuggling was common in the fourteenth century, but the scale on which it was carried on by the Lombards, and, in this instance no doubt, the circumstances which led to its detection, must have been out of the ordinary. Although references to alien merchants in England are rare in the chronicles of the period, the smuggling of the Lombards, revealed and punished in 1364, was sufficiently noteworthy to be

[1] See p. 56 below.
[2] See pp. 92 ff. below.
[3] An Alexander Flamme of Lucca was lending money to the king in 1345. *C.C.R. 1343–46*, pp. 537, 583, 598. See also p. 112 below.
[4] See Appendix G.
[5] *C.C.R. 1346–49*, pp. 81, 160; *C.P.R. 1345–48*, pp. 21, 330.
[6] PRO Exch. Plea Roll 179, m. 17.
[7] *C.C.R. 1349–54*, p. 605.
[8] A Lewis Bochel was also imprisoned in 1345. See n. 5 above.

mentioned by John of Reading and to have been set down in almost
identical terms in Walsingham, the *Polychronicon*, the *Eulogium*, the
Continuation of Murimuth, and the *Chronicon Angliae*. The fact that
John of Reading was a monk of Westminster may account for his
accurate knowledge of when the case was heard in London. His version runs:

Sequenti mense Maii Longobardi et quidam comes Londoniensis de minora-
tione regiae monetae ac transvectione lanarum aliarumque venalium non
solutis debitis consuetudinibus regiis ministris saepius convicti se miseri-
cordiae domini regis supponentes, non modica pecunia mediante cum
favore dominorum gratiam regalem invenerunt.[1]

The other version, probably from a St. Albans source, is as follows:

Eodem anno Longobardi mercatores sunt accusati per socios suos de magna
infelicitate in mercimoniis suis facta Regi; unde pars major illorum in
Turri Londoniarum recluditur, quousque finem Regi fecissent ad eius bene-
placitum.[2]

To an account substantially like this the *Eulogium* adds:

Dictum erat in populo quod defraudabant regem de tribus milibus librarum
argenti quolibet anno.[3]

We do not know what caused some of the merchants to inform
against their fellows, nor do we know how long the latter were imprisoned in the Tower; but the official records of the end of the case
supply supplementary facts which tend to confirm the date given
by John of Reading and prove that the Lombards made fine *non
modica pecunia mediante*. On 27 July, 1364, a group of merchants of
Lucca, who had been tried before the council, very possibly in May,
came before the barons of the exchequer and made fine with the king

---

[1] *Chronica Johannis de Reading et Anonymi Cantuariensis 1346–1367* (J. Tait, ed. Manchester: Manchester University Press, 1914), p. 161.

[2] *Thomae Walsingham Historia Anglicana* (H. T. Riley, ed., Rolls Series 1863) I, 300. For
similar versions, see Ranulf Higden, *Polychronicon* (C. Babington, J. R. Lumby, ed., Rolls
Series, 1865–86), VIII, 414; *Chronicon Angliae* (E. M. Thompson, ed., Rolls Series, 1874), p.
55; *Ypodigma Neustriae a Thoma Walsingham* (H. T. Riley, ed., Rolls Series, 1876), p. 309;
Adami Murimuthensis Chronica sui Temporis cum eorundem continuatione a quodam anonymo
(T. Hog, ed., English Historical Society, 1846), p. 200.

[3] *Eulogium historiarum sive temporis* (F. S. Haydon, ed., Rolls Series, 1858–63) III, 234.

for £1,000 for smuggling goods in and out of the country.[1] On the same day Anthonius de la Vale of Asti paid a fine of £200 for the same offence acknowledged before the council on 13 July,[2] and another group, some of whom at least were Florentines, came before the council on 9 July and declared that they wished to satisfy the king for all goods smuggled by them.[3] The fines are entered on the receipt roll for the Easter term,[4] 1368 as paid and on the pipe roll for the same year, where the merchants are quit.[5] The prosecution seems to have continued. On 13 July, Martin de Mere of Genoa acknowledged before the council that in 1361 he had imported pearls worth 400 florins without paying the customs of 16s. 10½d. He was permitted to pay a fine of 20s. On 13 July, also, Martin Palvesyn (Pallavicini?) of Genoa made fine for 100s. for smuggling jewels worth £400 into the country,[6] and Hugh Adelas of Asti, paid a fine of ten marks.[7] On 26 August, it was recorded on the receipt roll that Thomas Serland, through Simon Bochel, paid a fine of £133 6s. 8d., doubtless for the same offense.[8]

At least one member of the company, Nicholas Sardouche, continued these practises. His career was in many ways typical of an alien merchant in England. He seems to have come to England about the middle of the century. In 1359, he was acting as attorney for another merchant of Lucca.[9] He exported wool[10] and shipped other commodities in and out of England, carried on business throughout the country,[11] had financial connections in Bruges,[12] acted as main-

[1] They were Lazarus Guyneys, Simon Bochel, Nicholas Sardouche, Frederick de Guyngain, Paul Panyk, Andrew de Portyk, Kanalk Paf, James, his servant, Jarynus Morycon, kalandrer, and Bonecors Brankalyon. PRO K.R. Mem. 140 and PRO L.T.R. Mem. 136, Communia Trin. Fines; PRO Receipt Roll 477, 27 July, 1368.

[2] *Ibid.*, PRO K.R. Mem. 140, Communia Trin.

[3] They were John Gauchius, John Baldwin (Florence), Silvester Nicholas (Florence), Bartholomew Buoni, and Francus de Lipo. PRO K.R. Mem. 140, Communia Trin.

[4] PRO Receipt Roll 477, 27 July.

[5] PRO Pipe Roll 213, Item Lond. d.

[6] PRO K.R. Mem. 140, Communia Trin. d.

[7] *Ibid.*, PRO Receipt Roll 477, 13 July, where he is called a merchant of Venice.

[8] PRO Receipt Roll 477, 26 August.

[9] *C.P.R. 1358–61*, p. 197.

[10] PRO K.R. Customs 70/18.

[11] *C.P.R. 1367–70*, p. 39.

[12] *Cal. Plea and Mem. Rolls. London*, II, 10.

pernour and attorney for several of his compatriots,[1] and was himself a party in several suits. In 1368, however, complaint was brought against him by the silkwomen of London, and the investigation which followed showed that for eight years, at least, he had been engaged in all manner of corrupt trade practises, especially in the smuggling, forestalling, and regrating of mercery. The evidence brought forward during the trial, which will be examined in detail later,[2] explains why the Lombards were hated and attacked by the mercers, as well as Sardouche's own ill-repute and violent death. He was killed in 1370 in a quarrel which arose out of personal animosity, but which was undoubtedly inflamed by trade jealousy and ill-feeling. According to the confession of John de More to the coroner of Berkshire to whom he had surrendered, de More was indebted to Sardouche for £111, payable at Easter, 1371.[3] Sardouche, meeting de More in Cheapside shortly before Christmas, 1370, asked him to pay the money to one of his creditors, a certain Elui. De More agreed, and at the same time demanded that Sardouche retract his unseemly and insulting boasting, which had offended de More. Sardouche refused, and in the brawl that followed, was struck down by two men who had been passing and who had taken up the quarrel, although de More testified that he did not know them. De More, who had walked away, then returned and killed Sardouche who was attempting to escape. After a trial before the justices of gaol delivery,[4] in the course of which he claimed benefit of clergy although he was probably a mercer,[5] John de More was pardoned.[6] The two other assailants, Lawrence de Berkford and Simon de Daterden, were also pardoned, and it is significant that they, too, were mercers.[7]

The third notable company of alien merchants in England at this

[1] *Ibid.*, p. 82; *C.P.R. 1364–67*, p. 53.

[2] See p. 82 below.

[3] Cf. *Cal. Plea and Mem. Rolls, London*, II, 111, for payment of debts to Sardouche by mercers in July, 1369.

[4] PRO Coram Rege Roll 443, m. 33 Rex.

[5] For the extension of benefit of clergy to the laity, see L. C. Gabel, *Benefit of Clergy in England in the Later Middle Ages* (Smith College Studies in History, XIV, Northampton, Mass., 1928–29), pp. 76 ff.

[6] *C.P.R. 1370–74*, p. 159.

[7] *Ibid.*, p. 268.

period, the Hanse of Almain, was the outgrowth of a very old trade connection between England and the cities of the Empire. From Anglo-Saxon times, German merchants had come to England,[1] and by the middle of the fourteenth century, the Hanse of Almain had been established in England for almost a century. Much has been written about the early history of the Hanse. The documents relating to Hanseatic trade have been edited and discussed in the numerous publications of the *Verein für Hansische Geschichte;* the London Hanse in the Middle Ages has been the subject of the investigations of Lappenberg, Kunze, Keutgen, Daenell, and other contributors to the *Hansische Geschichtsblätter.* Yet the problem of how and when the Hanse of Almain developed out of the *hanse* of German cities, in particular those of Lübeck, Hamburg, and Cologne, is still unsolved.[2] The Hanse of Almain is first mentioned in the latter half of the thirteenth century; but early fourteenth-century evidence seems to show that the merchants of Cologne maintained at that time a separate organization and owed separate dues to the city of London. The distinction and antagonism between the two groups of merchants apparently diminished in the latter half of the fourteenth and in the early fifteenth centuries, but was still alive or was revived in the late fifteenth century.[3] To the merchants of the Hanse of Almain, the only organization of its kind in England,[4] successive kings

[1] J. M. Lappenberg, *Urkundliche Geschichte des Hansischen Stahlhofes zu London,* (Hamburg, 1851), p. 4.

[2] 1157, Protection was granted to men of Cologne who have a guildhall in London. *Hansisches Urkundenbuch,* i, 8. 1266, Hamburg was granted right to have *hanse* throughout England. *ibid.,* 219. 1267, Lübeck was granted *hanse* like that of Cologne. *ibid.,* 220. 1282, First mention occurs of the Hanse of Almain. *Liber Albus,* (H. T. Riley, ed., Rolls Series, 1859), 485.

[3] M. Weinbaum, 'Stalhof und deutsche Gildhalle zu London,' *Hansische Geschichtsblätter,* XXXIII (1928), 45–65.

[4] At an earlier time, there had been the Hanse Flamande de Londres, a capitalistic, interurban association of merchants, which can be traced back to the twelfth century, but it apparently perished in the democratic revolution in Flanders at the beginning of the fourteenth century. This is Pirenne's theory, which is supported by the fact that there is no trace of the Flemish Hanse in English documents of this period. Warnkönig, followed by Varenbergh, held that it was in existence until 1426. H. Pirenne, 'La Hanse Flamande de Londres', *Académie royale des sciences, des lettres et des beaux-arts de Belgique, Bulletin, Classe des lettres et des sciences morales et politiques,* I (Brussels, 1899), 65–108. L. A. Warnkönig, *Histoire de la Flandre et de ses Institutions Civiles et Politiques jusqu'à l'an 1305,* (Brussels, 1835–46). E.

granted and confirmed[1] important privileges, which had their proto-
type in the early privileges of the Hanse of Cologne. The Hansards
had their headquarters in their own guildhall, the *gildhalla Theutoni-
corum*, in Thames Street, while the merchants of Cologne were
probably occupying the adjoining land to the east, known as the
Steelyard.[2] All traces of their long occupation of the property have
now been obliterated by the Cannon Street Station. Upon this site
they had their own wharf and storehouses, as well as their hostel,
where most of the members lived an almost collegiate life under the
control of their own alderman and a committee of twelve. Membership in the Hanse was restricted to independent merchants not in
partnership with a nonmember. As in the Flemish Hanse, workmen
were excluded.[3] In the fourteenth century, the principal members of
the Hanse were still from Dortmund and Cologne, cities which owed
much of their prosperity to their trade connection with England.
Its members belonged, in many instances, to those commercial
families which had been and which were to be active in the London
Hanse for generations: the Sudermanns, the Clippings, and the Rev-
els. The connection between England and Lübeck and the cities of
the Baltic grew, however, and merchants of Prussia were mentioned
with increasing frequency.

It has been said that most of the difficulties which arose between
the Hanse and England toward the end of Edward III's reign were
caused by the Prussians,[4] whose attacks on English merchants in

Varenbergh, *Histoire des Relations Diplomatiques entre le Comté de Flandre et l'Angleterre au
Moyen Age*, (Brussels, 1874). W. Stein, 'hansa,' *Hansische Geschichtsblätter*, xv (1909), 102–
110. K. Hohlbaum, 'Ueber die Flandrische Hanse von London,' *ibid.*, ix (1898), 147–180.

[1] In 1327, Edward III confirmed the charter of 1317, which included charters of 1260,
1281, 1311. *Cal. Letter Book E*, p. 220.

[2] The site was occupied and known as the *Stalhof* as early as 1320, the date of the earliest
extant ordinances of the Hanse. It was distinct from the guildhall. For a discussion of this and
of the meaning of *Stalhof*, see J. Stow, *Survey of London*, (C. L. Kingsford, ed., Oxford, 1908),
ii, 318–20; W. Kurzinna, 'Der Name *Stahlhof*,' *Hansische Geschichtsblätter*, xviii (1912), 429–
461. A. H. Thomas doubts whether the houses of the *hanse* of Cologne and of the Teutonic
merchants were the same. *Calendar of Early Mayor's Court Rolls*, (Cambridge: Cambridge
University Press, 1924), p. 43, n. 1. There is fifteenth-century evidence to show that at that
late date the Steelyard was in the possession of the merchants of Cologne. Weinbaum, *op.
cit.*, 46–48.

[3] K. Engel, 'Die Organization der deutsch-hansischen Kaufleute in England im 14. & 15.
Jahrhundert,' *Hansische Geschichtsblätter*, xix (1913), 445–517; *ibid.*, xx (1914), 173–225.

Norway[1] brought retaliation upon Hansards in London.[2] The rights of the London Hanse were infringed and curtailed. Protests and negotiations between the English government and the Hanse failed, and the latter was forced, for the first time in its dealings with England, to abandon the autonomous position which was characteristic of Hanseatic organizations in foreign countries and appeal to the Hansetag for aid. The settlement of these difficulties and the further trouble which arose between Hansards and English merchants belong to the period later than the one which we are considering. During most of latter half of Edward III's reign, the Hanse maintained its position as the foremost mercantile organization in England, with no events or members of outstanding interest. There was, however, one short and almost unique period of financial activity among the Hansards, due very largely to the presence in England of Tidemann of Limberg, a merchant of outstanding financial ability, at a time when the failure of the king's Italian financiers and the inability of English merchants immediately to take their place gave the Hansards the opportunity of becoming the financiers of the king and of the English merchants, in whose name some of the great loans of the period were made.[3] Hanseatic historians see in Tidemann a financial genius far in advance of his times.[4] He was, rather, one of the great merchant-financiers, both English and alien, produced and usually almost ruined by Edward III's war needs. His career, however, was not so unusual that it cannot serve as an example of the fortunes of a successful merchant who undertook to finance a campaign, who became involved in the losses and litigation which inevitably followed Edward's financial schemes, and whose reputation, as was so often the case with alien merchants,[5] suffered because of rumored or actual misdemeanors.

[4] F. Schulz, *Die Hanse und England von Eduard III bis auf Heinrich VIII* (Berlin, 1911), p. 2.

[1] *Diplomatarium Norwegicum* (A. Bugge, ed., Kristiania, 1910–14), xx, 704.

[2] Schulz, *op. cit.*, pp. 21 ff. See p. 60 below.

[3] J. Hansen, 'Der Englische Staatskredit unter König Edward III und die hansischen Kaufleute,' *Hansische Geschichtsblätter* xvi (1910), 323–414; G. Grosch, 'Die Geldgeschäfte hansischer Kaufleute mit englischen Königen im 13. & 14. Jahrhundert,' *Archiv für Kulturgeschichte*, ii (1904), 121–71; 265–95.

[4] Grosch, *op. cit.*, pp. 156, 271.

[5] Grosch, *op. cit.*, p. 171.

When a comparatively young man of thirty, Tidemann of Limberg[1] first appears as a member of the consortium which farmed the customs in 1340. From then on he is found living in his own house in Thames Street, importing and exporting merchandise, lending money to the king and receiving in return the stanneries, the crown, assignments on the customs, and gifts. He was also holding land which may have been given in repayment of money lent to the king and others.[2] After 1350, he was involved in a series of law suits arising out of the last farming of the customs in 1348. The farmers had failed, and in 1352 proceedings were brought against them in the exchequer. An investigation was made of the whole transaction and interesting evidence as to the methods used and the persons involved came to light.[3] When Walter de Cheriton, Gilbert de Wendlyngburgh, and their associates guaranteed to lend the king 40,000 marks and were given the customs and the privilege of acquiring £20,000 of debts owed by the king,[4] they were by no means ready to advance the money themselves. Half the loan at least was secured through the Germans. It was said, when the loan was made, that that amount was advanced by Conrad Femol and John Conyng, but according to the evidence given in the subsequent suits, the merchants who lent to the farmers were John of Wesenham, a Londoner, and Tidemann of Limberg. John of Wesenham, realizing that the farmers were short of ready money and seeing an opportunity of making a good profit, proposed that he and Tidemann should lend them 20,000 marks and receive in return the allowance of one mark per sack on wool exported and 13,000 marks of the king's debts. The agreement with the farmers was drawn up in John of Wesenham's name at Tidemann's house in Thames Street. Later, an agreement was made between Wesenham and Tidemann whereby the latter was to receive £5,000 of the loan and £3,000 of the debts. An additional loan was subsequently made by Wesenham to the farmers for which Tidemann acted as broker. Henry Picard, acting for the farmers, had approached Wesenham for another loan, but he, 'cui predicti nuper firmarii irati fuerunt,'

---

[1] A brief biography is to be found in Hansen, *op. cit.*, pp. 402 ff.
[2] See pp. 62 ff below.
[3] PRO Exch. Plea Roll 77, 78; Kunze, *Hanseakten aus England*, pp. 113 ff.
[4] *C.C.R. 1346–49*, pp. 248, 249.

was unwilling to deal directly with them, and proposed that the matter be arranged through Tidemann, who, in Wesenham's name, lent 2,000 marks.[1]

After the failure, the king brought suit to recover the 13,000 marks of his debts allowed to Tidemann and Wesenham, as part of the £20,000 granted for the contract which had not been fulfilled. It was finally decided that they should restore the entire amount to the king. Unable to pay, they were put in the Tower and the stanneries were taken away from Tidemann. By 9 February, 1353, they were released, but by the end of the month Tidemann was again in prison because he had come into the exchequer and said that the farmers were false, and threatened them in various ways. He was released on mainprise the next day and eventually made fine for his contempt and trespass.[2] In July, 1353, the king agreed to accept £6,000 instead of 13,000 marks, and by July, 1354, Tidemann had paid his share.

When and why Tidemann left England it is difficult to say.[3] It was stated in parliament in 1386 during the impeachment of Michael de la Pole, Earl of Suffolk, to whom Tidemann had transferred his share in the annuity granted to him and John atte Wold from the customs of Hull,[4] that he had not been in the country for thirty years and that payment of the annuity had been discontinued for twenty or thirty years.[5] It was further stated that he had fled because 'un Neel Hakeneye fuist occis par sa femme et sa servant et le dit Tydman; pur quele felonie les ditz femme et servant fuerent ars et le dit Tydman s'enfuy.'[6] Additional evidence that his departure was in the nature of a flight is contained in an account of the grant of his land in Rotherhithe[7] to the abbey of Bermondsey in 1376. In that year the king gave to the abbey 'terras in le Breche in Retherhithe . . . quas sibi retinuit per escaetam ratione mesprisionis et offensionis factae

[1] PRO Exch. Plea Roll 78, m. 116 ff.

[2] *Ibid.*, m. 60.

[3] Grosch says that he intended to remain there permanently but there is no evidence for this, *op. cit.*, p. 271.

[4] PRO L.T.R. Customs Roll 8, m. 55. John atte Wold had died long before.

[5] *Rot. Parl.* iii, 216–219.

[6] *Ibid.*, 218.

[7] See p. 63 below.

per Tidemannum Lymberghe mercatorem Almannie.'[1] No direct evidence, however, other than that given in parliament thirty-four years after the event, connects him with the murder of Nigel of Hackney, who was not one of the Dortmund Hackeneys, as the editor of the *Dortmunder Urkundenbuch* suggests,[2] but the son of a prominent London wooldraper[3] Richard of Hackney murdered in 1352. In a hitherto unnoticed record of the appeal brought in the King's Bench in the Easter term,[4] 1353, by Nigel's brother, Richard of Hackney, the persons accused of the murder were Herman Mynter, a Hansard,[5] William de Kirkeby, and Nigel's mother-in-law,[6] Juliana, wife of John Hardyngham. Juliana and Herman Mynter were acquitted. William de Kirkeby did not appear. A second suit was brought against him and Mynter, who could not then be found. They should have been outlawed at the fifth county court at which they did not appear, but the sheriff could not proceed against them because the coroners were not present. One coroner was accounting at the exchequer as a collector of the fifteenth, and the other was at Harrow investigating another murder. There seems to be no further trace of the case. Tidemann was a business associate of Mynter's, but there is no evidence to connect him with the crime.

In June, 1353, just at the time the case was being heard, Tidemann was summoned with twelve alien and seventy English merchants to consult with the king.[7] In 1354 he was himself bringing an action of trespass against John Crulle in the King's Bench.[8] In 1357

---

[1] *Annales de Bermundeseia* (H. R. Luard, ed., Rolls Series, 1866), 479.

[2] K. Rübel, ed., Dortmund: 1881–99, II, 447.

[3] Richard of Hackney was an alderman in 1332 and died in 1343, leaving to his son Nigel money and land in the parish of St. Dunstan's toward the Tower and elsewhere, and the advowson of St. Mary atte Hull. *Finance and Trade under Edward III*, pp. 38, 61. *Cal. of Wills, London* (R. R. Sharpe, ed., London: 1889), I, 467.

[4] PRO Coram Rege Roll 371, m. 31*d*. Rex. A guardian (Sir Thomas Moraunt of Kent, her uncle) was appointed for Nigel's daughter Alice, aged four, on 13 September, 1352. *Cal. Letter Book F.*, p. 248.

[5] He had also lent money to the farmers of the customs in 1348. PRO K.R. Mem. 148, Brevia directa. In 1351 he was acting as attorney for merchants of Prussia. *C.C.R. 1349–54*, p. 387.

[6] In 1349 a grant of land was made to Nigel, son of Richard of Hackney, citizen of London and Margaret his wife, daughter of John de Hardyngham. *C.C.R. 1349–54*, p. 146.

[7] *C.C.R. 1349–54*, p. 605. *Report on the Dignity of a Peer*, iii. 596–8.

[8] PRO Coram Rege Roll 375, m. 16.

his lands in Rotherhithe were confirmed to him.[1] In July, 1359, he petitioned to be discharged of £5000 2s. assigned to him at the exchequer for the redemption of the king's crown, which he had redeemed with his own money.[2] In August he received a bond for 1,000 marks lent at the exchequer with the promise that it would be repaid at Christmas,[3] and on the same day his associates were granted an allowance of 43s. 4d. per sack on wool exported from Boston in satisfaction of the loan.[4] Payments of the annuity are recorded in the customs accounts for Hull until 1368.[5] This seems to be the last trace of him in the records, but it is impossible to say whether he transferred the annuity to Michael de la Pole then or earlier. The transfer was not confirmed until 1385.[6] There is evidence that he was in Dortmund[7] at least occasionally, from 1356 to 1370, because his name appears in the records as being involved in law suits, putting his seal to documents, and paying taxes. In 1358, he purchased a house in Cologne, became a burgess there in 1371, died in 1386, and was buried in the church of the Augustinian hermits.[8] The date given in 1386 for stopping the annuity is approximately correct; but the fact that his departure was probably not earlier than 1360, seems to lessen the possibility of his connection with the murder. Nothing else in the career of the foremost member of the London Hanse and the philanthropic merchant and burgess of Cologne, whose rent roll was the largest in the city,[9] suggests that the accusation was true. Whatever may have been the case, Tidemann of Limberg was largely responsible for the brief period of financial activity of the Hanse, during the decade before 1350. After his departure from England, great financial activity on the part of German merchants ceased, but the Hanse of Almain continued throughout

[1] *C.P.R. 1354–58*, p. 586.

[2] *C.P.R. 1358–61*, p. 228.

[3] *Ibid.*, p. 260.

[4] *C.C.R. 1354–60*, p. 590.

[5] PRO L.T.R. Customs Roll 8, m. 55.

[6] *C.C.R. 1381–85*, p. 542.

[7] *Dortmunder Urkundenbuch*, I, 513, 537; II, 59.

[8] J. Hansen, 'Der englische Staatskredit,' *Hansische Geschichtsblätter*, XVI (1910), 402–406.

[9] Hansen, *op. cit.*, p. 403. He had contributed to the building of a hospital in Dortmund, and made large gifts to the Carthusians in Cologne. In 1351, he had secured the right to carry an altar with him on his journeys.

the next centuries to be the foremost foreign commercial organization in England. Their competitors and rivals in the fourteenth century were primarily the Italians, and after them merchants from all other parts of the continent. The activities of the latter were less conspicuous than those of the merchants of Florence, Lucca, and of the Hanse of Almain, but they were to no small extent responsible, as we shall see later, for supplying England with the products of the continent and for exporting her greatly desired wool and woollen cloth.

II

THE PLACE OF ALIENS IN ENGLAND'S FOREIGN TRADE

THE clearest indication of the importance of alien merchants in England in the fourteenth century is the part they took in English foreign trade. They had, of course, other interests, especially in various kinds of financial activity. They lent money, supplied bullion to the mint,[1] and held office as masters of the mints[2] and wardens of the exchanges in London and other ports.[3] Lombard bankers were also authorized to hold private exchanges,[4] where, by royal authority, they changed money and issued letters of exchange, which travellers to the continent carried, and by which money was transferred to the papal court or to merchants on the continent.[5] Never-

[1] PRO K.R. Accounts, Various, Mint, 298/6.

[2] The most noted master of the mint during this period was Walter de Bardi, who held that office on into the reign of Richard II. *Foedera*, iii, 2, p. 727; *C.C.R. 1360–64*, p. 296.

[3] PRO K.R. Mem. 108, m. 355*d*.

[4] No English money could be taken out of the country without special permission. Because of its control over the exportation of money, the government had direct supervision over the changing of money and the issuing of letters of exchange. *Stat.* i, 322; *Rot. Parl.* ii, 338; *C.P.R. 1374–77*, p. 312. The royal authority to issue letters of exchange was given 'par nostre counge especiale, par lettres desouz nostre secre seal.' The licenses to travellers to take the letters out of the country were enrolled on the patent rolls and are our chief sources of information, in the absence of the actual letters. The licenses usually ran as follows: 'License for John de Mowbrey . . . to cross from the port of Dover with 20 horses and their harness, a letter of exchange of Reyner Dymenge, Lombard, for 800 marks and £100 for his expenses.' *C.P.R. 1367–70*, p. 53.

[5] Their business as papal bankers must have been somewhat curtailed by Edward III's repudiation of the tribute and the intermittant payment of Peter's Pence, but there was a constant transfer of money to agents suing at the papal court. There are many documents like the following: an acknowledgment of the receipt by the Strozzi of 20,000 florins from Simon Langham, Archbishop of Canterbury, to be repaid at Avignon, W.A.M. 9224; or the license to merchants of Pistoia, Lucca, and York to 'make letters of exchange to their fellows in foreign parts for £4,000, there payable to the papal chamber on behalf of Arnald Guarnerius, nuncio and collector of the said chamber in England,' *C.C.R. 1374–77*, p. 419; or the request of Richard de Fereby that the Strozzi transfer £30 through their continental agent to his agent who was suing at Rome for a benefice for his son, PRO Coram Rege Roll 451, m. 26 Rex.

theless, foreign merchants were primarily importers and exporters, and the most accurate estimate of their economic position in England between 1350 and 1377 is to be found in the documents which contain the record of goods imported and exported: the enrolled customs accounts. These records provide, furthermore, the material for a valuable comparison between the amount of trade in alien hands with that in native hands. Moreover an essential part of any estimate of the position of aliens must be derived from a consideration of the general course of trade in the four groups of commodities which we find on the customs rolls: wool, woollen cloth, wine, and general merchandise. The government's policy, for example, of creating a monopoly for aliens, especially in the exportation of wool, is an indication both of the profit the exchequer could obtain from alien merchants, and of the ability of the foreigners to take over a very large part of English commerce, when native competition was removed.

There were few years during the last half of the reign of Edward III when the wool trade was not interfered with by pestilence or parliament. When the period begins, the country was suffering from the ravages of the Black Death, which, among its other effects, worked the final ruin of the company to whom the custom and subsidy on wool and the petty custom had been farmed. This failure marked the end of the series of disastrous attempts made during the first decade of England's last long struggle to maintain her power in France[1] to secure unprecedented amounts of ready money by farming the wool customs. It is impossible to discover exactly to what extent the production and exportation of wool was affected by the plague, because there are no customs returns for the years when the customs were farmed except when an additional subsidy was imposed and was not farmed. The 2s. subsidy which began 28 February, 1350, ceased in the following June because of the truce with France. At the same time the

---

[1] The customs and subsidy on wool had been farmed in 1347 for three years to a company of English merchants, of whom the most important were Walter de Cheriton, Thomas de Swanland, and Gilbert de Wendlingburgh. Within a year they were in difficulties. The company was reorganized and the petty custom was added to the farm. In 1350 a receiver had to be appointed owing to the complete collapse of the company. John Malewayn administered the customs from 20 July, 1350, until the end of the three-year period. *C.P.R. 1348–50*, pp. 99, 145, 557; *C.C.R. 1349–54*, p. 98.

20*s.* subsidy which had run from 6 April also stopped. From the returns for the latter from eleven ports, it would seem that only four and a half sacks and 150 woolfells had been exported from April to June, and those were shipped from Sandwich by two English merchants.[1] The 4177 sacks on which the 2*s.* subsidy was collected must have been exported between 28 February and 6 April. The 2*s.* subsidy was reimposed in September, 1350, and ran until Michaelmas, 1351. We have therefore the returns for the last year of the farming of the customs. The amount of wool exported in 1350–51, 35,696 sacks, was well above the average for this time, which was 30,000 sacks. But in the two succeeding years there was a bad slump. In Ipswich, Sandwich, and Chichester, no wool was exported in 1352–53, and in other ports the quantity taken was greatly decreased. This decrease may have been due to the fact that in 1352 the exportation of wool was prohibited because of the danger to shipping arising from the war,[2] although this prohibition seems to have applied only to English merchants. Alien merchants were taking their normal amount[3] but were, perhaps, unable to absorb the native trade as well. The prohibition and the consequent holding of wool in England may also account for the surprising and sudden increase in the amount of wool exported during the next year when restrictions were removed. Two equally violent variations followed the return of the pestilence in 1361 and 1368.[4] Immediately following each of these years there was an increase in the quantity of wool exported and then a sudden decrease. In the latter year, this fluctuation chiefly occurred in the east coast ports. In Southampton alone the amount taken in the otherwise bad years was undiminished. The depression there came in 1355–56, which was also a bad year in Chichester and Sandwich.

Early in our period, the exportation of wool was put into the hands of the alien merchants. In 1352, English merchants were prac-

[1] PRO L.T.R. Customs Roll 5, m. 1; *ibid.* 12, m. 1.

[2] *C.C.R. 1349–54*, p. 506.

[3] Licenses were issued to aliens for the exportation of wool. *ibid.*, pp. 542, 544. For the amount of wool exported annually by aliens and by natives, see p. 160 below.

[4] All business in the exchequer and the courts was suspended in the summer of 1361 and the spring of 1368. PRO K.R. Mem. 137, Communia Pasch.; *ibid.*, 144, Brevia Pasch. *Coram Rege* rolls are lacking for Michaelmas 1361 and Trinity 1368, and the pleas for those terms were postponed until the following terms.

tically excluded from the carrying trade, but it was the establishment of home staples in 1353 which created a real monopoly for aliens.[1] The staples remained in England until 1 March, 1363, when a foreign staple was established at Calais.[2] The shipment of wool was suspended from Michaelmas, 1362, until the following February, doubtless to facilitate the change in the staple.[3] The alien monopoly had ceased in 1356, but it is impossible to separate alien from native shipments between 1356 and 1362 because natives were paying the higher customs rates of aliens for the privilege of exporting.[4] When, however, the wool trade resumed its normal course and English merchants again paid their normal customs,[5] we find them well in control of the trade, shipping over half the wool from all ports, save for occasional years, when in London, Boston, Southampton, and Yarmouth alien shipments exceeded those of native merchants. In 1365, aliens again had a brief monopoly of the export trade from 2 February to 17 May.[6] This was apparently the time when home staples were being established in addition to the foreign staple. In the parliament held in January, 1365,[7] it was conceded that home staples should be established in the towns where they had been set up in 1353, and in such additional parts as should be specified.[8] The additional ports were Ipswich and Melcombe.[9] There are several indica-

---

[1] The staple for wool was moved from Bruges, where it had been since 1340, on 2 August, 1353, and set up in ten English, one Welsh, and four Irish towns. *Rot. Parl.* ii, 246; *Stat.* i., 332. The accounts for Lynn and Melcombe stop because they were not staple ports. The accounts for Exeter begin with this year and continue for the next nine years but very little wool was taken by aliens. PRO L.T.R. Customs Roll 8, m. 27, 51.

[2] *Stat.* i. 390. Merchants were to give security that they would take wool to Calais. *Foedera*, iii, 2, p. 698. Export from Bristol ceases with the home staple and does not begin again until 1369. No wool seems to have been exported from there during the second period of home staples. PRO L.T.R. Customs Roll 8, m. 48*d*; *ibid.*, 14, m. 56.

[3] *C.C.R. 1360–64*, p. 424.

[4] For authorizations to export under that condition, see *Stat.* i, 351, 374; *C.P.R. 1358–61*, p. 564.

[5] A petition that native merchants be allowed to ship wool *saunz estre restreint* was granted in the parliament of October–November 1362. *Rot. Parl.* ii, 271.

[6] PRO L.T.R. Customs Roll 8 passim.

[7] The parliament was held during the Utas of Hilary, anno 38. In the printed Statute Rolls it is said to have met in 1363–64, while in the printed rolls of Parliament the same parliament is said to have met in 1364–65. The latter must be correct. Edward III's regnal year began 25 January and Hilary in the 38th year would be in January, 1365. *Stat.* i, 383; *Rot. Parl.* ii, 283.

[8] *Rot. Parl.* ii, 287; *Stat.* i, 384.

tions that the home staples were actually set up.[1] The stopping of the shipment of wool from 31 January to 2 February and the restriction of export to aliens when it began again point to a re-arrangement of some sort.[2] In addition, customs accounts for Ipswich and Melcombe, of which there are none after the establishment of the staples in 1353, begin in May and June, 1365.[3] Native merchants were allowed to export after 17 May,[4] and the system of double staples continued until 11 June, 1369, when the foreign staple was temporarily removed from Calais because of the war.[5] Several changes were made in the home staples at that time. Queenborough was substituted for Sandwich,[6] and Ipswich and Melcombe were again omitted.[7] The last two ports were again added in 1370.[7] The foreign staple in addition to the home staples was established once more at Calais in April, 1370, as is clear from orders to the collectors of the customs,[8] from the fact that in the customs records the shipments to Calais are entered separately from those to other ports, and from the imposition, first of additional customs on native shipments,[9] and later of 19*d.* per sack on all wool taken elsewhere.[10] There was, however, some difficulty in enforcing the use of Calais as a staple, a fact which destroys to a great extent the force of the reply to the Hanseatic protest against the collection of the 19*d.* per sack on

---

[9] *Rot. Parl.* ii, 288. *Fait a remembrer, qe est acorde et assentu qe une estaple soit a Melcombe de novel et une autre a Gippewicz, outre les plas limitez en l'Estatut de l'Estaple.*

[1] Cf. A. L. Jenckes, *The Origin, The Organization and the Location of the Staple of England* (Philadelphia, 1908), p. 49: ' There is no indication of the establishment of home staples at this time.'

[2] PRO L.T.R. Customs Roll 8, *passim.*

[3] Ipswich, 25 May, PRO L.T.R. Customs Roll 8, m. 52. Melcombe, 27 June, *ibid.*, 14, m. 52.

[4] *C.F.R. 1356–69*, p. 306.

[5] *Rot. Parl.* ii, 301; Stat. i, 390; *C.F.R. 1369–77*, p. 11.

[6] The staple had been moved from Sandwich to Queenborough 26 July, 1368. PRO Staple Roll 22. Cf. Appendix C. The staple towns were Newcastle, Kingston upon Hull, Boston, Yarmouth, Queenborough, Westminster, Chichester, Winchester, Exeter, and Bristol. *Stat.* i, 390.

[7] PRO L.T.R. Customs Roll 8, m. 52*d; ibid.* 14, m. 52.

[8] *C.C.R. 1369–74*, pp. 192, 434; *C.F.R. 1369–77*, p. 170.

[9] In 1371–72 English merchants paid at the same rate as aliens on wool taken to Flemish or other ports, although aliens paid no additional customs on such wool. PRO L.T.R. Customs Roll 8, *passim; C.F.R. 1369–77*, p. 151.

[10] PRO L.T.R. Customs Roll 8, *passim.*

wool taken elsewhere, for the reply asserted that the staples had been established at the request of the merchants, who therefore should not complain of additional fees imposed for the privilege of not using them.[1] In November, 1373, Lynn was made a staple port.[2] Calais remained the sole foreign staple until 1383,[3] although much of the wool, especially that of aliens, was not taken to Calais. Many licenses were issued, to Italians in particular, who found it more convenient, even when licenses cost 11s. per sack,[4] to take wool direct to Lombardy.[5]

During the first period of the alien monopoly, 1353–56, foreign merchants seem to have taken from all ports the amount of wool normally shipped by both alien and English merchants. During the year's monopoly of 1369–70, however, except in the four ports, London, Boston, Yarmouth, and Southampton, where the trade of aliens was greatest, shipments dropped considerably. This may have been due to the plague or to the fact that in so short a time aliens were unable to take over the trade of native merchants. Only in one year throughout our entire period, in 1368–69, did aliens carry more than half the wool exported. During the remainder of the period they shipped usually between a fourth and a third, their total annual shipments varying usually according to the general variation in the total amount exported.[6]

As the tables in the appendix show, the chief ports used by aliens for the exportation of wool were, in order of importance, London,

---

[1] P. 92 above.

[2] *Rot. Parl.* ii, 318.

[3] Location of the staple 1350–77:

1340–August 1353	Bruges
August 1353–March 1363	England
March 1363–February 1365	Calais
February 1365–June 1369	England and Calais.
June 1369–April 1370	England
April 1370–1383	England and Calais

There were, therefore, home staples for about ten and a half years, a foreign staple for five and three-quarters years and home and foreign staples simultaneously for ten and a half years.

[4] See p. 43 below.

[5] *C.F.R. 1369–77*, pp. 161, 171, 182, 193–95.

[6] Cf. p. 160 below.

Boston, Yarmouth, Southampton, and Hull. From the first four, where the trade of aliens was greatest, they shipped in some years more wool than English merchants carried. From Southampton for five years and a half, from Boston for five years, from London for three years, and from Yarmouth for two years and a half they exported more than half the wool.[1] In the other ports, the amount of alien shipments, when there was free competition with English merchants, was small and in most places almost negligible. From the south coast ports, with the exception of Southampton, and from Newcastle and Ipswich, aliens exported little wool after 1370. In fact during the last two years of Edward III's reign almost all the wool shipped by aliens was carried through London, Boston, Yarmouth, and Hull. In Bristol, however, at the end of the reign the trade of aliens was increasing. Although earlier in this period, as far as we can tell, they took almost no wool from that port, at the end of the period, the little which was exported from Bristol was taken by aliens.

Compared with the wool trade, the cloth trade was subject to little regulation. Efforts were made to restrict the exportation, of worsteds especially, and to compel the carriage of cloth to Calais, but these regulations seem to have had little effect.[2] In 1363, an attempt was made to restrict the exportation of woollens to Hansards and Gascons, the latter taking cloth in exchange for wine,[3] but this restriction seems not to have been strictly enforced. We are, unfortunately, unable to make an accurate estimate of the amount of cloth exported from England or of aliens' share in the shipment of it after 1362, because in that year the entire cloth custom in Yarmouth, an important port, especially for the export of worsteds, was farmed for the remainder of our period[4] and no returns were made by the farmers for the amount of customs collected or of the goods

[1] Southampton	Boston	London	Yarmouth
Mich. 1368–29 Dec. 1374	1362–63	1363–64	1370–71
	1368–69	1368–69	27 Nov. 1376–Feb. 1378
	1372–75	1371–72	

[2] *Rot. Parl.* ii, 275; *C.C.R. 1360–64*, pp. 436, 542; *C.P.R. 1374–77*, p. 441; *Cal. Letter Book H*, p. 31.

[3] *Rot. Parl.* ii, 276.

[4] *C.F.R. 1356–68*, pp. 214, 292; *ibid. 1369–77*, p. 133.

shipped. Although aliens carried a very small amount of cloth from Yarmouth during the years up to 1362, it is idle to speculate whether or how long this state of things continued. After 1377, the Hansards seem to have gained a predominating part in the Yarmouth trade,[1] but at what time after 1362 this occurred it is impossible to say. After 1372, records for all ports, except London, are lacking, because the cloth custom, together with the petty customs and the cloth subsidy, was farmed to Richard Lyons until 1376.[2] Whatever conclusions about the cloth trade in all ports we are able to draw must apply, therefore, only to the period from 1350 to 1362 when aliens carried between one-third and one-ninth of the cloth exported.[3] For the following decade we can consider the shipments from the separate ports only, and after 1372, there are no available figures for any part of the cloth trade.

From English ports as a whole, alien merchants shipped less cloth (as distinct from worsteds) than native merchants, but in Boston and London, where alien trade was greatest, and from Newcastle, where the total export was small, they shipped the greater part of the cloth. Their shipments predominated in London and in Boston after 1356, except for three years in each port. The cloth trade from Yarmouth and from the south coast ports was very largely controlled by English merchants. Aliens' trade, as we should expect, was concentrated in the east coast ports. It expanded less rapidly than the entire export trade in cloth, and seems to have been subject to less violent variations than the trade of native merchants. A large part of the aliens' trade was controlled by Hansards, in the east coast ports especially. In Boston, after 1362, Hansards' shipments equaled those of all other aliens and of English merchants together, the former, however, being few. From Hull Hansards exported more cloth than other aliens but the total alien export was small. From London and from other ports, they exported comparatively little.[4]

[1] H. L. Gray, 'The Production and Exportation of English Woollens in the Fourteenth Century,' *E.H.R.* xxxix (1924), 35, Table III.

[2] John Hedington was associated with him for the first year. *C.F.R. 1369–77*, pp. 197, 198, 227, 231, 273, 316; *C.P.R. 1370–74*, pp. 383, 384; *ibid. 1374–77*, pp. 48, 49, 206.

[3] Cf. p. 177 below.

[4] Cloth exported by Hansards was not always separated from what was imported when both were charged at the same rate.

It is impossible to find out the number of worsteds exported after 1361, because after that year Hansards paid only the 3*d.* in the pound of the petty custom on them, and this was accounted for with the remainder of the petty custom. The farming of the cloth customs in Yarmouth in 1362, moreover, leaves us without records for a port which was exporting more worsteds than any other, and therefore without any idea of the total number of worsteds exported exclusive of Hansard shipments. Until 1362, however, aliens shipped few worsteds from Yarmouth. London was apparently the only port from which they exported many worsteds and from it they usually carried more than English merchants exported. It is possible that the number of worsteds exported by Hansards from Boston might increase alien shipments considerably, because Hanseatic cloth trade centered there, but when they stopped paying the custom of 1347, their shipments of worsteds were customed with general merchandise. Until 1361, aliens exported between one-third and one-ninth of the worsteds.

The importation of cloth was naturally diminishing. Whatever cloth aliens brought, they carried principally to London and to Boston, bringing little to Yarmouth, Hull, and Sandwich, and almost none to other ports. The impossibility of separating the cloth exported by Hansards from that imported by all aliens, and the fact that English merchants paid no customs on imported cloth, prevents our finding out the total importation of cloth. It was, however, of little importance either in the trade or in the customs revenue of the fourteenth century. The exportation of English woollens was the growing trade of this period, and from its beginning it had been in the hands of English merchants. The Hansards alone were their serious rivals, but only in Hull and Boston. Aliens' share in the exportation of both cloth and worsteds was never large. From 1352 to 1362 alien shipments varied from one-third to one-ninth of the total.

In the wine trade, aliens enjoyed, in the matter of customs, a considerable advantage over English merchants,[1] which monopolies and trading privileges were constantly increasing. Throughout most of the period from 1350 to 1377, English merchants were put under

---

[1] See p. 54 below.

various restrictions. According to the frequently re-enacted law of 1353, they were permitted to go to Gascony only at the time of vintage and then only to certain ports, Bordeaux, Bayonne, and Libourne.[1] During two periods native trade was even more restricted. From 1363 until January, 1365, Englishmen were permitted to engage in only one kind of trade, with the result that all but vintners were excluded from the wine trade.[2] In May, 1368, English merchants were forbidden to go to Gascony,[3] and although the law was suspended in the next year, a very definite restriction was contained in the new law which provided that all Englishmen trading with Gascony must give security to import not less than one hundred tuns.[4]

In spite of these restrictions, however, English merchants' share in the wine trade increased during this period. By comparing the returns for the subsidies of 1350–51 and 1371–72, paid by aliens and natives, with the butler's accounts for alien shipments during the same years, it becomes evident that, whereas at the earlier date aliens carried about one-fourth of the wine, in 1371–72 they carried only one-fifth. A permanent decrease in their trade came after 1362. Aliens carried their wine chiefly to London, Southampton, and Sandwich, with only occasional large shipments to Bristol, Hull, and Boston, as in 1355–56, when there was not an increase in the whole amount imported, but when large quantities usually taken to one port were distributed among other ports. English merchants, on the other hand, seem to have taken large quantities to the east coast ports as well as to the more convenient ones in the south.

For general merchandise imported and exported, the enrolment of the petty custom is practically continuous from 1351 to 1372,[5] but there are very few particulars of accounts to supply details about the

---

[1] *Stat.* i, 331, 383, 384; Simon, *The History of the Wine Trade*, i, 212.

[2] *Rot. Parl.* ii, 278, 286.

[3] *Stat.* i, 389; *C.C.R. 1364–68*, pp. 75, 76.

[4] *Stat.* i, 391. Since the names of the merchants importing wine are not given in the returns for all ports for the subsidy of 1371–72, it is impossible to discover whether this was enforced. It would scarcely seem that it was, although a petition against it was refused in the parliament of November, 1372. *Rot. Parl.* ii, 315.

[5] The petty custom at Yarmouth was farmed in 1362, and at Ipswich in 1364. *C.F.R. 1356–68*, p. 214; PRO L.T.R. Customs Roll 9, m. 27.

trade. Furthermore, no comparison between alien and native shipments can be made. The petty custom was paid only by aliens;
therefore no record of the goods carried by English merchants was
kept, except when a subsidy was collected from both foreign and
native shippers.[1] Several such subsidies were imposed during this
period, but the information we have about them is of little use for
our present purpose. Returns for the subsidy of 1350–51 exist, but the
accounts for the petty custom for that year are lacking because the
customs were farmed. We can learn, therefore, from the subsidy returns only the total value of general merchandise carried by all
merchants. The subsidy of 1360 was granted to the mayor of London, who made no returns for it.[2] Since the subsidy of 1371–72 was
on cloth as well as on general merchandise,[3] it is impossible to separate the value of one from the other. After 1372, the petty custom
and the subsidy were both farmed,[4] although there are a few returns
for London in 1375.

In 1350–51, the merchandise imported and exported by English
merchants and aliens was valued at just over £47,500. Two years
later, aliens alone were carrying goods valued at £33,000, and the
value of general merchandise imported and exported by them seems
to have increased, as annual valuations at five year intervals show:

1357–58	£38,000
1362–63	£40,500[5]
1367–68	£51,500.[6]

The principal ports through which such merchandise was carried
were, in order of importance, London, Boston, Hull, Southampton,
and Newcastle. Very little was carried elsewhere.

The number of alien merchants trading in England at any time
during this period cannot be estimated, because of the lack of sources
from which such information can be obtained. It was, no doubt, usual

[1] For rates of custom and subsidies, see p. 52 below.

[2] See p. 44, n. 6 below.

[3] *C.F.R. 1369–77*, pp. 141, 210; PRO L.T.R. Customs Roll 5, m. 23.

[4] *C.F.R. 1369–77*, pp. 197, 198, 227, 231, 273, 316.

[5] This does not include the goods carried through Yarmouth. In 1359–60, before the Yarmouth customs were farmed, the total value of merchandise carried was £47,000.

[6] This does not include returns for Yarmouth and Ipswich.

for merchants to secure letters of protection as passports for enter-
ing the country,[1] but these were not always enrolled on the patent
rolls. Certificates of hosting, such as are found in the next century,
were apparently not made during this period, although we find evidence that, in spite of protests to the contrary,[2] the law that aliens
should not live where they would or keep hostels, but should go to
host, was not a dead letter. The *Letter Books* of London contain
fourteenth-century rules for hostellers.[3] Elsewhere there are orders
for hosts to seize the goods of an alien guest who has committed an
offense,[4] and complaints that a host had opened the goods of his
guest before the customs were paid.[5] The Hansards had their own
guildhall and hostels where they lived but some of them seem to
have gone to host, because in 1365 it was ordained that half of the
3*d.* per tun tax on woad payable by the merchants was to be given
to 'those hosts who are of the freedom of the city and in whose
houses the said merchants are received.'[6] The other half went to the
sheriffs. No records, however, of the number of aliens who went to
host seem to have survived, if indeed any were kept. The list of aliens
assessed for the fifteenth of 1343 would be an invaluable piece of evidence, if it existed. We have now only a few references to it and the
names of a very few merchants who protested against the taxation.[7]
Not until 1448 do we get such lists.[8]

The particulars of the customs provide some information concerning the number of merchants who shipped goods through the

[1] In 1342, ships of merchants of Estland, 'which is a friendly country and they lawful
merchants and of good fame,' were arrested because the merchants were aliens and did not
show letters of conduct. *Calendar of Inquisitions (Chancery) 1309–49*, p. 451.

[2] E.g., in 1376, the commons and the city of London protested that aliens stayed as long
as they pleased, kept hostels, and received whomever they pleased, including spies. *Rot. Parl.*
ii, 332, 347.

[3] *Cal. Letter Book G*, pp. 33, 149, 182.

[4] *C.C.R. 1354–60*, p. 367.

[5] *C.C.R. 1354–60*, p. 337.

[6] *Cal. Letter Book G*, p. 67.

[7] See p. 74 below.

[8] M. S. Giuseppi, 'Alien Merchants in England in the Fifteenth Century,' *Trans. Royal
Hist. Soc.* (New Series), IX (1895), 75–98. Even at this later date, these records are very incomplete. There are certificates of hosting for only three ports, and subsidy returns for four
ports.

various ports. The account for the custom on wool exported from London during the year from Michaelmas 1365, for example, gives the names of 129 aliens.[1] During the following year, twenty-five aliens brought wine to London;[2] and the account for the subsidy collected on wine in all ports in 1371–72 also gives twenty-five names, but the individual importers are not given for all ports and some are put down as *Johannes de Burdeux et socii sui*.[3] Not enough customs accounts of this kind have survived however, for the years between 1350 and 1377[4] to enable us to make even an estimate of the number of aliens importing and exporting, and it is also by no means certain or likely that all whose goods were customed came to England.

No lists of the members of foreign companies trading in England have been found, and since the personnel of the companies changed frequently, it is probable that no such registers were kept either by the companies or by the English government. The German Hanse either could not or would not give even a list of its member cities, although the English authorities asked repeatedly for one.[5] A few figures can be found throughout the documents of the period, but they are of more use as illustrations than as statistics. About thirty Hansards are mentioned in connection with the confiscation of their goods in 1351.[6] A letter of protection issued in 1352 to merchants of Lucca and their associates mentions fifteen by name,[7] and twelve of the same company appeared as mainpernours for Nicholas Sardouche in 1369.[8]

The number of merchants of whose nationality we can be sure

---

[1] PRO K.R. Customs 70/18. In 1443–44, according to the Mayor's certificates for hosting, there were 185 aliens in London, not including galley men. Between 1453 and 1471, there were from six to eighteen alien householders and twenty-eight to 105 non-householders, not including French and including only those aliens who remained more than six weeks. Giuseppi, *op. cit.* pp. 86–93.

[2] PRO K.R. Accounts, Various, Butlerage, 80/18.

[3] *Ibid.*, 80/22.

[4] See p. 139 below.

[5] W. Stein, 'Die Hansestädte,' *Hansische Geschichtsblätter*, XIX (1913), 239.

[6] *C.C.R. 1349–54*, pp. 321–23, 384–86; Kunze, *Hanseakten aus England*, pp. 147, 149, 151–52.

[7] *C.P.R. 1350–54*, p. 344.

[8] PRO Coram Rege Roll 433, m. 19 Rex.

is small. From documents of all kinds we learn the names of a considerable number of merchants, but seldom do we find both name and nationality given. Apart from those merchants who, like the Hansards and the Lombards, acquired something like individuality by reason of their connection with a famous company, or because of their services to the king, or because of the frequency with which their names and causes appear on the plea rolls of the period, few aliens can be identified even as of one country or another.[1] We are, furthermore, unable to discover what proportion of the alien merchants in England came from any one country. This can be shown by one typical example. Among the 129 aliens exporting wool from London in 1365–66,[2] only seventeen can be certainly identified. Nine were Italians, six were Flemish, and two were Germans. We find indications, however, that merchants from the Lombard and Hanseatic cities were the most influential and possibly the most numerous. When representatives of the merchants were summoned before the council in 1353, the group included, in addition to seventy English merchants, twelve aliens, of whom four were Germans and eight were Italians.[3] The Ordinance of the Staple, of the same year, provided that the body which was to settle disputes in the staples was to consist of two English merchants, two Germans, and two Lombards.[4]

Although we cannot even estimate the number of alien merchants in England in the fourteenth century, we have, in the enrolled customs accounts, a means of finding out what is more valuable—the

[1] Even with these aids, the task of identification has its pitfalls. Errors were sometimes made in giving the city from which a well-known alien came, as when Francis Bochel and Francis Bandini, both of Lucca, were said to be merchants of Genoa. PRO K.R. Mem. 130, Communia Pasch. Some Englishmen, moreover, whose families possibly were of foreign origin, retained a foreign surname, like Simon of Almain who was a prominent citizen of Norwich and not a German. Others had the same names as contemporary aliens, for John Fraunceys, sheriff and Mayor of London, and John Fraunceys of the society of the Bardi must have been different persons. Cf. also p. 13, n. 7 above.

[2] PRO K.R. Customs, 70/18.

[3] *C.C.R. 1349–54*, p. 605.

[4] *Rot. Parl.* ii, 251. The financial preeminence of the Lombards rather than their greater numerical strength is evident in recognizances and suits for debt, in which they appear more frequently than merchants of other nationalities. There are in these records a few Flemings, a few Gascons, and fewer Germans.

relative positions of alien and of English merchants in English foreign trade. The latter were well in control of the trade. Of the chief article of export, wool, aliens carried about one-third. They imported between one-fourth and one-fifth of the wine. During the decade from 1350 to 1360 they exported on an average of one-fifth of the English-made cloth which was taken to the continent. Alien competition[1] was salutory to trade, and the creation of alien monopolies, especially in the exportation of wool, was profitable to the government. Alien ships were useful, particularly in time of war, when they could be seized along with English ships to make up the English navy.[2] But at no time during our period did aliens threaten the supremacy of English merchants in the English foreign trade, although no great decrease or fluctuation in alien trade is apparent. The real value of any survey of this sort will be seen, however, only when it can be compared with conclusions drawn from other periods.

[1] Differences in customs rates and in commercial privileges for aliens and natives made partnerships between the two groups of merchants usually impossible. Their association in importing and exporting was confined chiefly to smuggling and the illegal avowal of each other's goods. Occasionally we find aliens and natives owning a ship jointly. Ship-masters and merchants were usually distinct groups, although merchants sometimes owned their own ships. One of these merchant ship-owners, John Bridport, citizen of London, who was part owner of a ship with John Gyles of Flanders, (*Cal. Mayor's Letters, London*, p. 81) also hired foreign ships. The indenture made on one occasion with the owner of a ship is preserved among the muniments of Westminster Abbey and is printed here, in the appendix, as an example of arrangements made in the fourteenth century for carrying goods. See Appendix D.

[2] Imports and exports were carried indiscriminately in native or foreign-owned ships. An attempt was made in 1367 to enforce a navigation act, but the order to use only English ships for carrying goods was revoked within a month. *C.C.R. 1364–68*, p. 319. Ships used in the carrying trade were usually from 20 to 200 tons burden, and shipments of any one commodity in one vessel were not large. Mention is made of two small ships under sixteen tons burden. *C.P.R. 1361–64*, p. 424. That ships much over 100 tons were not usual in the smaller ports seems to be implied in the order to allow the *George* of Exmouth of 140 tons burden to be unloaded elsewhere than at Topsham, because the entrance to that port was so narrow that the *George* 'could not come to the place without great detriment.' *C.P.R. 1364–67*, p. 167. The use of merchant ships for naval defense was one of the reasons why piracy throve to such an extent that the merchant was often indistinguishable from the pirate. The king was willing to come to terms with those who harried even his allies in order to secure their support against his enemies. This is seen in pardons issued to those who had robbed foreign ships. In 1342 pardon was granted to mariners and others of the realm who robbed ships coming to Flanders, for which deed the king had to make restitution of a great sum of money, if they 'will go at once with their ships with Robert de Morle, admiral of the fleet from the mouth of the Thames northwards, or not having ships will go in the company, well found for war at their own charges, for two months upon the sea in defence of the realm and offence of the king's enemies.' *C.P.R. 1340–43*, p. 469. During the next year, five individuals were pardoned because each had furnished two ships for the king's service, e.g., *C.P.R. 1343–45*, p. 21.

III

THE ECONOMIC PRIVILEGES AND DISA-
BILITIES OF ALIEN MERCHANTS

THE economic status of alien merchants in England was determined by the commercial privileges they enjoyed and by the
restrictions imposed upon them to make their presence profitable
to the government and less objectionable to English merchants.
Their legal status was defined by personal privileges and by the
right of access to various courts granted them in order to make
trade possible and attractive. We shall consider first their economic
position and see what opinions about alien merchants different
groups in the community held and how these opinions were reflected
in the regulation of aliens' trade, especially in the customs rates
levied on the goods they carried.

It was one of the axioms of fourteenth-century English commercial policy that the coming of aliens was for the good of the realm.[1]
This point of view was expressed and reiterated in statutes[2] and in
petitions in parliament,[3] on customs rolls[4] and in letters of protection
to the aliens themselves.[5] It can usually be interpreted to mean that
they were a financial asset. The king, parliament, and even the English merchants recognized the varied usefulness of alien merchants,
and were willing to encourage them as importers and exporters in
order to profit by them politically and financially.

Although Edward III had less need now than in the earlier part
of his reign for making commercial concessions to the merchants of
those countries whose aid he wanted in the war with France, his

---

[1] *C.P.R. 1354–58*, p. 594; *Memorials of London*, p. 270.

[2] *Rot. Parl.* ii, 251.

[3] *Ibid.*, p. 258; *Stat.* i, 347; *C.P.R. 1350–54*, p. 514.

[4] PRO L.T.R. Customs Roll 8, m. 1. 'Considerantes utile et expediens esse nobis et toti
regno nostro quod mercatores alienigene dictum regnum nostrum frequentantes in eodem
regno favorabiliter pertractentur ut habundancius merces suas deferant infra idem regnum.

[5] *C.P.R. 1354–58*, p. 594.

commercial treaties with Genoa and Venice and the special protection offered to their merchants were attempts to secure the support of their naval power. Financially foreign merchants were useful to the king in several ways. He exacted higher customs from them than from English merchants, in return for the privilege of trading in England, and he frequently increased the revenue from the customs still more by putting the entire trade in some commodity, usually wool, into the hands of aliens.[1] They were also the principal financial agents in the kingdom, both because they were still the chief money-lenders, although they no longer contributed enormous sums for the king's private and public needs as they had done in the earlier part of the reign, and because of their widespread connections on the continent. There was every reason why the king should find their coming 'for the good of his realm,' and should grant them protection and privileges.

Parliament, in its dealings with aliens, was usually dominated by the policy of the king and the non-municipal group, on whose favor foreigners were dependent for their privileges, which they were willing to procure by making loans to the magnates, by paying increased customs, and by various commercial services. In return, parliament granted them trading privileges within the country, and thus used them to offset the powerful local mercantile interests.[2] In addition, petitions for the improvement of conditions unfavorable to aliens were usually granted. Thus, when lawlessness and brigandage throughout the country caused complaints that trade was hampered, an order was issued that, 'considering the profit in the coming of aliens,' the Statute of Winchester should be enforced and offenders brought to justice within forty days.[3] Again, in 1369, after commissions had been appointed to make a census of aliens living in the country, they were recalled at the request of the commons, because they were annoying to the foreigners.[4] Only for brief periods did parliament heed the complaints of London, which had been recur-

[1] See p. 25 above. The alien monopoly from 1352 to 1356, for example, must have meant an increase of almost £16,000, if the customs were collected in full. Cf. tables of wool exported. Appendix C.

[2] See p. 56 below.

[3] *Stat.* i, 347; *C.P.R. 1350–54*, p. 514.

[4] *Rot. Parl.* ii, 300.

rent with every grant of privilege to aliens, and curtail the latter's rights.[1] Even London, however, had long found the coming of aliens useful, by arranging for the repair and part of the defense of Bishopsgate first by the Danes and more recently by the Hansards.[2] Furthermore, fifty marks had been remitted in the farm of the city on several occasions when the payment of that amount by the woad merchants of Amiens had ceased because of the war.[3] The mayor of London was said 'to receive his chief emolument from merchant strangers' and in 1339 Reginald de Conduit was granted the rent of certain properties in consideration of his losses in two years in which he was mayor because the war prevented foreigners from coming to the city.[4] The same attitude toward aliens is seen in connection with their coming to fairs. In 1363, it was said that the fair of St Ives had not been held for twenty years, and the arrears of tolls were pardoned because 'alien merchants by whose coming to fairs most of the profits of the same were derived, have kept away from fairs and still keep away and so they have taken no toll in that time.'[5] The fact that numerous people were indicted for riot at the fair of St Ives as recently as 1350[6] seems to belie this statement, but does not destroy the argument that aliens as transient merchants were welcomed in England by practically all groups. As the customs accounts prove, there was no real reason why English merchants should have feared alien competition.[7]

We may inquire what was asked of alien merchants in return for this friendly attitude which assured to them the privilege of coming to England and, as we shall see later, granted them justice in the king's courts and rights in private law sufficient to protect their persons and property. The answer can be found by examination of the customs rates and trade regulations imposed upon aliens. In general it may be said that after 1303, except for short periods during the

---

[1] *C.P.R. 1374–77*, p. 389.

[2] *Liber Albus*, p. 485; A. Bugge, 'Die nordeuropäischen Verkehrswege im frühen Mittelalter', *Vierteljahrschrift für Social- und Wirtschaftsgeschichte*, IV (Leipzig, 1906), 263.

[3] *C.C.R. 1339–41*, p. 29; PRO K.R. Mem. 116, Brevia directa Mich.

[4] *C.P.R. 1338–40*, p. 389.

[5] *C.P.R. 1361–64*, p. 428.

[6] *C.P.R. 1348–50*, p. 550.

[7] Cf. Chap II above.

reign of Edward II, when the *Carta Mercatoria* was suspended, no commodity was imported or exported by aliens free of customs duty, and throughout the latter part of Edward III's reign, there were few years when an additional subsidy was not imposed on all articles except woollen cloth.[1] Also, aliens usually paid duty at a higher rate than English merchants. Whether this distinction had any effect on aliens' trade in the fourteenth century, it is impossible to say. There seems to have been no contemporary objection to the practice, although it was necessary to take precautions to prevent one group from avowing the goods of the other. It was not until the next century that the deterrent effect which such inequalities must ultimately have on the coming of aliens was emphasized.

Articles of commerce fell, for purposes of taxation into four groups: wool, 'la sovereine marchandise et jewel de son Roialme de Engleterre,'[2] with its associated commodities, woolfells and hides; woollen cloth and worsteds; wine; and general merchandise, which included all other imports and exports from spices to live stock.[3]

On wool, woolfells and hides, aliens paid a triple duty. In common with native merchants, they paid the *antiqua custuma* of 1275: one half mark or 6s. 8d. on every sack of wool and every 300 woolfells, and one mark on every last of hides.[4] After 1303, according to

---

[1] Only once during this period was a subsidy imposed on woollen cloth imported or exported. Cf. p. 33 above. After 1353, a subsidy was collected on cloth sold within the country. A specific tax of 4d. per cloth on undyed, 5d. on partly dyed, and 6d. on dyed cloth was collected from alien merchants and English alike, in addition to the ulnage fee of ½d. This subsidy was usually farmed but some returns for it are found on the customs rolls. Only in the accounts for London were alien payments recorded separately from those of English merchants. See H. L. Gray, 'The Production and Exportation of English Woollens in the 14th Century,' *E.H.R.* xxxix (1924), 13–35, for an examination of these accounts and for tables of cloth sold.

[2] *Rot. Parl.* ii, 246.

[3] It included all cloth other than woollen and worsted, such as linen, silk, velvet, cloth of gold. Wax was taxed separately at the rate of 1 shilling per quintal, according to the *Carta Mercatoria*.

[4] PRO L.T.R. Customs Roll 8 *passim*. After 1368, 240 woolfells were considered the equivalent of one sack of wool. According to the *Assisa de Ponderibus et Mensuris*, a last of hides contained twenty dickers each containing ten hides (i.e., 200 hides) *Stat.* i, 205. Ducange, referring to this same source, has twelve dickers. According to a customs document of 1323, printed by Gras, p. 209, the last was 200 hides at that time. The *N.E.D.* gives the same, and also twelve dozen hides as a last.

the terms of the *Carta Mercatoria* to which native merchants refused
to subscribe, aliens paid an additional quarter mark or 3*s*. 4*d*. on wool
and woolfells and a half mark on hides.[1] They therefore paid 10*s*. in
customs on wool and woolfells and £1 on hides. In addition to this, a
subsidy, granted at intervals throughout the period by parliaments,
councils, or merchant assemblies, was imposed. The wool subsidy
had been, in origin, an emergency levy, imposed for a limited period
for some special purpose like financing a campaign or equipping of a
naval force to protect commerce. By this time, it had, like the war,
become practically continuous, but the controversy as to its legality,
and as to whose was the power to impose it still raged, with the advantage now definitely on the side of parliament.[2] Except for a few
unusual months during 1350 when it was 62*s*., the subsidy varied
from 20*s*. to 43*s*. 4*d*. per sack, making a combined customs and subsidy rate of 30*s*. to 53*s*. 4*d*.[3] Several small additional charges were
connected with the shipment of wool. For affixing the cocket seal,
the receipt for the customs, 2*d*. per shipment was paid by each merchant.[4] A fee was paid for weighing the wool, the tronage, which
varied in different ports from $\frac{1}{2}d$.[5] to $2\frac{1}{2}d$.[6] per sack. This, however,
does not always appear in the customs accounts since it was fre-
quently granted to individuals.[7] From 1371 to 1376, part of the time

---

[1] PRO L.T.R. Customs Roll 9 *passim;* Gras, p. 262, c. 15.

[2] In 1362 and again in 1371, parliament secured the sole right to impose a subsidy on
wool. *Rot. Parl.* ii, 271, 308. Stubbs, ii, 434.

[3] See p. 45 below for schedule of rates.

[4] PRO L.T.R. Customs Roll 8 *passim.* For examples of one kind of cocket, see Gras, p.
144, n. 2. In 1357, collectors of customs were ordered to put in letters of cocket their own
names, the names of subcollectors, 'inserting the nature of the things, the price or value
thereof, from what ship they were received, the class of goods and the amounts of custom so received, in true and full Latin phrases.' They were to have no additions after the date, no
erasures or interlineation and were to be sealed with green wax. *C.C.R. 1354–60,* p. 342. The
term cocket was also applied to receipts and indentures relating to other commodities than
wool. Hale, *Concerning the Customs,* p. 102; *Cal. Early Mayor's Court Rolls,* p. 184, n. 1. The
documents called cockets in the index to the K.R. Customs accounts include a great variety of
receipts, with various kinds of seals. The cockets for the petty custom were to be sealed with
the petty seal on the back of the cocket seal. *C.C.R. 1354–60,* p. 338. For examples of this for 8
Henry IV, see PRO K.R. Customs 72/16. There are no accounts for payments for cockets
other than those for wool, for our period.

[5] PRO L.T.R. Customs Roll 8, m. 63 New Castle.

[6] *Ibid.,* Roll 14, m. 27 Lynn.

that the staple was at Calais, 19*d.*, called 'Calais money,' was collected in England for each sack of wool or its equivalent number of fells taken elsewhere than to the staple. This was to recompense the staplers in Calais for the loss of port dues said to be equal to that amount.[1] During those years, as at other times when the staple was on the continent, wool could be taken elsewhere only by special license, for which, as was said in 1376, in the course of a parliamentary investigation, merchants, voluntarily and without compulsion, paid as much as 11*s.* per sack.[2]

There were few exceptions and no preferential rates in the payment of the wool custom. The king's wool, by whomever taken, was free of duty. Exemption from paying the whole or a part of the customs and subsidy was frequently granted in payment of the king's debts, or as recompense for damage done by the king's subjects.[3] The usual export duties on wool were high. As far as a cautious generalization is possible when port charges varied and subsidies changed, it seems that aliens paid on every sack exported approximately from $33\frac{1}{3}$ per cent, when customs and subsidy were 30*s.*, to 50 per cent when they were 53*s.* 4*d.*, if we take the average price of a sack of wool to be between £5 and £6.[4] If, however, as Knighton

---

[7] *Ibid.*, Roll 8, m. 55 Hull. In only two ports, Boston and Chichester, is it given on the customs roll for the entire period.

[1] They were 4*d.* for custom of entry, 10*d.* for custom of export and 5*d.* for profits of siegneurage of the mint. *C.F.R. 1369–77*, p. 145.

[2] *Rot. Parl.* ii, 326. See Appendix C for amount taken to Calais and elsewhere. Native merchants sometimes paid alien rates for the privilege of not going to the staple. Any increase in port charges was usually a matter for protest. In 1364 petition was made against the payment of 40*d.* per sack in Calais. *Rot. Parl.* ii, 287. Similarly, in 1376 objection was made to an increase in tronage and incidental charges in London, *ibid.*, p. 351. The reply to each petition simply condemned unreasonable and unusual customs. In 1376 Hansards had to protest against the taking of 6*d.* for every man in the ship as a fee for the cocket. *Hanserecesse*, iii, 304, c. 6.

[3] Customs were sometimes paid in advance as a loan and the wool was then exported free, e.g., *C.C.R. 1354–60*, pp. 160, 252. In 1350 exemption from the subsidy on merchandise brought from Norway was granted to the masters of four ships of Almain, to whom the king wished to show favor. *C.C.R. 1349–54*, p. 167.

[4] *C.P.R. 1334–38*, p. 480. Cheap wool, such as the three sacks seized at Pevensey in 1349 and said to be worth in all £8, might be subject to a duty of almost 100 per cent. PRO K.R. Mem. 136. Wool bought at Lincoln in 1375 was worth £10 per sack. PRO Controlment Roll 28, m. 31d. The price of Lincolnshire wool had not changed much since 1337 when it was put at 10 marks. *C.P.R. ut supra.*

says, wool was sold for as much as £20 per sack on the continent, a large profit was possible.[1]

RATE OF SUBSIDIES ON WOOL 1350–1377

Michaelmas, 1348–Michaelmas, 1362	40/–	[2]
28 February, 1350–28 June, 1350	2/–	[3]
6 April, 1350–28 June, 1350	20/–	[4]
24 September, 1350–Michaelmas, 1351	2/–	[5]
24 January, 1360–26 June, 1360	2/–	[6]
Michaelmas, 1362–31 January, 1365	20/–	[7]
2 February, 1365–Michaelmas, 1368	40/–	[8]
Michaelmas, 1368–Michaelmas, 1369	38/8	[9]
Michaelmas, 1369–end of reign	43/4	[10]

[1] *Chronicon Henrici Knighton* (J. R. Lumby, ed., Rolls Series, 1889–95), ii, 2.

[2] Granted by merchants alien and denizen for three years from Michaelmas, 1348. *Rot. Parl.* ii, 201; *C.F.R. 1347–56*, pp. 134, 241. Farmed with the customs in 1348. *C.P.R. 1348–50*, p. 145. *C.C.R. 1346–49*, p. 248. Granted by parliament for two years from Michaelmas, 1351, *Rot. Parl.* ii, 229; PRO L.T.R. Customs Roll 5, m. 16: *C.F.R. 1347–56*, p. 312. Renewed by great council for one year, or if war continued, for two years. *Rot. Parl.* ii, 252; *C.F.R. 1347–56*, p. 382. Renewed by parliament for six years. *Rot. Parl.* ii, 265; *Stat.* i, 351. Robert of Avesbury, *De Gestis Mirabilis Regis Edwardi Tertii* (E. M. Thompson, ed., Rolls Series, 1889), p. 431 has 50 shillings for six-years.

[3] Granted by merchants trading in the realm 'unanimously and spontaneously' for one year. *C.F.R. 1347–56*, p. 217. Ceased 28 June, 1350, because of truce. *C.C.R. 1349–54*, p. 241. It was combined with a subsidy of 12*d.* per tun on wine and 6*d.* in the pound on general merchandise.

[4] Granted by the council from 6 April until Michaelmas. *C.F.R. 1347–56*, p. 233; PRO L.T.R. Customs Roll 5, m. 1. Ceased 28 June because of truce. *C.C.R. 1349–54*, p. 237.

[5] Granted by merchants for one year from 24 September, 1350. *C.F.R. 1347–56*, p. 252. Extended to Michaelmas, 1351. *C.F.R. 1347–56*, p. 311. *Rot. Parl.* ii, 229; *C.C.R. 1349–54*, p. 327. It was combined with a subsidy of 40*d.* per tun on wine and 6*d.* in the pound on general merchandise.

[6] Granted by the magnates with the consent of merchants native and alien assembled for the purpose to be collected from December, 1359, until Michaelmas, 1360. It was levied for the protection of shipping and at first took the form of an *ad valorem* rate of 6*d.* in the pound on all merchandise. *C.C.R. 1354–60*, p. 600. In January, 1360, it was changed to 2*s.* per sack on wool, 2*s.* per tun on wine and 6*d.* in the pound on general merchandise. *C.C.R. 1354–60*, p. 601; *Foedera*, iii, 2, p. 496. Ceased 26 June, 1360, because of truce. *C.C.R. 1360–64*, p. 49. The accounts of this subsidy do not appear on the customs rolls because it was paid to the mayor and sheriffs of London, who were not required to render any account. *C.C.R. 1354–60*, p. 600.

[7] Granted by parliament for three years from Michaelmas, 1362. *Rot. Parl.* ii, 273; *C.F.R. 1356–69*, p. 251; *Chronicon Anglie*, p. 52. Ceased when all export ceased between 31 January and 2 February, 1365.

RATE OF CUSTOMS AND SUBSIDY ON WOOL
PAID BY ALIENS, 1350–1377

January, 1350–28 February, 1350	50/–
28 February, 1350–6 April, 1350	52/–
6 April, 1350–28 June, 1350	72/–
28 June, 1350–24 September, 1350	50/–
24 September, 1350–Michaelmas, 1351	52/–
Michaelmas, 1351–24 January, 1360	50/–
24 January, 1360–26 June, 1360	52/–
26 June, 1360–Michaelmas, 1362	50/–
Michaelmas, 1362–31 January, 1365	30/–
2 February, 1365–Michaelmas, 1368	50/–
Michaelmas, 1368–Michaelmas, 1369	48/8
Michaelmas, 1369–end of reign	53/4

After wool, woollen cloth was the most important article of commerce. It was divided into two classes for the purposes of taxation: cloth of foreign manufacture imported into or re-exported from England, and cloth, sometimes called cloth of assize, and worsteds made in England and carried abroad. Both, when taken by aliens, had, since 1303, been subject to the following customs:[1]

undyed cloth	1s. per cloth
partly dyed cloth	1s. 6d. "
dyed cloth	2s. "
worsteds	3d. in £.

In 1347, a new custom had been imposed on English woollens and worsteds exported by all merchants. For the first time native mer-

---

[8] Granted by parliament to be collected from 2 February, 1365 until the following Michaelmas and then for three years. *Rot. Parl.* ii, 285; *C.F.R. 1356–69*, p. 302.

[9] Granted by parliament to be collected from Michaelmas, 1368, for two years. *Rot. Parl.* ii, 295; *C.F.R. 1356–69*, p. 386. Ceased with the new grant in 1369.

[10] Granted by parliament to be collected from Michaelmas, 1369, for three years. *Rot. Parl.* ii, 300. Renewed for two years from Michaelmas, 1372. *Rot. Parl.* ii, 310, 317; *C.F.R. 1369–77*, p. 189. Renewed again for two years (for one year unconditionally, for two years if the war lasted). *C.F.R. 1369–77*, p. 260. Renewed again for three years *Rot. Parl.* ii, 322.

Note: The subsidies on wool and fells were doubled on hides, except that from Michaelmas, 1368 to the end of the reign the subsidy on hides was £4.

[1] Gras p. 263, cc. 16, 17, 18, 20.

chants were now asked to pay a cloth custom, but at a lower rate than aliens. The rates for aliens were as follows:[1]

undyed cloth	21*d*. per cloth
partly dyed cloth	2*s*. 7*d*. " [2]
dyed cloth	3*s*. 6*d*. "
worsteds	1½*d* and 3*d*.
bed cloths, single	7½*d*.
bed cloths, double	13½*d*.

It was no doubt the intention of the council which put the export custom on English cloth in 1347 that it should be for aliens an addition, not an alternative to the custom of 1303.[3] That it was not so regarded by the Hansards is well known, but the details and the length of the struggle to make good their claims have not always been emphasized. For that reason it is worth while to consider the question in detail here. The customs on three kinds of cloth were involved: cloth of assize, on which aliens were supposed to pay the custom of 1303 and the cloth custom of 1347; narrow cloth or short lengths and pieces, which, after 1347, were taxed proportionately according to the rate for whole cloths, in addition to the 3*d*. in the pound custom of 1303; and worsteds which were taxed at a specific rate after 1347 in addition to the *ad valorem* rate of 1303.[4] In 1348, shortly after the new cloth custom was imposed, the king issued an order to John Wesenham, the king's butler, and at that time the collector of the cloth custom, that worsteds exported by Hansards should be taxed at the rate of 3*d*. in the pound only.[5] In the customs account for London for Michaelmas 1358–59; it is specifically stated that there are no returns for worsteds taken by Hansards because

[1] *C.P.R. 1345–48*, p. 425; *C.P.R. 1348–50*, p. 201.

[2] This, according to the letters patent, should be 2*s*. 7½*d*. since it was said to be the moiety of the customs on dyed and undyed cloth, but the ½*d*. is ignored. Hale, *Concerning the Customs*, p. 167, gives 2*s*. 1*d*. as the rate for partly dyed cloth.

[3] Hale, *op. cit.*, p. 170. Customs collectors were appointed to collect the new customs of 1303, the customs on wool, hides and fells, the subsidy on wool, hides and fells and the 'customs on cloths of wool and worsted made in England for export.' *C.F.R. 1356–68*, p. 325: also pp. 21, 389.

[4] Cf. rates of customs on cloth, p. 45 above.

[5] Brit. Mus. Nero B x fo. 372. This is dated 20 January 1348. It was confirmed 3 February, 1348, *C.P.R. 1348–50*, p. 6.

such customs are contrary to their privileges as contained in the
Carta Mercatoria.[1] In the very next year, however, they were paying
1½*d.* on worsteds in London along with the additional custom on
narrow cloths.[2] The whole matter seems to have been under discussion at this time. On 16 May, 1358, it was stated that Hansards
should pay only 3*d.* in the pound on narrow cloths,[3] and on 16
October the collectors in Boston were ordered to take from them
only the 21*d.* of 1347 on cloth of assize and not the 12*d.* of 1303.[4]
That they paid only the later cloth custom on cloth of assize at least
from then until 1361 is evident from an entry on the customs rolls for
Hull in 1360,[5] and from an order to the treasurer and barons of the
exchequer to that effect, dated 7 February, 1361.[6] These rates received further confirmation in the decision in a case tried in the exchequer in the following April. The sheriffs of London had sued the
collectors of customs, holding them accountable for 12*d.* on cloth of
assize, 1½*d.* on worsteds, and 21*d.* on narrow cloths exported by Hansards.[7] The collectors maintained that according to the orders of 1358
and 1361, Hansards should pay 21*d.* on cloth of assize, 2*s.* on scarlet,
1*s.* 6*d.* on cloth of half grain and 3*d.* in the pound on narrow cloths
and worsteds. This they had collected as their rolls showed. They
were upheld in their position by the court.[8] Before this case was
heard, however, the whole question of the rate of customs paid by
the Hansards had been finally settled. An order of 8 February, 1361,
to the collectors in London stated that they were to pay only 12*d.* on
cloth of assize and not the additional 21*d.*[9] On 20 February, the treasurer and barons of the exchequer were informed that according to a

[1] PRO L.T.R. Customs Roll 7, m. 9.

[2] *Ibid.,* m. 9d.

[3] *C.C.R. 1354–60,* p. 448; *Hansisches Urkundenbuch,* III, 179.

[4] *C.C.R. 1354–60,* pp. 467, 518. *Hansisches Urkundenbuch,* III, 190. The merchants of
Aquitaine seem to have made a similar attempt to avoid paying double customs on cloth, but
were unsuccessful. *C.F.R. 1356–68,* p. 29; *C.C.R. 1354–60,* p. 287.

[5] PRO L.T.R. Customs Roll 7, m. 9d.; *ibid.* 9, m. 29.

[6] *Hansisches Urkundenbuch,* IV, 1; Kunze, *Hanseakten aus England,* p. xl.

[7] £58.7*s.* 6½*d.* was demanded of them for the year 1358–59. PRO K.R. Mem. 137, Communia Pasch.

[8] *Hansisches Urkundenbuch,* IV, 4.

[9] PRO L.T.R. Customs Roll 7, m. 9d, 10; *C.C.R. 1360–64,* p. 151; *Foedera,* iii, 2, p. 600;
Hansisches Urkundenbuch, IV, 1.

writ of 16 May, 1358, Hanseatic merchants were not to pay at the rate of 21*d*. on narrow cloths and pieces.[1] On 25 February, they were further informed that worsteds were to be taxed only at 3*d*. in the pound.[2] This exemption from the entire cloth custom of 1347 was hardly questioned for the rest of the reign.[3] It is interesting that after fourteen years of uncertainty the rates of the *Carta Mercatoria* should have been the ones decided upon, even when the Hansards would have paid the higher custom of 1347, their chief objection having been to paying twice on the same commodity.[4]

An examination of the enrolled customs accounts, reveals further variations, not noted elsewhere, in the amounts collected on English cloth, which were apparently not according to the nationality of the shippers, but according to the practice in the several ports. Whether this be due to the incomplete enrolment of the returns, or to incomplete returns by the collectors, or to uncorrected irregularities in the ports, the difference in customs on English cloth offers the sole example in this period of a variation in customs rate from one port to another.

The two cloth customs had not yet been consolidated. Both in the particulars sent up from the ports and in the exchequer enrolments, the custom of 1303 was accounted for with the petty custom,[5] while the cloth custom, properly so called, of 1347 was accounted for separately and enrolled for the most part on a separate roll.[6] If aliens had paid both customs, the amount of cloth which appears on roll 7, which contains returns for the cloth custom, customed at 21*d*. should also appear on roll 9, the enrolment of the petty custom, cus-

[1] PRO K.R. Mem. 137, Communia Pasch.

[2] Loc. cit.

[3] In Kingston 1369–70, 1371–2 Hansards are said to be paying 7½*d*. on single bed cloths, but this seems to be the only instance although one cannot be sure whether their worsteds and bed cloths are being accounted for among those taken by aliens or in the accounts of the 3*d*. in the pound custom. PRO L.T.R. Customs Roll 8, m. 57; *ibid*. 9, m. 31. One of the protests which received a favourable answer in 1375 was against paying at the higher rate on lengths of cloth. *Hanserecesse*, III, 302, cl. 4.

[4] PRO L.T.R. Customs Roll 9, m. 29.

[5] E.g., PRO K.R. Customs, 7/10.

[6] PRO L.T.R. Customs Roll 7. London, as usual, is the exception. The two customs are united in the enrolled accounts from 1361. Cf. p. 161 below.

tomed at 12*d*.[1] In the accounts for Newcastle, Yarmouth, Sandwich, Melcombe, and Ipswich there is no record of the collection of the 12*d*. of 1303. Except at Yarmouth, little cloth was exported from these ports and in all of them alien shipments were small. In the other ports, the 12*d*. custom was collected only in the following years:[2]

Hull	1352–1355; 1361–1362.
Boston	29 January, 1354–Michaelmas, 1354.
Lynn	1352–1353.
Chichester	1354–1361
Southampton	1353–1354; 1356–1360; 1361–1362.
Bristol	1352–1354.

In several instances it is specifically stated in the account for the 1303 custom that no cloth was exported during a period for which there are returns for the cloth custom.[3] In London both the 12*d*. and the 21*d*. customs were collected throughout the period but only 3*s*. 6*d*. was collected on dyed cloth and the unusual amount of 3*s*. 1½*d*. on partly dyed cloth.[4] In Southampton, moreover, from 1370 to 1372 English merchants paid 17½*d*. on undyed long cloth and 2*s*. 2¼*d*. on partly dyed long cloth and 2*s*. 11*d*., on scarlet long cloth, while aliens paid 2*s*. 2¼*d*. on long cloth and 3*s*. 6*d*. on scarlet.[5]

It may be that the controversy between the Hansards and the government over the payment of the new cloth custom, and the policy adopted before 1362 in some ports of allowing the Hansards to pay only one custom, (in this instance the new and greater custom),[6] was extended to all aliens. There is nothing to support this theory in the writs issued to the customs collectors,[7] but on the other hand, there seems to be no explanation of the apparent omission to collect the 12*d*. custom. That objections were raised to paying both customs is seen in the following order, which, however, shows that the con-

[1] Undyed cloth is used as an example because it was exported in the greatest quantity. The discussion is intended to apply to the other kinds of cloth.

[2] Cf. PRO L.T.R. Customs Roll 9.

[3] E.g., *ibid*. m. 22, Bristol, Mich. 1359–60.

[4] *Ibid*., m. 35.

[5] PRO L.T.R. Customs Roll 7, m. 14.

[6] Cf. pp. 46 f. above

[7] PRO Fine Roll 169, m. 8.

sidered opinion of the king and council was that both should be collected:[1]

To the collectors of the petty custom in London; notwithstanding a previous order to the collectors of the custom on woollen cloths made in England for export to stay the demand which they have made against merchants of the Duchy of Aquitaine for the payment of an additional custom of 12*d.* for . . . cloth of assize . . . exported by them provided the merchants pay 21*d.* for each such whole cloth to receive the said custom of 12*d.* in accordance with the tenor of their commission as the king and council have decided that it is not just nor consonant with reason that payment of that custom should now cease by pretext of the above order, seeing that the custom was granted by alien merchants in the time of the king's progenitors in return for certain privileges and exemptions within the realm.

The intention of the king and the council was carried out only in London during this period and it was not put into effect generally throughout the ports until 1381.[2]

As a result of such irregularities, it is impossible to draw up a uniform schedule of rates paid on English-made cloth and worsteds between 1350 and 1377. Up to 1362 there was great variation. After that year, until 1381, Hansards usually paid only the custom of 1303 on both cloth and worsteds. All other aliens seem to have paid only the custom of 1347 on the same goods, except in London, where they paid the combined customs, but only on undyed cloth. On partly dyed and dyed cloth, they paid there, as in the other ports, only the custom of 1347.[3]

The customs on wine and on general merchandise, and the subsidies imposed simultaneously on both offer no difficulties. In 1302 the ancient prise of wine, which was still exacted from English merchants,[4] was commuted for the Gascon merchants into a duty of 2*s.*

[1] *C.F.R. 1356–68*, p. 29.

[2] Cf. PRO L.T.R. Customs Roll 14.

[3] Undyed cloth was worth about £2 per cloth. H. L. Gray, 'Woollen Industry and Export,' *E.H.R.* xxxix (1924), 25. n. 6. Scarlet was worth about three times as much. In 1374, an ell of scarlet (to be given to the king at his coronation for land held in sergeanty) was valued at 6*s.* 8*d. C.P.R. 1374–77*, p. 81. Narrow grey cloth of Cornwall was worth 3*s.* per cloth at this time. PRO K.R. Customs, 158/34.

[4] The Barons of the Cinque Ports (1278), the citizens of London (1327), and the citizens

per tun, and in the following year the commutation was extended to all aliens.[1] Occasionally during the latter half of the reign of Edward III the rate was doubled[2] by the imposition of a subsidy, which was the origin of the later tonnage. Collected in 1350 and 1351 and again for a few months in 1360, the subsidy became practically continuous from November, 1371.[3] Even with a subsidy as large as the custom, the tax on wine was not a heavy one. If we take the average price of wine to be £7 per tun,[4] the custom was about $1\frac{1}{2}$ per cent, the combined custom and subsidy 3 per cent.[5]

General merchandise, which included all commodities except wool, woolfells, hides, wine, woollens, and wax,[6] was, after 1347, the only group of imports or exports on which natives did not pay customs. Aliens paid 3d. in the pound on the value of such articles.[7] The imposition of a subsidy, which became the later poundage, removed this distinction between aliens and native merchants, for

---

of York (1376) were exempt. F. Sargeant, 'The Wine Trade with Gascon,' *Finance and Trade under Edward III*, (G. Unwin ed.), p. 282.

[1] Gras p. 262, c. 14. For slight variations, see Appendix C.

[2] In 1350 the rate was 12d. and in 1351 it was 40d. Cf. p. 44, n. 3; p. 44, n. 5 above.

[3] Granted by the great council for one year from All Saints, 1371. PRO L.T.R. Customs Roll 5, m. 23, PRO K.R. Customs 150/24. Granted for one year from Mich. 1372. *Rot. Parl.* ii, 310. Granted for one year from Mich. 1373. *ibid.* ii, 317. Granted for one year from Mich. 1374. *C.P.R. 1374–77*, p. 48. In 1373 a second subsidy was apparently imposed to pay the expenses of a convoy for the protection of wine ships. An alien who had not come with the convoy protested successfully against the payment of it. PRO K.R. Customs 137/22, 23, 158.

[4] A. Simon, *The History of the Wine Trade in England* (London, 1906), I, 331 ff. In 1375 Hansards valued a tun at 10 marks, *Hanserecesse*, III, 307.

[5] In addition to the customs there was the ancient toll of pence varying from 2d. to 6d. and the gaugers fee which in London was 1d. per tun. Gras, p. 36; Sargeant *op. cit.*, p. 282; *Cal. Letter Book G.* p. 56.

[6] In at least one instance customers tried to collect 3d. in the pound on wine imported by aliens but this was declared unlawful. *C.C.R. 1369–74*, p. 275. Personal property was not free from customs. A bed with curtains and points for fastening armour which had been seized because uncustomed through a misunderstanding about this, were released on payment of the customs. *C.C.R. 1360–64*, p. 497.

[7] Gras p. 263, c. 20. The value of the merchandise was to be determined from letters carried by the merchants stating the value, or was to be declared by the merchant on oath. Gras p. 263 c. 21; *Rot. Parl.* ii, 262. In 1375 the Hansards complained that their oath was not accepted and received the reply that it had been found false. *Hanserecesse*, III, 313, c. 5. Goods were not to be examined and appraised by mayors, sheriffs or other officials not connected with the collection of customs. *Rot. Parl.* ii, 251. It is not stated on what value of the goods the customs were to be assessed.

both paid the subsidy at the same rate of 6*d*. in the pound. The subsidy was collected between 28 February and 28 June, 1350; 24 September, 1350 and Michaelmas, 1351; 24 January and 26 June, 1360, and from All Saints, 1371, until Christmas, 1376[1] with the subsidy on wine.

Rate of Custom and Subsidy on Wine and Merchandise Paid by Aliens
1350–1377

	Wine	Merchandise
January, 1350–28 February, 1350	2/– per tun	3*d*. in £
28 February, 1350–28 June, 1350	3/– " "	9*d*. "
28 June, 1350–24 September, 1350	2/– " "	3*d*. "
24 September, 1350–Michaelmas, 1351	5/6 " "	9*d*. "
Michaelmas, 1351–24 January, 1360	2/– " "	3*d*. "
24 January, 1360–26 June, 1360	4/– " "	9*d*. "
26 June, 1360–1 November, 1371	2/– " "	3*d*. "
1 November, 1371–Christmas, 1376	4/– " "	9*d*. " [2]
Christmas, 1376–end of reign	2/– " "	3*d*. "

Except in two instances, one of which no doubt was unintentional, rates paid by aliens on all goods were higher than those paid by natives on the same imports and exports. The difference lay in the customs rather than in the subsidies. Since the latter during this period fell equally upon English and alien merchants, it is obvious that the brunt of Edward III's war subsidies was borne by aliens only in so far as monopolies of exporting wool were thrust upon them by parliaments which believed that commercial and financial prosperity came with home staples, and the encouragement of aliens by the exclusion of native merchants from the carrying trade. When subsidies were equal, the difference in the rates paid by aliens and native merchants was proportionately much less than the original difference which was the result of the agreement to the *Carta Mercatoria* by aliens. The *nova custuma* had not been in intention a discrimination against aliens. Edward I, had it been possible, would have collected it from English merchants, as Edward III did for seven years be-

---

[1] See p. 44, n. 3, 5, 6; p. 51, n. 3, above.
[2] See p. 33 above.

tween 1350 and 1377.[1] They paid it then in return for the privilege of taking wool elsewhere than to the staple, or for permission to export when trade was restricted to aliens.

For short periods natives seem to have paid the 3*d.* in the pound custom on general merchandise[2] and unless it was a slip on the part of the clerk who made up the rolls, the cloth custom of 1303.[3] These, however, seem to be isolated instances and there is no evidence of a general exaction of the petty custom as there was of the *nova custuma* on wool.

The two examples of aliens or groups of aliens paying at a lower rate than English merchants were the result of the exemption of the Hanseatics from the cloth custom of 1347, and of the rise in the price of wine while the amount paid per tun for the king's prise remained fixed at 20*s.* On cloth of assize, on which natives paid 7*d.* less export duty than aliens, Hanseatics paid 2*d.* less than natives and 9*d.*[4] less than other aliens. Although the 20*s.* per tun paid by the king for his prise of wine[5] probably originally represented fairly the actual price of the wine, by 1303 it was considerably less than that price, so that the prise constituted a tax,[6] and one which, on shipments up to twenty tuns, fell more heavily upon natives than the 2*s.* per tun customs duty paid by aliens.[7] The price of wine increased during the fourteenth century, and if we take £7[8] as the average

---

[1] 1356–62; 1371–72. Cf. Appendix C.

[2] London | 19 Nov. 1366–Mich. 1367 | PRO L.T.R. Customs Roll 9, | m. 34d.

	Mich. 1369–70	*ibid.*	m. 34d.
Boston	Mich. 1352–3	*ibid.*	m. 23
Hull	Mich. 1369–71	*ibid.*	m. 29d.
Exeter	Mich. 1355–6	*ibid.*	n. 26
Southampton	Mich. 1359–60	*ibid.*	m. 42
	10 Aug. 1370–Mich.	*ibid.*	m. 45
	Mich. 1371–24 Dec. 1372	*ibid.* 14,	m. 1.

There are other cases where goods are said to have been taken by divers merchants but these may well be all alien.

[3] Boston Mich. 1371–24 Dec., 1372, PRO L.T.R. Customs Roll 7, m. 14.

[4] This figure is based on the theory that aliens were not paying the 12*d.* custom on cloth.

[5] Gras, p. 41; one tun from vessels carrying ten to nineteen tuns and two tuns from vessels carrying twenty tons or more.

[6] Gras, p. 42.

[7] Gras, p. 42, n. 9. The price of wine in 1303 is taken as 50*s.*

[8] See p. 51 above.

price per tun after 1350, it is evident that aliens had a considerable advantage over natives in shipments of all sizes:

Shipment of:	10 tuns	20 tuns	40 tuns
Aliens paid	20s.	40s.	80s.
Natives lost	120s.	240s.	240s.[1]

A question arises concerning the legality of increasing established customs rates by new customs or subsidies. As far as the imposition of new customs or subsidies was concerned, aliens were in much the same position as natives. The royal power to levy increased taxes was theoretically bound, in one instance by the *Carta Mercatoria*,[2] and in the other by the growth of the taxing power of parliament. In neither was the restriction wholly effective, although in parliament natives possessed more effective means of defending their rights than aliens, because the question of subsidies was bound up with the larger question of general taxation. Alien merchants lacked any permanent general organization through which they could maintain their privileges. The Hanseatics alone were able to make a successful protest against new impositions, and they were successful only against the cloth custom which could scarcely be called a war measure or tax intended to raise money for the protection of shipping. Other aliens, while doubtless relying on the *Carta Mercatoria* for protection against royal exactions, tacitly fell in with the policy of native merchants, who had ceased to make grants in their own assemblies and accepted those subsidies which parliament voted.[3] Thus that body

[1] This represents the difference between the value of the one or two tuns of wine taken as prise and the £1 to £2 paid to the merchant for it.

[2] Gras, p. 264, cl. 25. 'Volumus autem ac pro nobis et heredibus nostris concedimus quod nulla exactio prisa vel prestacio aut aliquod aliud onus super personas mercatorum predictorum mercandisas seu bona eorundem aliquatenus imponatur contra formam expressam superius et concessam.'

[3] There is no evidence that alien merchants protested against the wool subsidies. In 1375, the Hansards objected to some incidental charges on wool, including the 19d. 'Calais money.' The king replied at that time that their privileges antedated the staple, and since the latter had been established at the request of alien and native merchants, the charges in connection with it were not customs, but payments for acts of special grace. *Hanserecesse*, III, p. 301, cl. 3. At the same time, they protested against the poundage of 1373, 'la quele ils ne soleient unqes pajer avant ces heures et encontre lour franchises et privileges', but they were told that it was a war measure to raise money for the protection of commerce and must be borne by aliens and English alike. *Op. cit.*, p. 300, cl. 2.

which had taken little share in the imposition of early customs on aliens, became the arbiter of commercial taxation for them as well as for English merchants.

For the right to engage in trade within the country, to buy and sell by wholesale and retail, and to act as financial agents, alien merchants were dependent on both the central and the borough governments, and in the conflict between these two authorities, they sometimes found their position a difficult one. There are various indications as to how widely alien merchants travelled or had land or business connections throughout the country. Objections to them as competitors in trade came most frequently from the commercial cities on or near the coast, from London in particular. Their head-quarters must almost always have been in the ports, but they travelled about the country, going to fairs, and buying wool, cloth, and other English products. Nicholas Ploket recovered from merchants of Brabant thirty shillings for his expenses in going from London to Wales to buy cloth and wool.[1] The woad merchants of Amiens bought cloth from a citizen of London in Gloucester, and the terms of their agreement were sent to the mayor of London.[2] Early in the reign the Bardi had been freed from murage and pavage in Oxford.[3] A letter of protection and safe-conduct issued to Nicholas Sardouche and others describes them as bringing from Nottingham and Boston to London goods which they had received in payment of debts.[4] In 1347, Hansards had warehouses in Huntingdon and when the goods of the Hansards were seized in 1351, orders for arrest and returns were made for Hereford, Warwickshire, Wiltshire, Hampshire, Somerset, Gloucestershire (Bristol), Norfolk, London, York, and Lincoln.[5] Much the same distribution of aliens can be seen from the cases which were heard in the royal courts.[6] Aliens are occasionally found as burgesses in inland towns, especially in the south, at Bath,

---

[1] *Cal. Plea and Mem. Rolls, London,* II, 33.

[2] *Cal. Mayor's Letters, London, 1350–70,* p. 146.

[3] H. E. Salter, *Munimenta Civitatis Oxonie* (Devizes, 1920), 83.

[4] *C.P.R. 1367–70, p. 39.*

[5] PRO Pipe Roll 197, m. ii, iv; *ibid.* 198, Item London, d.; PRO L.T.R. Mem. 126, Communia Pasch.; PRO K.R. Accounts, Various, Foreign Merchants, 128/7. *Hanserecesse,* I, 153–57.

[6] See Appendix E.

Wells, and Winchester.[1] They must, however, always have been most numerous in the ports and commercial centres from Hull around to Southampton but the representatives of the greater companies especially must have visited frequently and perhaps been established in the wool growing and cloth making centres.

Wherever foreign merchants went throughout the country, they could sell by wholesale and sell mercery by retail,[2] but selling by retail and selling to other aliens was the cause of most of the city antagonism toward alien merchants. The situation was made more difficult by the action of the central government. The control of local trade, chiefly through gilds, was one of the privileges granted and repeatedly confirmed to the towns, who reserved the rights for their freemen, to the exclusion of all outsiders, English or alien. Yet, throughout this period, except for only four years, aliens could, according to statute, sell by retail and sell to other aliens. In 1351, the Statute of York of 1335, which gave aliens these rights, was re-enacted,[3] and it remained in force for the rest of the reign except for short periods. In 1363 and 1364 the statute restricting merchants to one trade and the charters issued to some of the companies interfered with the trade of aliens.[4] In 1368,[5] for one year, and again in 1376,[6] the right of aliens to trade by retail was temporarily withdrawn, as the result of petitions. How far aliens were ever able to exercise this right it is difficult to say. The grants to them were usually modified by a saving clause for London, although on the other hand, concessions to natives contained statements: 'Et est l'entention du Roi qe nul prejudice soit fait as aliens q'ont Franchises par Chartres des Rois.'[7] Privileges granted to the woad merchants of Amiens, in return for a substantial contribution, included

---

[1] See Appendix G.

[2] Gras, p. 260, c. 3. Cf. *ibid.*, p. 137 where it is erroneously stated that 'they were not to sell spices or mercery in small quantities, a trade of course reserved for the privileged burgesses of the towns.'

[3] *Stat.* i, 315; *Rot. Parl.* ii, 231. Cf. petition for the re-enactment, *ibid.* p. 229: *Quele chose serroit grant profit pur notre Seigneur le Roi et pur tote la Commune.*

[4] *Rot. Parl.* ii, 277, 278. Repealed 1365. *Stat.* i, 383, 384; *Rot. Parl.* ii, 286.

[5] *Stat.* i, 389.

[6] *Rot. Parl.* ii, 332, 347, 367; *C.P.R. 1374–77*, pp. 389, 391; *Cal. Letter Book H*, p. 53.

[7] *Rot. Parl.* ii, 296.

the right to sell by retail and to whomsoever they chose,[1] but the Hansards were refused the right to sell wine by retail, because it was not explicitly mentioned in their charters.[2] There are other instances which show that the saving clause for the towns was effective. In 1354, aliens were forced to petition that the statute re-enacted in the preceding year be enforced.[3] In 1371, the servant of a smith was put on the pillory in London for saying that aliens traded as freely as citizens.[4] In 1374, a vintner of Bordeaux sought a license to sell wine by retail in Colchester, which he dared not do because he was not a freeman of the town.[5]

A part of the question of the right to trade by retail and to sell to other aliens was the right to act as a broker. London itself seems to have been inconsistent in the matter of allowing aliens this privilege. In 1345 brokers who were not of the freedom of the city were to be investigated,[6] and in 1376 it was one of the complaints of the Londoners that aliens were acting as brokers.[7] In 1366, a list of those forbidden, at the request of the masters of the gild of grocers, to act as brokers of the gild, includes one Venetian, Nicholas Nigrebon, and Venturus Alisaundre and other aliens.[8] In 1373, however, it was enacted that strangers should be admitted as brokers upon payment of a fine of forty shillings and on the finding of two or three sureties,[9] and a list of those sworn as brokers in that year contains the names of aliens, most of whom were Lombards. In 1376, two Lombards were tried for acting as brokers in an usurious loan.[10]

Another question connected with rights of retail trade, and one which was a matter of perpetual dispute and complaint on the part of the towns was the length of time aliens might remain in the country. The *Carta Mercatoria* is vague on this subject, which was so

[1] *Liber Albus*, p, 418.

[2] *Cal. Plea and Mem. Rolls, London*, I, 151.

[3] *Rot. Parl.* ii, 262

[4] *Cal. Letter Book G*, p. 283.

[5] *C.P.R. 1374–77*, p. 3.

[6] *Cal. Letter Book F*, p. 129.

[7] *Rot. Parl.* ii, 347.

[8] *Cal. Plea and Mem. Rolls, London*, II, 58.

[9] *Cal. Letter Book G*, p. 313.

[10] *Cal. Letter Book H*, p. 23.

much under the control of local authorities, who would have restricted the stay of alien merchants to sufficient time to dispose of their cargo and to secure another, but not long enough to permit them to take part in local trade. Forty days was the usual period. It seems unlikely that this limit could ever have applied to members of the great commercial and financial companies, and letters of protection were often granted for a year or more. For what may be called the transient merchant, however, the towns tried to enforce it. The towns raised another objection to allowing aliens an unlimited stay, and on that point they had some support from the central government. Aliens maintained, with some success, that if they paid customs as aliens, they should not pay taxes, local or national, as natives. The resident alien, who might acquire property and enjoy trading privileges in the town, would therefore, enjoy some of the privileges of the native-born merchant, without sharing his burdens. The central government was not averse to taxing aliens who remained longer than a given time, although it was not altogether successful or consistent in collecting the taxes on the few occasions on which they were levied.[1]

The question of the rights of aliens in local trade as against their exercise of the same cannot be answered dogmatically now any more than it could have been in the Middle Ages. Grants to one side or the other, to the towns or to the aliens, or to the nobles that they might buy from whom they would, must, at all events, have added legality to the attempts of one enfranchised group to assert its rights at the expense of another group conflictingly enfranchised. The king was willing to grant the right of retail trade to aliens and used it as a curb on the independent spirit of the towns. How far aliens were able to exercise that right depended on the strength of local opposition. They could, however, by becoming citizens of the towns, overcome the bars raised against them in local trade, as they could, by securing letters of denization from the crown, obtain the privilege of paying customs at the lower rate paid by native merchants.[2]

[1] See Chapter IV below.
[2] See Chapter IV below.

IV

THE DENIZATION OF ALIEN MERCHANTS

ALIEN merchants who traded with England enjoyed certain privileges there which made trade possible and desirable. They were assured the protection of life and goods, in general terms, by *Magna Carta*,[1] the *Carta Mercatoria*,[2] and treaties between England and their native countries, and more specifically, by personal letters of protection, issued under the great seal.[3] They could claim to be liable for only those customs, taxes, and impositions which were specifically designated in the *Carta Mercatoria* as charges on aliens.[4] They were not responsible for debts of which they were not principal debtors or sureties,[5] but this privilege was difficult to maintain. It was looked upon with suspicion by English creditors, who felt that alien companies could disclaim responsibility for the debts of defaulting members for which they were morally, and perhaps actually,

[1] cc. 13, 14.

[2] Gras, p. 260, c. 3. See also the Ordinance of the Staple. *Rot. Parl.* ii, 247.

[3] These were of three kinds: general letters of protection and safe-conduct; protections *cum clausula volumus;* and protections *cum clausula nolumus.* The first was a kind of passport to admit an alien to the country and to protect him while going about in pursuit of his business. Safe-conducts were usually granted only to aliens, for in 1328, when they were sought for an Englishman, it was said 'though it was not customary for kings in part to issue such letters to their subjects in the realm, nevertheless at the request of the Queen Mother, prelates etc. the king granted them in the form demanded.' *Cal. Plea and Mem. Rolls, London,* i, 82. The second prevented the bringing of suits against the holder, especially by his creditors. Fitzherbert divides this class of protections into four groups: *quia profecturus; quia moraturus;* for the king's debtor; and for those in the king's service beyond the seas or in the marches of Scotland. *La Novelle Natura Brevium* (London, 1687) p. 62. Protests were frequently brought against the abuse of this kind of protection. *Rot. Parl.* ii, 242, 332, 359; *Stat.* i, 323; *Cal. Letter Book G,* p. 302. The third protected land and possessions from seizure or levy. These were rarely granted to laymen or to individuals, but usually to religious houses. There are some examples of their issue to alien merchants. See Appendix B; *C.P.R. 1317–21,* p. 42; *ibid., 1330–34,* p. 429; *ibid., 1343–45,* p. 320.

[4] See pp. 71 ff. below.

[5] This privilege had been granted to individuals and the Hanse at an earlier time. It was granted to all aliens in 1353. *Rot. Parl.* ii, 250. The same rule held at the staple at Bruges. *Cartulaire de l'Ancienne Estaple de Bruges,* (L. Gilliods van Severen, ed., Bruges, 1904–1906), I, 229. For earlier joint responsibility, see *Stat.* i, 324; *Rot. Parl.* ii, 240.

responsible. Arrests for the debts of others were not uncommon during this period. For example, in 1375, two Lombards fled from Boston, owing, it was said, £10,000 for goods bought there. The matter was brought before the king and council in parliament, and the goods of the members of the societies of the Albertini and the Strozzi were seized, although they disclaimed all responsibility. Not until five years later, after a long suit, in course of which their goods had been seized and released several times was an agreement made and they were released from all claims and actions brought against the fugitives.[1]

Alien merchants were not responsible for trespasses committed by their countrymen, but the English government reserved the right to enforce the law of marque and reprisal upon aliens of a city or country where English subjects could not secure justice.[2] Under such circumstances, an investigation was made, following an appeal for aid from the English subject, and a request for reparation or a warning was sent to the authorities of the place where the injury was done or where the offenders lived.[3] The request failing, the goods of all the merchants of that place and sometimes the merchants themselves were seized and held until reparation was made.[4] In one instance, two sons of a merchant of Normandy were given as hostages until the stolen goods of an English merchant should be restored.[5] If reparation was not obtained by these means, goods to the value of the damage done were seized in England from merchants of the place where the offense was committed, and handed over to the injured Englishman.[6] Reprisals were not always swiftly carried out. On one occasion an Englishman had been robbed and imprisoned on the shores of the

---

[1] *C.C.R. 1374–77*, pp. 172, 252, 440, 472; *ibid. 1377–81*, p. 460; *C.P.R. 1374–77*, p. 196; *C.F.R. 1369–77*, p. 357; *Rot. Parl.* ii, 350, where the amount of the debt is said to be £20,000 to £30,000.

[2] *Rot. Parl.* ii, 250.

[3] After money and wool of Henry Picard had been seized by Jacobus Gerardi Gentilis of Florence, while they were being taken from England to Tuscany, the mayor of London wrote to the authorities in Florence, reminding them that a request had already been made for the return of the goods, and urging action 'lest reprisal should be taken from their folk repairing to London.' *Cal. Mayor's Letters, London*, p. 1. Also *ibid.*, p. 163.

[4] Cf. p. 11 above for arrest of merchants of Lucca.

[5] *C.C.R. 1354–60*, p. 47.

[6] *Ibid.*, p. 139.

Baltic. Two inquests were held and orders given for the arrest of the goods belonging to men of the Baltic towns. Five years later, however, the Englishman was compelled to petition parliament to secure execution of the orders for arrest. He was then advised to sue in chancery where the reports of the inquisitions would be viewed and the arrest granted according to the law and reason.[1] Swift and thorough action was taken, however, against the privileged Hanse of Almain when an Englishman had been murdered in Lescluse, under circumstances which made the crime seem an insult and an attack upon the English. In July, 1351, orders were issued to seize all the goods of the Hansards, except those of Tidemann of Limberg and Alvin de Revele, because Richard Curteys of Bristol had been murdered,[2] as it was afterwards said, at the instigation of Hildebrand Suderman who had also been spreading the report that 'all Englishmen are false and maintainers of homicide and are not to be believed.'[3] Within a fortnight the Hansards were being taken into the king's protection and allowed to go to Flanders to consult with members of the Hanse there.[4] By the middle of September, their goods, with the exception of Hildebrand Suderman's, were being de-arrested.[5] There is no evidence of the outcome of the matter, except that in 1354, Suderman's goods were transferred to John de Colonia.[6]

The wills of aliens could be proved in England, their executors could bring suit for the collection of their outstanding debts, and their heirs could inherit their personal property.[7] The fact that an alien could not inherit land, or acquire it save by the favor of the king to whom it escheated at his death was for the merchant no

---

[1] *Rot. Parl.* ii, 207.

[2] *C.F.R. 1347–56*, p. 303; *Cal. Letter Book F*, p. 233. *C.C.R. 1349–54*, pp. 322, 386, 475. The object of the king can scarcely have been to replenish the exchequer at the expense of the Hanse, as is suggested in *Cal. Letter Book F*, p. xxx.

[3] *C.P.R. 1350–54*, p. 257.

[4] *C.P.R. 1350–54*, p. 141; *Cal. Letter Book F*, p. 236.

[5] *C.C.R. 1349–54*, pp. 322, 385, 586, 475.

[6] *C.C.R. 1354–60*, p. 16. Suderman was now dead.

[7] PRO K.R. Mem. 136, Brevia directa Mich.; *C.P.R. 1361–64*, p. 250; *Cal. of Wills, London, passim*. Non-freeman could not dispose by will of a greater estate than a term of years. *Memorials of London* p. 151. For examples of aliens bequeathing tenements of land, see *Cal. of Wills, London*, I, 488; *C.P.R. 1343–45*, p. 546.

great disability. He could obtain land by purchase, lease, or gift, and he could rent shops and tenements in which to conduct his affairs and reside.[1] He seems actually to have been able to rent a number of houses, which he let to other aliens.[2] Land throughout the country, also came into his hands, usually because the owner or tenant, frequently the king himself, was financially bound to him. Such land was generally held for a short time, until the debt was paid or some other arrangement was made.[3] The merchant in some cases was little more than the administrator of the land, as when Francis Bache of Genoa held the Templars' lands at Cressing and Wytham in Essex,[4] or Anthony Pessaigne, also of Genoa, held Dinsley, Lannock and Temple Chelsin in Hertfordshire[5] before they were transferred to the Hospitallers. In 1348, the abbot and convent of Grestain in Normandy demised, with the king's license, to Tidemann of Limberg the manors of Norton in Somerset, Connok in Wiltshire, Ramridge in Southampton, Marsh Gibbon in Buckinghamshire,

---

[1] Pollock and Maitland, i, 459. The Bardi had houses in Lombard Street, which they released to the king for £700. *C.C.R. 1327–30.* p. 362; PRO Chanc. Misc. 9/6. One of the company, Nicholas Marini, had a tenement in the parish of St Stephen, Walbrook, with access to Budge Row and Bucklersbury, which John Donat held in 1376. *Cal. Letter Book H*, p. 26. Nicholas Bulietti of Florence held tenements in the same parish in 1352. *Cal. Letter Book G*, p. 249. Bartholomew Guidonis of Florence held half a messuage in the parish of St Nicholas Acon in 1357. *Cal Letter Book G*, pp. 93, 96. Anthony Provan of Turin had his own house in the parish of St Antolin in 1352. PRO Exch. Plea Roll 77, m. 65d. Hildebrand Suderman and Tideman of Limberg had houses in Thames Street. PRO Ancient Petitions, File 140, no. 6985; PRO Exch. Plea Roll 78, m. 116.

[2] Bertrand of Florence, the king's banker, held two houses in St Nicholas Lane, where he conducted his own business, and others where various aliens lived, among whom were Nicholas Nigrebon and Silvester Nicholas. He had a tenement in Lombard Street, where John Baldewyn of Florence lived, and five shops in St Nicholas Lane. PRO K.R. Mem. 139, Communia Hil.; *C.F.R. 1356–68*, p. 177.

[3] In this way, the Bardi held land in Essex and Kent belonging to Richard Grey of Codnore. *Cal. Ancient Deeds*, iii, 160; PRO K.R. Writs, 33. Eleanor, widow of Hugh le Despenser, and her second husband, William, lord Zouche de Mortimer, alienated to Anthony Citeron of Genoa and Nicholas de Salvo, for their lives, land at Great Marlow in Buckinghamshire, Stanford in the Vale in Berkshire, and other land in Oxfordshire and Northamptonshire. *C.C.R. 1330–33*, pp. 563, 593; *V.C.H. Bucks.*, iii, 70; *Year Book, 18–19 Edward III* (L. O. Pike, ed., Rolls Series, 1904), p. 302; *ibid.*, *19 Edward III* (L. O. Pike, ed., Rolls Series, 1905), pp. 236–40.

[4] PRO K.R. Mem. 104, m. 217; Lay Subsidy Rolls 107/10, 13; Ancient Petitions, File 95, No. 14674; *C.C.R. 1318–23*, p. 485.

[5] *C.F.R. 1307–19*, p. 170.

Grafton in Northamptonshire, Dernford in Cambridgeshire, Creeting and Mickfield in Suffolk belonging to the alien priory of Wilmington. They were granted 'to him, his heirs and assigns for a thousand years, with the knights' fees, advowsons of churches, liberties, franchises and other profits and emoluments pertaining to the manors, saving always to the king during the war with France as much farm as the prior would render yearly for the manors and other profits pertaining to the king, and to the chief lords of that fee their services.'[1] He was exempt from the payment of fifteenths or tenths or taxes on these lands, but there was always some difficulty in maintaining this right.[2] Whether his heirs would have inherited the lands it is impossible to say, for two years later[3] the king granted him the right 'to grant the same to whatsoever Englishmen he will, so long as it be not in mortmain, to hold to these same persons, their heirs and assigns, of the king by the service of one knight's fee. Furthermore for a sum of money paid in hand at the receipt of the exchequer and because Tidemann has acknowledged that he does homage for the manors and holds them of the king and his heirs by the said service, the king has pardoned to him and those to whom he will grant the manors, the farm aforesaid, amounting to £86 11s. 9½d. yearly, saving as above.' The manors were granted to the de la Poles in 1354 on the same terms on which Tidemann held them.[4] He also held the manor of Charlton[5] in Kent, and in 1348 was given a marsh in Rotherhithe by the prior and convent of Bermondsey. It was to be held by him and Geoffrey de Wychingham, citizen and mercer of London during Tidemann's life and for five years more.[6]

The terms of the grants of land to Tidemann of Limberg and the careers of other important alien merchants seem to show that, through the favour of the king, aliens who apparently received no formal grant of what we may call denization, attained a position

---

[1] *C.P.R. 1348–50*, p. 221. It is stated in the *V.C.H. Sussex*, II, 123, that almost all the manors of the priory outside Sussex had been granted to him by 1370, but he had left England long before this. Cf., pp. 19 ff. above.

[2] PRO Exch. Plea Roll 76, m. 103d.

[3] *C.P.R. 1348–50*, p. 513.

[4] *C.C.R. 1354–60*, p. 659.

[5] PRO K.R. Mem. 147, Brevia directa and Communia Mich.

[6] *V.C.H. Surrey* IV, 1; v. 84, Cf. p. 19 above.

not always easily distinguishable from that of a subject. Anthony Pessaigne, Anthony and Francis Bache, all of Genoa, spent most of their lives in the service of Edward II and Edward III. Anthony Pessaigne was knighted,[1] became the king's counsellor,[2] and Seneschal of Gascony.[3] Anthony and Francis Bache served as purveyors to the wardrobe,[4] as diplomatic and financial agents and in the many ways implied in the title 'the king's merchant.'[5] All were exempt from aids, tallages, and all manner of contributions for their lands and goods and from holding office.[6] Yet in 1352 and in succeeding years, Anthony Bache claimed exemption from the subsidy on moveables because he paid customs as an alien.[7]

The basis of Bache's claim to exemption from a tax which should have been covered by the preceding grant of exemption and which, as we shall see,[8] was probably not as a rule collected from aliens, supplies an important clue in the problem of the status of alien merchants in England in the fourteenth century and of their naturalization or denization. For the non-commercial alien the process of naturalization was still the feudal one of doing liege homage to the king. But for the alien merchant, the question was not simply one of feudal relationships. His interests were commercial, not tenurial, and his position was determined by his commercial rights. Some commercial privileges of native merchants, desirable for aliens who were resident in England, such as the payment of customs at the lower rate, were in the king's gift. Others, like the rights of citizens of the towns, were under the control of local authorities. It may be argued that the latter rights should not enter into the question of naturalization, which was a matter of the king's favor, but it will be seen that the possession of certain local rights by an alien affected his status in the eyes of the king and the exchequer. The problem is how

[1] *C.P.R. 1330–34*, p. 223.

[2] *C.C.R. 1330–33*, p. 581.

[3] *C.P.R. 1317–21*, p. 58.

[4] *C.P.R. 1307–13*, pp. 412, 433, 459.

[5] *C.C.R. 1337–39*, pp. 298, 372; *ibid., 1339–41*, p. 510.

[6] *C.P.R. 1307–13*, p. 459; *C.P.R. 1327–30*, p. 416; PRO K.R. Mem. 113, Brevia directa Mich.; *ibid.* 127, Brevia directa Hil.

[7] PRO K.R. Mem. 128, Brevia directa Pasch.; *ibid.*, 129, 130, Brevia directa Trin.

[8] See p. 75 below.

and to what extent an alien merchant might acquire the privileges of a subject and a citizen.

In the early part of the fourteenth century, letters patent were first issued by which the king granted to alien merchants certain commercial privileges enjoyed by native-born merchants. These grants were the forerunners of the letters patent of denization, which conferred on aliens a limited kind of naturalization and were more easily obtainable than the act of parliament, which became necessary for complete naturalization. The fact that in the early fourteenth century the letters patent, which we may call letters of denization, were issued only to merchants,[1] implies that non-commercial aliens had other means, probably by doing homage, of securing denization or naturalization, for the terms are synonomous at that period.[2] Not until the reign of Richard II do letters of denization begin to resemble the later typical ones. The early fourteenth-century letters make no mention of rights of land holding or of the courts in which the recipients might sue. They contain grants of commercial privileges and, as the most important clause and the one which survived in later letters of denization, a statement as to the rate at which customs shall be paid. That this was the most desirable privilege is evident from the character of the letters patent and from the period at which they appear. We begin to find grants of this kind after alien customs had been definitely fixed at a higher rate and the clause which grants a relaxation of that rule soon becomes the important one. In 1324, Conrad Broke, Hildebrand Suderman, and Ludekin le

---

[1] Later in the century letters of denization were issued to the alien priories.

[2] Pollock and Maitland, i, 463. The distinction between naturalization by act of parliament and denization by letters patent, and the resulting distinction between a naturalized subject who has been admitted to practically all the rights of the native-born, and a denizen who has been admitted to certain rights only, cannot be drawn in the fourteenth century. Not until the next century, when parliament began to ratify the king's letters patent of denization, did that body take any part in the process of naturalization, save that in 1351, it settled the question of who should be considered natural-born subjects, which had been raised by English conquest of French territory in the Hundred Years' War. *Rot. Parl.* ii, 231. The fourteenth century had no equivalent for 'denizen' in its legal sense. An alien who had been admitted to certain privileges was simply said to pay customs *sicut indigena* or to be heard in the courts *sicut purus Anglicus*. PRO Patent Roll 262, m. 20; *Rot. Parl.* i, 135. Not until after 1660 does there seem to be a clear distinction made between those who were naturalized and those who were made free denizens. *Stat.* v, 246; *ibid.* vii, 637.

Long, all Hansards, were given the right to trade throughout the realm as the king's merchants and as denizens (*sicut indigene*); they were freed from the payment of local tolls and from the liability of having their goods seized for the debts and trespasses of others for whom they were not sureties.[1] Added to the grant for Hildebrand Suderman is the following clause: 'ita tamen quod nichil nobis decidat de custumis nobis debita in hac parte.'[2] The privileges were renewed for Hildebrand Suderman in the next year but no mention is made of the customs.[3] The attitude of the customs collectors toward a grant in such general terms introduced explicitness if not uniformity. They were willing to recognize only such privileges as were specifically mentioned, for nine years later Hildebrand Suderman petitioned for a confirmation because 'some collectors, on the ground that in the said letters patent there is no express mention of the customs which he should pay, compel him to the payment of those customs' which aliens pay.[4] The confirmation[5] and similar letters patent issued throughout the reign have as their principal clause exemption from alien customs.

The grant made to Benedict Zacharie in 1365 is worth giving in full, because it is as typical a fourteenth century letter of denization as is possible in a period when there was not complete uniformity, and because an important phrase is omitted in the calendering.[6]

Rex omnibus ad quos etc. salutem. Sciatis quod cum Benedictus Zacharie mercator London de partibus Lumbardie oriundus liber homo eiusdem[7] civi-

[1] *C.P.R. 1321–24*, pp. 402, 434.

[2] Kunze, *Hanseakten aus England*, p. 58.

[3] *C.P.R. 1324–27*, pp. 128, 194; *ibid. 1327–30*, p. 448. The translation of the grant of 1325 in the *Calendar of Patent Rolls* is rather misleading, for it reads that Hildebrand Suderman 'shall be as one of the king's merchants . . . and a denizen,' whereas it is worded exactly like the previous grant and refers only to trading privileges.

[4] *C.P.R. 1334–38*, p. 192.

[5] *C.P.R. 1334–38*, p. 192. In 1350, Hildebrand Suderman was subject to the same treatment as other members of the Hanse. p. 61 above.

[6] PRO Patent Roll 271, m. 21; *C.P.R. 1364–67*, p. 103.

[7] In some other grants it is stated that the merchants have lived many years in a city, that they have a house, a wife and children, and that they contribute to the charges on citizens, without any mention of their citizenship. *C.P.R. 1350–54*, p. 22; *ibid. 1364–67*, p. 234. In such cases it is often granted that the alien shall enjoy the privileges of the city within the city and throughout the realm.

tatis existat perpetuumque domicilium ac uxorem et liberos ibidem habeat et lotto et scotto ceterisque omnibus ipsam civitatem tangentibus una cum aliis eiusdem civitatis contribuat et porciones de decima et quintadecima ac aliis quotis nobis per cives dicte civitatis aut communitatem regni nostri Anglie concessis una cum aliis hominibus dicte civitatis nobis soluit *unde nobis facta est plena fides.*[1] Nos ea consideratione volentes ipsum Benedictum favore prosequi grosere concessimus eidem Benedicto quod ipse quamdiu civis dicte civitatis extiterit de tribus denariis de libra et de omnibus aliis prestationibus et custumis quas alienigene de bonis et mercandisis suis tenentur solvere de propriis bonis et mercandisis ipsius Benedicti infra idem regnum nostrum Anglie adducendis et ab eodem educendis ultra id quod cives civitatis predicte pro bonis et mercandisis suis solvere tenentur solvendum exnunc ad totam vitam eiusdem Benedicti sit quietus et quod plus quam alii cives dicte civitatis indigene pro custumis mercandisarum et aliorum bonorum suorum nobis solvunt solvere non teneatur nec ad hoc aliqualiter compellatur. In cuius etc. Teste Rege apud Wyndesore viii die Aprilis per breve de privato sigillo.

The interesting thing in this letter is the connection between citizenship and the king's grant of freedom from alien customs. The former was wholly in the control of the towns, so that the king's grant to an alien that he may enjoy all the privileges of a citizen of London in the city and throughout the realm[2] must have been little more than a formula of small value as far as enjoying those rights in London itself was concerned, unless it was supplemented by the grant of citizenship. City authorities looked upon all non-citizens as *extranei,*[3] and their right to admit outsiders to the freedom of the city was jealously guarded. They were willing to admit aliens to citizenship but they made their own terms.[4] The king, nobles or influential men might recommend persons for citizenship but it lay wholly within the power of the city authorities to confer it or not. In 1312, the mayor and aldermen of London removed an alien from citizenship although he had been admitted at the request of great men of the realm.[5] The

---

[1] This clause, which is omitted in the calendering, is also found in the grant to Bartholomew Myne, PRO Patent Roll 262 m. 20; *C.P.R. 1358–61*, p. 550.

[2] *C.P.R. 1364–67*, p. 234. For similar thirteenth century grant see *C.Ch.R. 1226–57*, p. 407.

[3] *Liber Albus*, p. 495.

[4] Men 'of strange land and respectability' might enjoy the franchises of the city but they must answer as citizens in all charges. *Liber Albus*, p. 287.

[5] *Cal. Letter Book E*, p. 14.

authorities in Cork refused to recognize as a denizen or citizen, John, son of Thadeus Donat of Lombardy, although he had been born in Ireland and had a house and a family in Cork and contributed to all the charges of the town. Their reason was that his father was an alien and no alien had ever been received into the liberty of the city since its foundation.[1] In 1326, all aliens who had been admitted to citizenship in London were removed from it and it was ordained that henceforth in addition to the requirements laid down in 1319 that citizens should be admitted only in the Husting with the consent of the commonalty,[2] an alien could be made a freeman only on the security of six reputable men of his trade. There is evidence, however, that at this time, citizenship was a prelude to the grant of denization and that an alien was regarded as a denizen in the matter of customs and taxes only as long as he was a citizen or contributed to city taxation as such. The clause to that effect appeared in letters of denization and occasionally the phrase *unde facta est plena fides* was added which, referring to the admission as a freeman, seemed to indicate that the taking of the freeman's oath of fealty was regarded as a sufficient act of homage to the king. It is probably the forerunner of the clause in later letters of denization which stated that the alien had done liege homage.[3]

Some who were made denizens in the matter of paying customs but of whom there is no evidence that they were also made freemen, seem to have continued to pay customs as aliens. Hildebrand Suderman, in spite of the confirmation of his privileges with a definite statement that he was to pay customs as a native merchant, was in 1350 upheld in his complaint in the exchequer that he was unjustly assessed for contributions to fifteenths collected from 1334 to 1341 because he was paying alien customs during those years.[4] Simon

---

[1] PRO Chanc. Misc. Bundle 10 19/18 (it should be numbered 17).

[2] *Cal. Letter Book E*, p. 214; *Liber Albus*, p. 142. In 1312 the commonalty had petitioned the mayor and aldermen that unknown strangers, native or foreign, should be admitted only on certificate of merchants whose trade he wished to enter. *Cal. Letter Book E*, p. 13.

[3] For freeman's oath, see *Cal. Letter Book D*, p. 195; *Cal. Letter Book H*, pp. 178, 314; J. H. Round, *The Commune of London* (London, 1899), p. 236. A German was said to have lived in Lenton, Notts, for twenty-six years *ad fidem nostram* and to have borne the same burdens as citizens, although it is not stated that he was a citizen. PRO K.R. Mem. 114, m. 33.

[4] PRO Pipe Roll 18, Item Lond.; K.R. Mem. 126, Brevia directa Mich.; PRO L.T.R. Mem. 123. Communia Mich.

Bochel of Lucca, although he was granted freedom from alien customs in 1361,[1] was paying the *nova custuma* on wool in 1365,[2] apparently without protest. Not until 1369 is he spoken of as a citizen of London.[3] On the other hand, those who were citizens but who had apparently received no grant from the king, protested successfully against the payment of alien customs. In 1330, Hermann le Skipper,[4] citizen of London complained that the collectors in London demanded customs on general merchandise 'si mercator extraneus et non civis civitatis predicte fuisset.'[5] The king ordered that he should be quit of the demands provided he paid such customs as citizens paid. In 1366, Thomas Serland of Lucca made a similar complaint. The king ordered an investigation as to whether other aliens who had been made citizens were free of alien customs for that reason. The record of the search in the particulars of the customs accounts[6] breaks off abruptly, but it had been found that in 1329 the collectors of the new custom in London had been quit of certain amounts levied on the goods of Ponche Portenare[7] and Nicholas Citeron 'pro eo quod ipsi fuerunt commorantes in civitate Londonie et non soluit novam custumam propter libertatem civitatis predicte.'[8] The criterion here is clearly citizenship, but when the matter touched the king's revenue, his acceptance or confirmation of its privileges was necessary. Hale, in his admirable chapter on the payment of customs explains the situation thus: a freeman of London or of the Cinque

[1] *C.P.R. 1361–64*, p. 42.

[2] PRO K.R. Customs 70/18.

[3] *C.P.R. 1367–70*, p. 244. The lack of a freemen's list for London makes it impossible to know when any freeman was admitted.

[4] He was a German but not a Hansard. Kunze, *Hanseakten aus England*, p. 53.

[5] PRO K.R. Mem. 106, Brevia Directa Mich.; PRO Exannual Roll 1.

[6] These particulars have disappeared.

[7] Portenare had been made a freeman in 1327 (*Cal. Plea and Mem. Rolls, London*, I, 27) and had been formally accepted by the king as such in 1330 (*C.P.R. 1327–30*, p. 553). Orders to cease demands on him for aliens customs had been made for several years. PRO K.R. Mem. 104, m. 39d. *ibid.* 107 m. 98; *ibid.* 109 m. 22; *ibid.* 106 m. 41d, 66.

[8] *Ibid.* 142, Brevia directa Trin. Similar demands were made on John Wynand of York. *C.P.R. 1350–54*, p. 374. On the Exannual Roll there are records of the new custom on wool, wine and general merchandise due from aliens who were citizens of London. These were Pouche Portenare, Nicholas Citeroun, Hermann le Skipper, Tidemann Coufot, and Torus Oddy. In the light of the statement above, it seems probable that they would all have been quit had they protested. PRO Exannual Roll 1.

Ports was free from the payment of prisage on wine but since no mention was made in the grant of the 2s. custom paid by aliens, an alien who became a freeman of these places was not freed from payment of butlerage unless specially exempt by the king, whose custom it was.[1] Not all freemen seem to have become denizens in the matter of paying customs. In the absence of freemen's lists for London[2] for this period it is impossible to tell how many aliens were made citizens, but of those known from other sources and of those on freemen's lists of other cities, only a few seem to have paid native customs.[3] Some of the aliens admitted to citizenship may not have been engaged in importing and exporting and were content with the privileges in retail trade, in having apprentices,[4] in being free of toll throughout England and with certain legal rights which citizenship gave them.[5]

The rule was made to work both ways. Alien merchants protested against paying customs as aliens and taxes as natives. The payment of the 3d. in the pound became the standard for judging liability for taxes although city tax collectors regarded residence, with or without citizenship, as the qualification. In 1355, Octavian Fraunceys, merchant of Florence, complained that although he and others paid customs as aliens and although he had the king's writ in his behalf, they had been unlawfully compelled to contribute toward the expenses of archers sent by London to the French war, and had been assaulted by the collectors. The latter, however, said that Fraunceys resided continually in London, carried on business there in wholesale and retail and 'that he ought to contribute with the rest of the citizens and that they continued to detain his chattels until he should pay the quota, as they were accustomed to do in such cases.'[6] In the following year the king repeated his order for the release of Fraunceys from this obligation for the rather confusing

---

[1] *Concerning the Customs*, p. 126.

[2] The only surviving lists are for 1309–12, *Cal. Letter Book D*, pp. 35–96.

[3] Cf. Appendix G.

[4] William le Monoier, apprentice to Peter le Monoier of Amiens, citizen of Wells, *C.P.R. 1345–48*, p. 441.

[5] *Letter Book D*, p. 153; *C.C.R. 1349–54*, p. 235; *Cal. Mayor's Letters, London*, pp. 74, 171; *Cal. Plea and Mem. Rolls, London*, ii, 19.

[6] *Cal. Letter Book G*, p. 46.

reason that he paid 3*d*. in the pound as an alien and was of the franchise of the city and in scot and lot with the citizens. The mayor and sheriffs replied that he held a hostel in Langbourne Ward, and carried on business there as a citizen and for that reason they refused to surrender his goods.[1]

Concerning taxes on moveables the same conflict is seen, which is really one between the attempt of alien merchants to maintain the privileges granted to aliens in the *Carta Mercatoria* and the tendency of the government to collect taxes from as many people as possible. There seems always to have been uncertainty concerning the incidence of the tax on moveables. Madox says that these subsidies were paid by citizens and burgesses[2] and the protests brought against unfair assessments seem to prove his statement, but they also show that contemporary assessors in cities were inclined to regard residence as the standard. Aliens who held land throughout the country were, of course, liable for all charges on that land.[3] At the beginning of Edward III's reign cases were repeatedly brought into the exchequer by aliens who had been assessed for the subsidies, in particular the sixth of 1323. The Peruzzi protested in 1328, as did six merchants of the Duchy of Aquitaine.[4] Two years later two merchants of Spain, Anthony and Edward Citeroun, protested against an assessment of £10 in Vintry Ward, and two of Genoa, Bartholomew de Chirio and Francekin Novelli, against 4*s*. 9*d*. in Bread Street Ward.[5] Two years later still three more merchants of the Duchy brought a suit.[6] The sole record of the case of the Peruzzi is a writ on the memoranda roll, which directs the barons of the exchequer to ascertain whether or not the merchants are citizens and if they are not, to cease de-

---

[1] *Ibid*., p. 54. In 1347, two Hansards were awarded damages against collectors of wool in Huntingdon, who had assessed them because they had houses in the city. The court decided that the properties were warehouses for storage and not shops where goods were bought and sold and were therefore not domiciles. PRO Coram Rege Roll 350, m. 20*d*.

[2] T. Madox, *The History and Antiquities of the Exchequer of the Kings of England* (London, 1711), p. 504.

[3] Francis Bache paid on his goods in Molsham in Essex. PRO Exannual Roll 1; PRO Lay Subsidy Roll 107/10, 13.

[4] These were Gosbert Cobel, assessed at £4, John Dosynoun, £1, Peter Massan, £2, John de Gout £2, Peter Beran, and Bertrand de la Tour £10.

[5] PRO Exannual Roll 1.

[6] These were Gosbert de Tro and Gerard Garembal, £4, and Michael Campenar, £2.

mands upon them, in accordance with the grant in the *Carta Merca-toria* that aliens should be quit of all tolls and taxes except those agreed to in the charter. The Peruzzi acknowledged that they had houses in Walbrook Ward and the record of the case ends there.[1] The suits of the other merchants are recorded in full on the plea rolls of the exchequer. The men of the Duchy admitted that they had goods and chattels in Vintry Ward but said that they were 'mercatores extranei et alienigene' and should pay no more than the *Carta Merca-toria* specified, whereas the collectors had assessed them as if they were citizens. On 17 June, 1329, the king issued a writ to the treasurer and barons of the exchequer to investigate the matter.[2] The subcollectors of Vintry Ward were summoned. They said, on oath, that they had acted according to orders received from the chief collectors, although they were well aware that the merchants were aliens and not citizens. It was decided that the merchants should be quit but the record goes on to say 'Postea predictis mercatoribus insistentibus curie hic pro exoneracione sua . . . habitaque super hoc deliberacione . . . visum est Baronibus non debere procedere ad exoneracionem quousque plenius inquiratur.' The inquisition was finally held at St Martin le Grand in July, 1332. It was found that the merchants were not citizens at the time the sixth had been levied,[3] neither did they contribute with citizens nor have a dwelling or taxable goods in the city. They were therefore quit of the demands. At the same time the other cases, which had been dealt with in the same way, were decided and all were quit.[4] In the record of the inquisition in the case of Michael Campenar we get the explanation of this assessment and possibly of the reluctance of the barons to press the matter. The sub-collectors, when asked why they had taxed the merchants, replied 'quod iniuncti fuit eis ex parte Regis per principales taxatores eiusdem sexte eosdem mercatores taxari.'

Later in the reign the taxation of aliens became a definite policy

[1] PRO K.R. Mem. 104, m. 94.

[2] PRO Exch. Plea Roll 56, m. 25d.

[3] By 1332 Anthony Citeroun was a citizen. *C.C.R. 1330–33*, p. 593. PRO Pipe Roll 181, Item Bed. d.

[4] PRO Exch. Plea Roll 56, m. 25d; *ibid.* 57, m. 21, 22; *ibid.* 59, m. 23d; PRO Exch. Writs 32, 33; PRO K.R. Mem. 107, m. 41; *ibid.* 108, m. 132d.

but one that was inconsistently carried out. In connection with the grant of the ninth sheaf, the ninth fleece, and the ninth lamb in 1340, it was decreed 'in the right of merchants foreign, which dwell not in cities nor boroughs, and also of other people that dwell in forests and wastes and all that live not of their gain nor store by the good advice of them which shall be deputed taxers, shall be lawfully set at the value of the fifteenth without being unreasonably charged.'[1] In 1342, the question of the taxation of aliens was considered by the parliament which the Black Prince held for the southern counties.[2] It was said that they had agreed when the king was in Brittany to pay tallage in aid of the king for the time they stayed in England. It was shown that they 'se coevrent par une Chartre grantee par le Roi l'aiel as Marchandz Aliens . . . par laquele Chartre ils ne deveroient mye estre eidez mes pur lour demure de 40 jours pur lour descharger et recharger.'[3] The final decision was that if they remained in the country they should aid as merchants denizen as long as they stayed. The act seems to have been retroactive, for in June, 1343, William de Cusance, the treasurer, and others including the mayor of London were ordered to 'assess all merchants and other strangers and aliens in London their portion of any aids, prests and grants made to the king by the commons of the realm or of the city from the time of his assumption of the governance of the realm . . . having regard to the length of stay in the city and upon all their goods and chattels there, pursuant to an ordinance made by the counsel of parliament.'[4] It seems to have been another of those attempts to increase the burdens of aliens in defiance of the *Carta Mercatoria* which was not wholly successful. Some collections were made. In a view of accounts in 1343 the sheriffs of London were said to be in arrears £58 13s. 10d. of the amount due from the assessment of aliens. Two merchants of Lucca who owed £46 were said to have paid and the arrears were thus reduced to £12 13s. 10d.[5] John de Coleyne, alien, was quit, after payment, on the pipe roll for 1343 for £8 6s. 8d. assessed for fif-

---

[1] *Stat.* i, 288. Cf. assessments on PRO Exannual Roll 1.

[2] *Stubbs*, ii, 411.

[3] *Rot. Parl.* ii, 137.

[4] *C.F.R. 1337–47*, pp. 307, 311, 331. Cf. PRO Exannual Roll 1.

[5] PRO K.R. Mem. 119, Status and Visus Comp. Trin.

teenths of various years from 1332. On the same roll the sheriffs answered for the following payments:[1]

Hildebrand Suderman	£7 out of £38. 1 mark.
Society of the Busdrake	£20 8*s*. 11*d*. out of £20 8*s*. 10¾*d*.
Henry and John Brake	£2 out of £20. 1 mark
John Werle	£3 6*s*. 8*d*. out of £6 6*s*. 8*d*.
Henry Bukke	£2 12*s*. 2*d*. " " £10.

At the same time Tidemann of Limberg was said to owe £46 1 mark; John Wolde £20; Nicholas Bartholomew of Lucca £333 6*s*. 8*d*.; John de Portenare, Lombard, £54. The opposition of the aliens to this taxation seems to have stiffened at this point and the policy of the government to have changed, very possibly because the king was borrowing large sums from them and found it politic to overlook the smaller tax in view of the larger loans. In 1344, a respite was granted to Nicholas Bartholomew and his fellows, merchants of Lucca, to the Bardi, the Peruzzi, Tidemann of Limberg, John de Portenare, Martin of Pistoia and others, chiefly because the king owed them more than their assessments.[2] The unpaid accounts and the residue of the partly paid ones became bad debts on the exannual roll until in 1350 the Hansards protested successfully against payment, on the grounds that the taxation was contrary to the *Carta Mercatoria*. In that year the barons of the exchequer were ordered to search the customs rolls to discover whether they paid the 3*d*. in the pound custom. If they did, they were to be quit of the demands for the subsidies.[3] The pipe rolls, the exannual roll, and the roll of the assessment of aliens in 1343 were examined as well as the customs rolls, where it was found that they paid alien customs.[4] Tidemann of Limberg was quit on the pipe roll for 1345,[5] and on the pipe roll for 1350 the sheriffs were quit of the sums due from other Hansards.[6] The assessments of the Lombards and of eleven other aliens con-

[1] PRO Pipe Roll 188 Lond.
[2] PRO K.R. Mem. 119, Communia Trin.; *ibid*. 120, Communia Trin.
[3] PRO K.R. Mem. 126, Brevia directa Trin.; PRO L.T.R. Mem. 123, Communia Mich.
[4] PRO Exch. Plea Roll 78 *passim;* PRO L.T.R. Mem. 123, Communia Mich.
[5] PRO Pipe Roll 190, Lond.
[6] *Ibid*. 195, Lond.

tinued to be recorded on the exannual roll with no indication that they were ever paid.[1]

The assessment of aliens does not seem to have been repeated during the rest of the reign and it seems safe to conclude that alien merchants were not expected to contribute to the taxes on moveables except when they held land, or had become citizens.[2] They seem to have been able by persistent effort to maintain very nearly the position established for them by the *Carta Mercatoria*. Those who wished to acquire the rights of denizens probably found little difficulty in so doing, provided they were willing to assume the burdens as well. The normal procedure at this period, which does not seem to have been continued in the next century, was first to secure citizenship, which was cautiously but willingly granted by the city authorities. The king, in accordance with his liberal policy toward aliens, confirmed these privileges by granting them the right to pay customs at the lower rate at which English merchants paid. Some aliens who had received both citizenship and denization seem to have preferred to pay alien customs to avoid internal taxation. When possible they undoubtedly chose the most advantageous financial position. At least one alien who was both citizen and denizen was put on a jury *de medietate lingue* as an alien.[3] Those aliens who were citizens and who could trade and pay customs like English merchants, (and the two seem to have been interdependent at this time) and who, by the king's favor, could hold land, must have occupied a position very like that of a naturalized subject of later centuries. In one way at least they were more privileged for naturalization did not carry with it the privileges of citizenship.

[1] A writ had been issued in 1346 ordering that Raimannus de Bologne be not molested by demands for payments other than those provided for in the *Carta Mercatoria*. PRO K.R. Mem. 122, Brevia directa Hil. In 1355 he appears on the Exannual Roll as owing £3.

[2] They sometimes made gifts to the king in aid of the war. In 1369 the Hanse gave 100 marks 'spontaneously' on the condition that it would not prejudice their rights. *Cal. Letter Book G*, p. 254.

[3] See p. 198, n. 7 below.

V

ALIEN MERCHANTS IN THE KING'S BENCH

FOURTEENTH century letters of denization, unlike later ones, contained no formal statement of the legal rights secured by the partially enfranchised alien.[1] It is possible to overemphasize such an omission in a period of development in the process of denization, but it is perhaps not without significance when we are considering the legal status of alien merchants and their right of access to the king's courts. Were the legal disabilities of an alien merchant less than his economic ones, so that the essential thing to be secured by denization was a remission of customs duties rather than a removal of bars to the bringing of actions in the royal courts?

Two general principles lay at the foundation of the legal position of alien merchants in England considered from the point of view of their access to the king's courts. In the first place, no merchant, native or alien, possessed a special status or was judged by a special law. The law merchant was a law of mercantile transactions rather than of merchants,[2] and it was administered principally in fair and market courts. The common law judges may have been willing to have merchant law used in their courts,[3] but it was highly specialized, and no one but a merchant was expected to know it. In 1354, after the enactment of the Statute of the Staple, providing that all cases falling within the jurisdiction of the staple should be tried by law merchant, whether the persons concerned were merchants or not, the commons petitioned that the laws and usages of the staple were unknown and should be set forth in writing. The king was pleased that this should be done, and decreed further 'que nul homme autre que Marchant denizein ou alien qi ne conissent mye les Usages,

---

[1] See Chapter IV above.

[2] Pollock and Maitland, I, 467.

[3] *The Commercial Laws of Great Britain and Ireland*, I (F. Pollock and others, ed., London, 1913), 12.

soit chargez par cel point tant que les dites Usages soient declarez en Parlement.'[1] It is unlikely that this was ever done. Merchants who came into the king's courts seem to have been satisfied with the common law or whatever means of justice was provided.

There was one privilege which aliens enjoyed in all courts: a jury made up half of their own countrymen, if enough could be found, in all cases except criminal cases involving the death penalty.[2] From being a custom practised in London even earlier,[3] it became universal by the royal charter of 1303,[4] and was enforced in local and central courts. In a suit in the exchequer between Tidemann of Limberg and John of Wesenham, the latter objected to a jury *de medietate lingue* on the grounds that the privilege applied only in local and fair courts, not in the king's courts. The records were searched for precedents and the objection was disallowed.[5] In the King's Bench such juries were usual but do not seem to have been a matter of course in cases involving aliens.[6] They were used also in inquisitions and in cases before mayors and commissioners, in spite of London's protest in 1357 that it was contrary to the franchises of London that matters done in the city should be tried by men of foreign countries.[7] According to the Ordinance of the Staple, cases in staple courts in which both parties were aliens were to be decided by juries made up wholly of aliens.[8] In a case in the King's Bench in which the defendant was an alien and in which four triers were appointed, two of the four were aliens.[9]

In the second place, no special courts were set up in England for aliens, and no enactments made concerning the means of legal redress available for alien merchants in the king's courts. The Statute

[1] *Rot. Parl.* ii, 261.

[2] *Ibid.*, ii, 262. See p. 134 below.

[3] *Cal. Plea and Mem. Rolls, London*, II, 53, n. 1, (1285). *Cal. of Early Mayor's Court Rolls*, p. 119 (1301).

[4] Gras, p. 261, c. 10.

[5] PRO Exch. Plea Roll 77, m. 82d. PRO K.R. Mem. 128, Brevia directa Trin.

[6] Cf. Appendix E.

[7] *C.C.R. 1369–74*, p. 26; *C.P.R. 1358–61*, p. 218; PRO Coram Rege Roll 433, m. 19 Rex. *Cal. Letter Book G*, p. 86.

[8] *Stat.* i, 336; *Rot. Parl.* ii, 262.

[9] PRO Coram Rege Roll 433, m. 19 Rex.

of Acton Burnell and the Statute of Merchants,[1] which dealt exclusively with debt, and the Ordinance of the Staple, which dealt with local mercantile matters,[2] applied to native as well as to alien merchants. The legal provisions of the *Carta Mercatoria* were concerned only with the treatment of foreigners in the local courts of fairs and towns and did not affect their position in the central courts.[3] It was, in fact, frequently stated that aliens should sue in the ordinary courts. In a grant of free trade to the Flemings in 1339, the king guaranteed to make good all injuries suffered by them in whatsoever court they might sue.[4] Again, in 1347, a case arising from the plundering of Flemish ships off the Isle of Wight was brought before the council and examined and the parties were told to sue at common law if they saw fit.[5] No special judicial system had been established for alien merchants, and, under the circumstances, access to the ordinary courts could scarcely have been denied them.

It is true, however, that the fact that merchants were aliens played some part in the selection of the court into which their suits were taken, when several courts were available. They were, for the most part, members of a transient group and few of them could devote the years to the pursuit of justice, which a suit in the common law courts sometimes demanded. They were dependent for protection on the king, whose diplomatic, financial, and economic interests were dependent on them. For these two reasons, we find, as we shall see later, many cases involving aliens brought before the council, or taken by special privilege into the exchequer. But alien merchants, although they were not expected to know the common law of England, were not denied access to it. This conclusion is confirmed by the plea rolls of the courts of Common Pleas and King's Bench. The *De Banco* rolls yield, as we should expect, chiefly cases of debt and account, since aliens were not likely to be concerned in cases arising out of the ownership or possession of land. The most interesting and

[1] See p. 105 below.

[2] In 1362, when the jurisdiction of the mayor of the staple in cases of felony and trespass was abolished, aliens were still permitted to have their cases of trespass arising in the staples tried either by common law or by merchant law, as had been provided in 1353. *Stat.* i, 336, 373.

[3] Gras, p. 260, cc. 5, 6, 8.

[4] *Foedera*, ii, 2, p. 1073.

[5] *C.C.R. 1349–54*, p. 48.

important evidence about the kind of actions and the courts open to aliens, however, is on the *Coram Rege* rolls.

Into the King's Bench were brought pleas of the crown, personal actions, and cases involving the king's interests or his officers. To all of these alien merchants were parties. The interest in criminal cases is more social than legal, although the number of appeals among this comparatively small number of cases is worthy of notice. Actually obsolete in the fourteenth century only in cases of arson, the process was rapidly being replaced in other felonies by indictments on the one hand, and by an action of trespass on the other.[1] But in the cases we are considering, there are almost as many appeals as indictments.[2] Murders were not infrequent, as the cases on the *Coram Rege* rolls and the coroners' rolls,[3] as well as the pardons on the patent rolls, show.[4] Very rarely was the accused punished. In most cases, he had fled and could not be found. In many others, he was pardoned because the deed was done in self-defence, or for no apparent reason. Conclusions drawn from legal, and particularly from criminal records are likely to be exaggerated and biassed, but it seems to be a fact that there were few of the outstanding merchants of this period, who were not connected in one way or another with acts of violence, or imprisoned for long periods, although it may have been for debt, not crime. Hildebrand Suderman and Tidemann of Limberg, the most important Hansards of the period, were both accused of murder, and may have left the country for that reason.[5] Nicholas Nigrebon of Venice and Venturus Alisaundre were parties to criminal cases or actions of trespass which arose out of assault.[6] William Pouche of Florence was killed in a brawl in Fleet Prison, where he had been confined eleven years for debt,[7] and Anthony Bache, one of the foremost Genoese merchants, died shortly after he had been released at

---

[1] W. S. Holdsworth, *A History of English Law* (3rd. ed., London: Methuen, 1922–26), II, 361 ff.

[2] Cf. Appendix E.

[3] E.g., PRO Coroner's Roll, Lincoln, 67, m. 17, 25, 26; *Cal. Coroners' Rolls, London, passim.*

[4] E.g., *C.P.R. 1350–54*, p. 100; *ibid. 1354–58*, pp. 284, 543; *ibid. 1364–67*, pp. 49, 88.

[5] See pp. 61, 19 above.

[6] See Appendix E.

[7] See p. 116 below.

his own petition, because his health had been impaired by long imprisonment.[1] The merchants of Lucca were involved in affrays in London, and Nicholas Sardouche was murdered.[2] The numerous unexplained actions for trespass would doubtless, if we had the statements of the parties concerned, shed further light on the economic and social activities of aliens. We get, however, one glimpse into their recreations, in the account of the murder of a Fleming by a fellow-countryman in a quarrel which began during a game of *tenes*.[3]

Actions of trespass have a greater significance, however. Coke's interpretation of Littleton's statement that an alien could not bring a personal action is probably not so 'bold a treatment of a carefully worded text' as has been suggested.[4] Coke maintained that the disability applied only to alien enemies, and that 'an alien whose sovereign is in league with ours may bring personal actions.'[5] Maitland agrees that this may be ancient common law, but thinks that it had 'little chance of asserting itself because of the opposition of the burghers.'[6] Whether Littleton and others were led to their conclusion because of their emphasis on real actions,[7] or whether, as may be possible, a diminution of the legal rights of aliens took place in the fifteenth century, the *Coram Rege* rolls of the latter part of the fourteenth century support Coke's interpretation, and show that aliens had practically the same rights in private law as subjects had, excluding, of course, real actions. Personal actions involving aliens brought in the King's Bench were numerous enough to show that they were a usual means of seeking redress, and not exceptional privileges enjoyed by a few. Among the personal actions, there were three in particular to which alien merchants were parties: trespass, debt, and account. Actions of assault, abduction, trespass to land and chattels, and of undefined trespass occur with aliens as plaintiffs or defendants, and occasionally as both. There are two instances of Hansards suing other Hansards on pleas of trespass in the King's

---

[1] PRO K.R. Mem. 133, Communia Mich.
[2] See p. 14 above.
[3] See Appendix E (Galfridus Webster of Brabant).
[4] Pollock and Maitland, I, 459.
[5] *Coke on Littleton*, 129b.
[6] Pollock and Maitland, I, 465–66.
[7] Holdsworth, *History of English Law*, IX, 94.

Bench.[1] Very occasionally actions of trespass involving aliens were brought in the Common Pleas.[2]

The King's Bench was one of the courts in which cases touching the king's officers were heard: complaints against customs collectors, cases arising out of attacks on collectors of subsidies, or the intimidation of juries.[3] When William Elys, farmer of the petty custom in Yarmouth, was accused in parliament of having robbed German merchants, it was said 'qe celles Billes touchantz la matire de feer et or fussent mandez el Bank le Roi pur trier.'[4] Cases concerning the seizure of goods for non-payment of customs, for exporting contrary to prohibitions, as reprisals, or as enemy property, as well as suits concerning the importation of counterfeit money or the exportation of gold and silver might also be heard *coram rege*.[5]

Many cases of this sort, except criminal cases, might have been and frequently were brought into the local courts as local records show, for the franchises of the towns were jealously against the encroachments of the king's courts. Among the cases here cited, however there were few in which this conflict of jurisdiction arose. In the action of trespass brought by Richard de Lynne, glover, of Coventry, against Henry Pouchemaker of Brabant, the mayor of Coventry claimed jurisdiction, how successfully it is not stated.[6] The trial of Nicholas Sardouche, merchant of Lucca, for many misdemeanors is an important example of this conflict, both because of the persons and interests involved, and because of the fulness of the records. On 29 November, 1368, the silkwomen[7] of London protested, by petition

[1] See Appendix E.

[2] E.g., Andres Peveral v. Nicholas Donet, Lombard and William Gervays, goldsmith. PRO De Banco Roll 419, m. 227d; Walter de Bardi v. Boneface Lapyn, moneyer. *ibid*. 433, m. 189; John Lubek de London, saddler v. Volmornus Gloyonen de Almain, merchant. *ibid*. 393, m. 274.

[3] See Appendix E.

[4] *Rot. Parl.* ii, 328.

[5] PRO Coram Rege Roll 436, m. 7 Rex; *ibid*. 459, m. 14 Rex; PRO Controlment Roll 25, m. 23. Cf. PRO Assize Roll 526, m. 3d. (Lincoln) for the indictment of aliens for using false weights.

[6] PRO Coram Rege Roll 389, m. 52d, Cf. Appendix E.

[7] Cf. *Rot. Parl.* v, 325 (1455) for similar petitions against aliens, also *Stat.* ii, 664 c. 21, act in favour of 'silkwymmen.' In 1363 'silkwymmen' were exempt from the statute restricting handicraft workers to one trade. *Stat.* i, 380.

to the mayor and aldermen, that Sardouche, by embracing all the silk he could find in London, had forced the price from fourteen shillings to eighteen shillings per pound.[1] The city authorities took action immediately. They summoned Sardouche to appear on 2 December, when he acknowledged buying 139 pounds of raw and colored silk from two Lombard merchants, Paul Penyk and Dyne Sanouche. He said that he had done this on the advice of his partners abroad, who had informed him that the loss of bales of silk and other merchandise on their way to Bruges would increase the price of silk. He pleaded ignorance of trespass and said that he was prepared to sell the silk for sixteen shillings per pound. He also confessed to having weighed the silk on his own balance in his house and not on the common balance or Small Beam of the city, by which, according to ordinance, fine goods and spices were to be weighed.[2] After two postponements, to 4 December, then to 11 December on both of which occasions Sardouche found mainpernours for a later appearance, he came before the mayor and aldermen on 11 December, pleaded guilty and, because of lack of mainpernours, was imprisoned to ensure his appearance two days later. He had apparently, however, been taken into custody on 9 December on another charge. On 5 December, the city authorities, making inquisition into the non-payment of customs on imports, found that Sardouche had avowed certain goods shipped to London by Thomas Serland, a merchant of Lucca but a freeman of the city, as Serland's property, whereas they actually belonged to other aliens. The sheriffs had, therefore, been defrauded of the additional customs due on the goods of aliens. In answer to summons issued after these findings, Sardouche had appeared on 9 December, pleaded guilty and had been committed to prison because of lack of mainprise until 13 December when the jury was to be called.[3] About this time the case was further complicated by royal intervention. The attention of the king had been drawn to it by the following undated petition of the silkwomen:

A notre tresredoute lige seigneur le Roi prient les poures femmes appellez

[1] *Cal. Plea and Mem. Rolls London,* II, 99, 100.
[2] *Cal. Plea and Mem. Rolls, London,* II, 100, 101, n. 1.
[3] *Cal. Plea and Mem. Rolls, London,* II, 103, 104.

Silkwymmen de Loundres qe come ils neient dount vivre fors soulement de cel mestier et come un Nicholas Sarduch par long temps avaunt ces heures eit priveement useez de forstaller et regrater et unquore use toute la soie crue et colore ouesqe tout plein des autres merchandises queux merchaunz aliens ameynent a la dite citee en greuous enhancement du prys ducelles sicome est maintenant ouertement menez en preeue par sa confession demeisne devaunt maire et Aldermans qar toute la soie qil poet trouer avendre en meisme la citee il ad ore tard privement achatee et enhancez la pris de chescune livre a iiiis. et plus desterling a commune damage sibien de vous seigneur et de toute la commune de la terre come de les femmes susditz. Qe plese par dieu et par profit de vous notre seigneur le Roi et de votre poeple graunter as ditz poures femmes brief direct as maire et Recordour de faire ent deue remedie et aussint par le profit de vous notre seigneur le Roi especial denque de autres sutils compassementz par le dit Nicholas encountre la commune profit du Roialme controuez et miesmes de vos custumes notre dit seigneur le Roi par lui souent concellez et nient paiez.[1]

The writ sought was granted on 8 December and during the two following months the case became a contest between royal and city jurisdiction. Five writs[2] were sent to the city authorities ordering them to send their records of the case to chancery, and two inquisitions[3] were taken which uncovered the details of a long career of smuggling, forestalling, exporting bullion, embracing, in fact the infringement of almost all ordinances concerning trade. Meanwhile another charge had been brought against Sardouche for when, on 15 February, the king ordered that he should be brought into chancery, reply was made that he was imprisoned for debts due Andrew de Porche, Dyny Rapound, Blaisius Carouch, all of Lucca, and Walter de Bardi.[4] Royal authority won out, however; Sardouche appeared *coram rege* although the city authorities still protested that they would send only such records as touched the king's interests. Sardouche pleaded not guilty and put himself on the country. A jury *de medietate lingue* was to be summoned in the Easter term and Sardouche was mainprised for the amazing sum of £21,600, which rep-

---

[1] PRO Coram Rege Roll 433, m. 19 Rex.

[2] January 3, 17, 21. *Cal. Plea and Mem. Rolls, London*, ii, 104, 106. January 27, February 9. *Cal. Letter Book G*, pp. 236, 237.

[3] December 19, January 10. *Cal. Plea and Mem. Rolls, London*, ii, 102, 105.

[4] PRO Coram Rege Roll 433, m. 19 Rex.

resented the amount of his frauds. The case was finally heard at *nisi prius* on the Saturday after Ascension at St Martin le Grand. On that occasion, Sardouche challenged the array of the panel of the jury on the grounds that part of the charges belonged to the jurisdiction of the sheriffs rather than to the king's court. In the course of the discussion of the validity of his claims the record breaks off.[1] On 16 June a pardon for all his misdemeanours was granted on payment of a fine of £200, but because of the plea of debt still pending in the sheriffs' court, he was returned to their custody.[2] He was apparently freed soon after this, for on 22 June he appeared before the mayor and aldermen to exhibit a writ of protection from the king, ordering them to protect him and his property. The writ was dated 15 June, and was the result of his complaint to the king of threats and charges brought against him.[3] His need of protection seems to have been real, for eighteen months later he was killed.[4]

There appears in this case, as in others of which we have a full account,[5] one of the reasons why cases which might fall within the jurisdiction of local courts were brought into the king's courts. The plaintiffs were dissatisfied with or distrustful of the action of the local courts. The same reason, doubtless, caused many to bring their actions directly into the king's courts. Sixty cases in the course of twenty-seven years is perhaps not a large proportion of the number of cases to which alien merchants were parties during that time. They are enough to indicate, however, that the bringing of actions by or against aliens in the King's Bench, most of which were personal actions, was neither unusual nor exceptional. The suits for debt and account heard in the Common Pleas and criminal cases in other courts would considerably increase the number of cases involving aliens in the common law courts. In over half the cases in the King's Bench during this period to which aliens were parties, they were defendants. In about a third of the cases they were plaintiffs, or in

---

[1] PRO Coram Rege Roll 433, m. 19 Rex.

[2] *C.P.R. 1367–70*, p. 279. See also W. Illingsworth, *An Inquiry into the Laws Antient and Modern respecting Forestalling, Regrating and Ingrossing* (London) 1800, pp. 235–36.

[3] *Cal. Plea and Mem. Rolls, London*, II, 109.

[4] See p. 14 above.

[5] Cf. Lombards v. Mercers, pp. 92 f. below.

criminal cases where an indictment was brought, the injured persons. In the remaining cases both parties were aliens. There seems to be no basis for the statement that aliens had no rights as plaintiffs in the king's courts.[1]

In general, it may be said that the ordinary courts were open to aliens. Englishmen, injured by aliens, had the same means of redress against them as they had against other Englishmen, although there was probably greater difficulty in finding aliens and in distraining them because frequently they had no property. The lack of time to carry on a long suit, the king's interests, lack of jurisdiction or of action on the part of other courts sent many aliens to the council,[2] but there was no bar against aliens in the common law courts.

[1] *Select Cases before the King's Council, 1243–1482* (I. S. Leadam, J. F. Baldwin, ed., Selden Society, xxxv, 1918), p. xxvii.

[2] See Lombards v. Mercers of London, pp. 92 f. below. Inaction on the part of the city authorities may have been responsible for the petition of Hildebrand Suderman for redress after men of London had broken into his house in Thames Street and carried away his goods, and for the reply which ordered an inquest instead of an ordinary action for trespass which might have been expected. PRO Ancient Petitions File 140, No. 6985.

VI

ALIENS BEFORE THE COUNCIL

THE particular interest which the king had in the legal entangle-
ments of aliens and the peculiar nature of some of the cases
account for the number of pleas which came before him and his council. These cases were of such variety that it is difficult to classify
them. They included, in general, cases which arose out of the violation of the king's letters of protection, of his diplomatic relations
with other countries, or of his own particular interests; and cases
which could not readily be settled elsewhere, because local feeling
would intervene to the prejudice of aliens, because they arose out of
flagrant acts of aggression on the part of the king's officers, or because they fell outside the scope of the common law. For one or another of these reasons many cases involving aliens were brought by
petition at one stage before the council.

The council received petitions from foreign rulers on behalf of
their injured subjects. For example, Flemish merchants, who had
been attacked at sea, brought petitions from the count of Flanders
and the commonalty of the land, which were exhibited to the king
and council, who replied to them.[1] On another occasion, a native of
Rouen was arrested on a charge of piracy and brought before the
council where he testified that he was a Spanish merchant and had
been in Lisbon at the time of the outrage. The king wrote to Alfonso
of Portugal, and to the merchants of the Spanish and of the English
staple at Bruges for verification of this statement.[2] When merchants
of Lescluse had been robbed within the jurisdiction of the bishop
of Durham, and had failed to receive reparation in the bishop's court
for the loss of their wool, the authorities of Bruges appealed to the
king, who ordered the bishop to make speedy restitution 'knowing

---

[1] *C.P.R. 1367–70*, p. 470.

[2] *C.C.R. 1349–54*, p. 470. He was acquitted of the charge 'by trial thereof made at Brugges
in Flanders by the king's command and returned into the chancery,' *C.P.R. 1350–54*, p. 251;
C.C.R. 1349–54, p. 418.

that the king would provide remedy notwithstanding the bishop's liberty.'[1]

Since violation of his letters of protection or of those of his representatives was the king's special concern, he was prepared to uphold the validity of such letters. Three merchants of Brittany, driven by a storm into the port of Shoreham, were arrested, but when in chancery they showed a safe conduct from the captain in Brittany, they were released and taken under the king's special protection while going to Flanders and back to Brittany.[2] There was reason for the decree that anyone convicted of having grieved merchants under the king's protection should be punished for contempt done to the king, by paying, as a fine, as much as he should be judged to have damaged the merchants and paying double damages to the merchants,[3] but we may doubt the efficacy of the decree as a preventive measure. One example is recorded of merchants who were set upon within the king's lordship and power, although they were relying on his special protection and safe conduct, who were taken and killed by 'some of the king's subjects who paid no heed to the king's letter patent of protection and safe conduct when it was shewn to them.' Their goods were stolen and their ships were burnt. A commission was appointed to do justice according to maritime law.[4] There are similar instances of cockets being torn up by the king's officials. Merchants of the society of the Leopardi were about to cross from England with money to redeem Henry of Lancaster, who was held in the Low Countries for the king's debts to the Flemings, when their cockets were taken from them by officials of the port and destroyed. They appealed to the king, who ordered the cockets and any other goods taken from them to be restored.[5] The dangers which beset aliens' goods in the course of importation and exportation were many and gave rise to much litigation, which usually began with an appeal to the king under whose protection they were. The oath of the merchants as to the value of general merchandise was not accepted; the goods were ille-

---

[1] *C.C.R. 1346–49*, p. 12.

[2] *C.P.R. 1358–61*, p. 181; *C.C.R. 1354–60*, p. 557.

[3] *Rot. Parl.* ii, 250.

[4] *C.P.R. 1374–77*, p. 410.

[5] *C.C.R. 1341–43*, p. 13.

gally opened by the mayor and sheriffs and left exposed and in danger of perishing.[1] Goods on which customs had been remitted for one reason or another were seized by the collectors for non-payment of customs, in disregard of the king's license.[2] Goods in ships driven into port by storms were constantly being seized for customs, although they had not been unloaded, and in spite of repeated orders from the king that no customs were to be collected under such circumstances.[3] Cases of this sort usually began with an appeal to the king or the council.

Cases of piracy[4] were frequently brought in their early stages before the council. An action of trespass might have been brought in the King's Bench, or in the latter part of the reign the case might have been heard in the court of Admiralty, but in both courts the course of justice was too slow for foreigners and often those against whom action was brought were royal officials. The king's captains in Brittany were frequent offenders, both in refusing to do justice and in engaging in piracy themselves. In 1350 Thomas Dagworth, who is described by Robert of Avesbury as 'strenuum militem . . . verum utique elegantem,'[5] connived at the theft of wine from a ship of Piacenza, shared in the spoils and refused to do justice to the merchants thus robbed. The case was brought before the king who ordered Dagworth to explain the theft and commanded that the wine

---

[1] *Rot. Parl.* ii, 251.

[2] *C.C.R. 1349–54*, p. 532.

[3] *C.C.R. 1369–74*, pp. 10, 263; *ibid. 1374–77*, p. 402; *C.F.R. 1369–77*, p. 151; *Foedera*, iii, 2, p. 611.

[4] The king considered himself bound to recompense aliens under his protection for losses sustained in piratical attacks but reparations were difficult to secure. Customs were sometimes remitted until the merchants had been satisfied. *C.C.R. 1349–54*, p. 548. Special trading privileges were sometimes granted (*ibid. 1333–37*, p. 687) or payment of damages might be made through the king's bankers (*C.P.R. 1374–77*, p. 505). But orders for reparation are few. Even the return of a stolen ship must have been far from adequate reparation. It might have changed hands several times since the seizure and depreciated from use and from attacks. During the reign of Edward II a ship of John Seriez of St Jean d'Angeli was seized in Brittany and brought to England by pirates of Bayonne, taken into custody in 1324. In 1327, when the French king sought restitution, the career of the vessel was traced. It had been taken to Bordeaux and given to Peter Galicien, who had been robbed by the same pirates. He had given it to Edward II, who gave it to Richard Fille. Originally valued at £160, it was now worth £60 when returned to John Seriez as a gift. *C.P.R. 1327–30*, p. 168.

[5] *De Gestis Mirabilis Regis Edwardi Tertii* (E. M. Thompson, ed., Rolls Series, 1889), p. 352.

be sought in all cellars and other places in London and safely kept. Finally after Dagworth's attorneys had appeared in chancery and undertaken to satisfy the merchants for the wine, if the king and council decided that it belonged to them, the mayor and bailiffs of Sandwich were ordered to dearrest the wine and deliver it to Dagworth.[1]

One of the cases preserved in unusual detail resulted from the plundering of a Genoese ship by William de Rouceby, acting under orders from John Avenal, the king's captain in Brittany, in 1353.[2] It must have been a particularly awkward occurrence, because a treaty had been made with Genoa only a few years before after long negotiations which had been delayed by just this sort of attack. In February, 1353,[3] Anthony Compaignon of Genoa, lately come to London, was granted protection and safe-conduct while going to his own or other parts for merchandise to bring to England. On 27 December his ship and goods were captured. He appealed to the king, accusing William de Rouceby. The latter, a retainer of the captain in Brittany, was summoned to chancery, where he made his defense. The ship, he said, had come to the Race of St Matthew in Brittany and had remained there for three ebbs and flows of the tide and had departed without paying customs. Therefore, acting under orders from John Avenal, he had pursued and captured it near the Scilly Isles. Avenal was ordered to appear before the council on the octaves of Holy Trinity (15 June). In the meantime, on 22 January, the king, acting on this information, ordered the sheriff of Somerset and his sergeant at arms to arrest the five ships which made the attack and to bring the masters and mariners with all speed to the council because the king was bound to help the petitioners, especially since they were under safe conduct and because of an ordinance,[4] newly made by him and the council, that swift justice be done to merchant strangers coming to England.[5] No mention was made of William de Rouceby. The theft was said to have been committed by the 'master

[1] *C.C.R. 1349–54*, pp. 3, 54.
[2] *Selden Society*, xxxv, pp. lxxiii, 37–41.
[3] *C.P.R. 1350–54*, p. 400.
[4] Ordinance of the Staple, 1353.
[5] *C.P.R. 1350–54*, p. 543.

of a ship of Plymouth and others sent from the fleet.' The prosecution was made in the king's name because of the new ordinance. On 4 March the judiciary and chancellor in Ireland were ordered to arrest the men named in the report of an inquisition held by the mayor of the staple at Bristol, the mayor of Bristol, and the sergeant-at-arms, and to bring them in custody to the king.[1] On 15 June John Avenal came before the council and repeated substantially William de Rouceby's account, adding that the mariners had landed and that therefore he had tried to collect the customs, but that the ship left during the night. Rouceby was then ordered into custody to appear when needed. About a year later John Avenal came before the council to hear the judgment of the court, which having collected evidence by hearings in chancery, in the council itself and by inquisitions, delivered the verdict to the defendant in the presence of the chancellor, the treasurer, the justices of both benches and others of the council, procedure more in accordance with common law than equity.[2] It was decided that he should be imprisoned in the Tower and his goods and chattels seized. He had apparently foreseen this verdict and had tried to distribute his goods, for on 6 May a commission was appointed to arrest his goods which had been sent into various counties.[3] During the next few years account were made by those holding his lands,[4] which were released 17 July, 1360. Avenal had died and no one was suing for restitution.[5] The case is one of the few in which actual testimony given before the council is preserved. Concerning the Genoese, it is said that 1000 sacks of wool were granted them July, 1354. There is record of a grant, but it is to merchants not concerned in this affair and to others in general who had sustained damages, a grant made in accordance with a treaty.[6]

The number of cases in which petition was made to the king and the council either in the first instance or because justice could not

---

[1] *C.P.R. 1354–58*, p. 56.

[2] *Selden Society*, xxxv, p. lxxiii.

[3] *C.P.R. 1354–58*, p. 207.

[4] PRO L.T.R. Mem. 157, Communia Hil.

[5] *C.C.R. 1360–64*, p. 49.

[6] *C.P.R. 1354–58*, p. 92. Similar cases, when officials, in doubt whether customs should be collected or not from ships driven into harbour by storms, came up in the exchequer when there was no charge of piracy or attack. PRO K.R. Mem. 148, Communia Mich.

be secured in other courts was great, but the chief interest lies in
the methods used by the council in dealing with them. A few cases,
probably those in which evidence could be secured with comparative
ease, were heard and decided by the council. In 1360, the mayor and
bailiffs of York were ordered to dearrest two foreigners and to return
to them one seal and two rings and permit them to go where they
would. They had been found wandering in the city for three days and
because no one understood their idiom they had been arrested. One
of them was sent in custody to the council to ask what should be
done. Citizens of London and several merchants, native and alien,
testified that they were lawful merchants of Lombardy, come to
England solely for the purpose of trading.[1] A case between merchants
of Genoa and a Spanish ship-owner which arose when the ship was
compelled to put into Bristol because of a storm was heard and decided by the council.[2] It was more usual for the petition or the hearing before the council to be only one stage in the proceedings. The
complaint was often referred to a commission which was ordered
'to make diligent scrutiny and inquisition . . . touching the goods so
taken which are not yet put in safe keeping, compel those who can be
proved to have any to make restitution thereof, levy the said goods if
they exist or the value of them if they do not exist from the goods of
those into whose hands they have come, arrest and commit to prison, those refusing to make restitution, keep in prison until further
order and deliver the goods or their value to the said merchants as
restitution is made.'[3] Equally often the commission or an individual
was ordered to make inquisition[4] or to arrest the goods of the male-
factors and to await further orders[5] or to make a return to the council or chancery or to send there the parties concerned on a certain
day.[6] The council might then decide to whom the goods were to be

[1] *C.C.R. 1354–60*, p. 608.

[2] *C.P.R. 1350–54*, p. 441.

[3] *C.P.R. 1374–77*, p. 148; see also *ibid.*, pp. 159, 218; *ibid. 1350–54*, p. 520; *ibid. 1361–64*, p. 136.

[4] E.g., Command to the sergeant at arms 'to go about within the liberty of the Cinque
Ports and elsewhere as shall be expedient, to inform himself by lawful means or by inquisition
of the names of those who have done this and to arrest their goods, certifying the king of what
he does herein with all possible speed.' *C.P.R. 1350–54*, p. 165.

[5] *C.P.R. 1354–58*, p. 120; *ibid. 1370–74*, p. 485.

[6] *C.P.R. 1350–54*, p. 166; *ibid. 1354–58*, pp. 68, 450; *ibid. 1367–70*, p. 65.

restored or what reparation should be made,[1] or it might transfer the case again to another court.

Not infrequently cases were transferred to the common law courts. For one reason, the processes of those courts were better suited to cases which were postponed from term to term because of the non-appearance of the parties. A collector who had been exacting unauthorized customs from aliens had not appeared when summoned before the council and the writ for his taking was sent to the justices of the King's Bench, who issued a *capias*, with, however, no better result.[2] More efficient means, however, of securing the appearance of parties before the council were being devised just at this time, as is illustrated by one of the most interesting and important cases which came before the council—that of the Lombards against the mercers of London. Interesting because it concerns a group of London merchants and their alien rivals in trade, it is important because of the completeness of the record which has survived and because there was issued in the course of the proceedings one of the newly devised chancery writs, the *subpoena*. The writ and the petition which led to its issue are well-known, and have been published, together with a very incomplete account of the case, as far as it has been hitherto traced, in *Select Cases before the King's Council*.[3]

A summary of this account is as follows: Before November, 1357, an attack had been made on some Lombards in London, and, as a consequence, Adam de Wroxham and Thomas Everard, mercers, were to be taken by the sheriff, and Nicholas Sharpenham and Thomas Malden, also mercers, had been imprisoned in the Tower. They were all released or the order for their seizure superseded by March of the following year. The cause of the affray was unknown but was probably trade rivalry, and the fact that Nicholas Sharpenham was not a London mercer, but was from Surrey and had been brought to the Tower by Henry Cove, a mercer later accused, seems to indicate that the Southwark mercers were aiding the Lombards. Sharpenham does not appear again. The imprisonment of some of the

[1] *C.P.R. 1374–77*, p. 62; *C.C.R. 1374–77*, p. 292.

[2] PRO Controlment Roll 11, m. 10; *C.P.R. 1350–54*, p. 463; PRO Coram Rege Roll 362, m. 11; *ibid*. 364, m. 20 Rex.

[3] *Selden Society*, xxxv (1918), pp. lxxvi–lxxxii, 42–47.

mercers in the Tower, the statement made by the Lombards in their petition that some of their assailants had confessed before the council and the fact that all the mercers were bound over to appear before it 'when anyone wishes to speak against them,' show that the case had already been heard before the higher court which was prepared to take action later. Not until a year later, however, was the writ issued, summoning the mercers to appear. Action was no doubt stimulated by the undated petition of the Lombards, which named eight mercers as principal aggressors and sought that the entire company be bound over to keep the peace. Three months later, the city authorities, directed by writ from the king, held an inquisition and found that Thomas Malden, Henry Forester, John Meleward, and Richard Phelip, a servant, were guilty of having attacked Francis Bochel and Reymund Flamy in Old Jewry in the ward of Colmanstreet on Monday after the feast of St John the Baptist, 1357. Here the records apparently ended and it was assumed that the mercers accused fled and that 'from such a finding the complainants must have reaped but meagre satisfaction.'

The facts given above are, however, far from being almost all the details of the outbreak which have been preserved.[1] A record of the case is to be found in unusual completeness on the *Coram Rege* and Controlment Rolls, and for that reason it has been printed in full in the appendix. From it we can fill in the gaps in the account given above and arrive at a satisfactory and far from conjectural conclusion. In 1357,[2] the mercers of London made a malicious and premeditated attack upon Lombard merchants. The immediate cause of the outbreak is not specifically stated, but it was undoubtedly trade rivalry, aggravated by such practices as led to the prosecution of the merchants of Lucca and of Nicholas Sardouche, in particular, a few years later.[3] There is no evidence that the council took charge of the case until complaint was made to it by the Lombards, and we may assume that the actual affray was quelled by the city authorities, who then refused or delayed to do justice. If the writ

[1] *Selden Soc.* xxxv, p. lxxvi.
[2] Probably on 28 June. See p. 96, n. 3 below.
[3] See pp. 11–14; 81–84 above.

of 3 August,[1] summoning all Lombards before the council has any connection with the case, it may be that the matter was brought to the attention of that body within a month after the outrage. Then or later, an appeal was made by the Lombards and a hearing granted sometime during the summer of 1357.[2] The identity of one of the injured Lombards, Francis Bochel, was established, and according to the later petition of the Lombards, one of the mercers, Thomas de Maldon confessed his guilt and named Geoffrey Bernham, servant of Henry Cove, mercer, as leader of the attack.[3] The city authorities were then ordered to do justice, and to aid them, some of the mercers 'quos fama quasi publica inde reddidit culpabiles' were imprisoned in the Tower or orders were issued for their arrest.[4] These were, according to the orders for their release and according to the statement of the Lombards in their petition, Thomas de Maldon,[5] Henry Forester,[6] Adam de Wroxham,[7] William Cove,[5] William de Woodford,[5] and Thomas Everard.[8] Nicholas Sharpenham, who seems to have been a Southwark mercer and probably a supporter of the Lombards,[9] was also released at this time. He had been given into custody by Henry Cove, one of the mercers accused by the Lombards, and the constable of London. The constable of the Tower could give no other reason for his imprisonment.[10] It may have been an attempt on the part of the London mercers to divert suspicion from themselves and to attack their Surrey rivals. Nothing more, however, is heard of Sharpenham after his release in February, 1358. His arrest and the fact that the London mercers were warned against doing harm to other mercers as well as to alien merchants[11] show the

---

[1] They were summoned to inform the king on certain matters. *Cal. Letter Book G*, p. 91.

[2] Cf. dates of orders for the release of the mercers, p. 95 below.

[3] Document A. *Selden Soc.*, xxxv, 42.

[4] The account of these early proceedings is contained in the writ of 7 October, 1359, which is given in PRO Controlment Roll 17, m. 24d. Cf. Appendix F. It had been noted but not given in full in *Cal. Letter Book G*, p. 112.

[5] *C.C.R. 1354–60*, p. 432.

[6] Petition of Lombards. *Selden Soc.*, xxxv, 42.

[7] *C.C.R. 1354–60*, p. 432.

[8] *Ibid.*, p. 495.

[9] *Selden Soc.*, xxxv, p. lxxx.

[10] *C.C.R. 1354–60*, p. 498.

[11] See Appendix F, pp. 190, 194 below.

jealous restrictiveness of local trade directed against English as well as alien competitors.

The order for the arrest of Adam de Wroxham was superseded by mainprise on 1 November, 1357,[1] and that of Thomas Everard on 4 March, 1358.[2] Thomas de Maldon was released from the Tower on 1 December, 1357.[3] The rest, who seem to have been imprisoned, were probably also released about this time. The release of the mercers was made at the request of the mayor and sheriffs and other worthy men of the city and in the hope that reparation would thereby be more speedily made. The action of the council in transferring the case to other authorities after a preliminary hearing is quite consistent with its usual methods; but it did not relinquish all hold upon the case for the mainpernours were bound to have the mercers before the council if anyone wished to appear before them. The hope of prompt action on the part of the mayor and sheriffs was vain. A year and a half later the Lombards were compelled to make a second petition to the council. In it they accused six mercers and the servant of one of them, and asked that the company, who are named in the petition, be summoned before the council and compelled to give surety that they will do no further harm.[4] Though the petition is undated, it must have preceded shortly, and have been the cause of the issue of the writ of *subpoena* on 8 July, 1359, which commanded the sheriffs to summon the seven accused by the Lombards, and the company of mercers,[5] to appear before the council on the following Tuesday. The action of the council on this occasion is recorded on the *Coram Rege* rolls and resembles the procedure followed at the first hearing of the case. The company of mercers[6] was warned against molesting other mercers or alien merchants. The mercers who had been released on mainprise were again imprisoned and a writ was issued on 7 October, 1359 ordering the city authorities to hold an

[1] P. 94, n. 7 above.

[2] *Ibid.*, n. 8.

[3] *Ibid.*, n. 5.

[4] *Selden Soc.* xxxv, 42.

[5] *Ibid.*, pp. 43, 44.

[6] All appeared except Adam Everard who had nothing in the city whereby he could be summoned, and Nicholas Bedyngton who was dead. *Ibid.*, pp. 44, 45.

inquest.[1] If, as seems likely, those who were imprisoned at this time were those who were brought from the Tower into the King's Bench after the return of the inquisitions had been made, they were a slightly different group from that named by the Lombards as having been imprisoned before and presumably now free on mainprise, or mentioned in the previous orders for release. The Lombards said that William Cove, Thomas de Maldon, Henry Forester, Adam de Wroxham, Thomas Everard, and William de Wodeford had been released on mainprise, but the group brought into the King's Bench included Henry Cove and John Meleward but not Thomas Everard.[2]

This time the city authorities acted promptly. On the following day, 8 October, two inquisitions were held. By the first it was found that on Monday after the feast of St John the Baptist[3] Henry Forester, Thomas Maldon and John Meleward, abetted by Richard Phelip, attacked Francis Bothel and Reymund Flamy in Old Jewry in Colemanstreet Ward. Phelip did not strike the Lombards. The result of the second inquisition was substantially the same, except that it did not implicate Phelip.[4] The findings of the inquisitions and the writ of 7 October, 1359, were brought by the chancellor into the King's Bench which now took charge of the case. The mercers imprisoned in the Tower were brought into court. Henry Forester, Thomas de Maldon, John Meleward were immediately asked how they would clear themselves. They each confessed their guilt and put themselves upon the king's grace, and begged to be allowed to make fine. Because it could not then be decided how heavy the fine should be, they were released on mainprise, to appear at the octaves of Trinity following. The Coves, Adam de Wroxham, and William de Wodeford were then bound over for good behavior under

---

[1] Appendix F, p. 191 below. In the introduction to the case in *Selden Society*, xxxv, p. lxxx, it is unaccountably stated that this took place six months after the release of Sharpenham on 1 February, 1358.

[2] Cf. Appendix F, p. 193 below.

[3] The feast of St John the Baptist was probably that of 24 June, making the date of the attack 28 June. Had it been the feast of the Decollation (29 August), the date would be 2 September. The later date is adopted by Riley in the *Memorials of London* (p. 488) but it would leave less than two months for the investigation by the council, the imprisonment and release of the mercers and the writ for the release of Thomas de Maldon says he has been imprisoned a long time. *Selden Soc.*, xxxv, p. lxxx, n. 27.

[4] Cf. Appendix F, p. 193 below.

penalty of 400 marks each and released. The sheriffs were ordered to bring Phelip before the court at the octaves of Hilary. He was not found and was eventually outlawed. The other three came on the appointed day to hear the decision about their fine and found mainpernours to answer for it. They appeared from term to term until Hilary, 1362, when they made fine, as is recorded on the roll of fines for that year, for twenty marks each and found pledges 'quod amodo se bene geret erga dominum Regem et populum suum sub pena C librarum.'[1]

There is still one problem unsolved: the identity of John Meleward and his connection with the mercers. He was not included among the company of mercers nor is he accused by the Lombards.[2] He did not appear in the case until he is mentioned in the inquisitions of 8 October, 1359. Yet he was apparently imprisoned with the mercers, for he was brought from the Tower to the King's Bench. It is barely possible that he was arrested between the time when the results of the inquisitions were sent to the council, and when they were sent to the King's Bench. Moreover Thomas Everard, who was imprisoned the first time, who was accused by the Lombards and summoned before the council 1359, was not bound with the company of mercers to keep peace nor does he seem to have been arrested the second time. He drops out of the case about the time that John Meleward enters it.

The case is interesting as an illustration of the difficulty which alien merchants experienced in attempting to secure justice from the city authorities even when the identity of their assailants was fairly well established, and when they were never beyond the reach of the law.[3] It is also an illustration of the slow and intricate workings of justice, even when the injured parties are alien merchants, who had appealed to the council and had been generally promised speedy justice. It is a typical example of the practice of the council of transferring to local authorities and to the King's Bench routine matters

[1] Appendix E, p. 196 below.

[2] The fact that one of his mainpernours was from Wiltshire supports the suggestion that he was not a London mercer. *Selden Soc.*, xxxv, p. lxxx.

[3] The evidence of the Coram Rege Rolls destroys the supposition that Forester, Maldon, and Meleward fled. Cf. *Selden Soc.*, xxxv, p. lxxxi.

like the collection of evidence or fines, while maintaining supervision of the case by the arrest or mainprise of those accused. The second part of the case alone, from the petition of the Lombards to the end, is as complete an example of proceedings[1] before the council as we have for this period. There is first the petition, accusing the mercers and asking for redress of a definite kind, followed by the *subpoena* of 8 July, summoning the mercers before the council. Then on the *Coram Rege* rolls we find the record of the action taken, partly by the council complying with the request of the Lombards and partly by the King's Bench at the command of the council.

The peculiar importance of the case however, is, derived from the writ issued 8 July, 1359. During this period special writs were devised for the use of the council and chancery. They differed from other writs in that they contained no mention of the charges to be brought, and in that they eventually became writs of privy seal, of which no record was kept and which were unauthorized by parliament. Palgrave calls them writs of jurisdiction, and distinguishes them from writs of grace and favor issued by the king. They were the writ of *premunire*, addressed to the sheriff, and the writ of *quibusdam certis de causis*, addressed to the defendant. Both compelled attendance before the council by such phrases as *sub periculo quod incumbet* or *sub gravi indignatione*.[2] About the same time a third writ came into general use. In it appearance was commanded *sub pena centum librarum* or any other sum. The writ of privy seal known as the *subpoena* was supposed to have been invented by John Waltham, who was Master of the Rolls from 1381–1386,[3] but it was known before that time, and was the result of the combination of the penal clause, long in use, with new chancery writs, rather than of any deliberate act of invention. The penal clause had been used as early as 1232,[4] and is frequently found in writs and orders of the fourteenth

---

[1] See *Select Cases in Chancery, 1364–1471* (W. P. Baildon, ed., Seldon Society, x, 1896), pp. xii–xv for description of chancery proceedings.

[2] F. Palgrave, *An Essay on the Original Authority of the King's Council* (London, 1834), p. 131; Holdsworth, *History of English Law*, i, 486; J. F. Baldwin, *The King's Council in England during the Middle Ages* (Oxford: Clarendon Press, 1913) pp. 288, 289.

[3] *Rot. Parl.* iv, 84; *Selden Soc.*, x, p. xiv.

[4] *Selden Soc.*, xxxv, p. xxxviii, n. 6.

century. In 1341, for example, in a writ issued at the request of merchants of Brittany, who, while under the king's protection, had been plundered by the English, the sheriff of Devon was ordered to have certain men of Plymouth before the king and council in chancery and 'not to omit to do this under pain of £100 which the king will cause to be levied of his lands and chattels.'[1] In 1367, the governor of Calais, the mayor, and treasurer of the staple were ordered to settle a dispute between merchants and Lombards, or if they were unable to do so, to send them to the council under penalty of £200.[2] But the insertion of a penal clause of this sort into the writ of *quibusdam certis de causis* or of *premunire* was the first step in the evolution of a new writ, which in its early forms was issued either under the great seal or the privy seal, and was addressed either to the sheriff or to the defendant. In fact, the writ of 1359, issued against the mercers, is given by Palgrave as an example of a *premunire*[3] but it contains the essentials of a *subpoena:* the absence of any indication of the charges to be brought and the penal clause. In the next reign, possibly under John Waltham, the formal writ of *subpoena* had developed: a writ of privy seal, of which no record was kept, addressed to the defendant, written in French, commanding appearance before the chancery to answer unspecified charges under a money penalty for non-appearance.[4]

It is stated in the introduction to *Select Pleas before the King's Council*[5] that the *subpoena* was used in the exchequer, but that none have been seen. Dr Holdsworth says it 'was certainly known in the exchequer as early as Henry IV's reign and was generally used in 1574.'[6] In the memoranda roll of the king's remembrancer for 1367 there is the following entry among the writs returnable for Hilary term:

Ebor. Mandatum est Willelmo de Whixle uni executorum testamenti Willelmi de Acastre mercatoris et civis Eboraci defuncti quod omni dilacione et

[1] *C.C.R. 1341–43*, p. 356.
[2] *Foedera*, iii, 2, p. 839.
[3] *Op. cit.*, p. 131.
[4] F. W. Maitland, *Equity, also The Forms of Action at Common Law* (A. H. Chaytor, W. J. Whittaker, ed., Cambridge University Press, 1926), p. 5; *Selden Soc.*, x, p. xiv.
[5] *Selden Society*, xxxv, p. xxxix.
[6] *History of English Law*, i, 241.

excusatione postponitis sit in propria persona sua hic in quindenis Pasche
ad respondendum informandum et deliberandum curiam Regis super diversis articulis Regis commodem Regis tangentibus ei ex parte Regis
obieciendis et imponendis et ad ulterius recipiendum quod curia consideravit
in hac parte. Et hoc sub pena centum librarum quas de terris et catallis
suis si ad diem predictum non venerit levari faciet nullatenus omittat.[1]

In the roll for the next year there are similar writs issued to various merchants ordering them to appear before the treasurer and
barons *sub pena centum librarum.*[2]

About this same time there are evidences of a tendency to assign
certain kinds of cases to what seem at first to be parts of the council,
but which were soon to develop into the separate courts of Chancery
and Admiralty. Records of proceedings in the council and in the
chancery at this period are fragmentary and it is difficult to trace
cases brought before them, but it seems certain that until the fifteenth century there was no clear-cut distinction between the courts.
The chancellor was the chief legal authority of the council and to him
as such petitions were frequently addressed.[3] The court over which
he presided was essentially the council. The beginnings of a differentiation between the council and the chancery appeared in the fourteenth century, however, in the transference of certain cases to the
jurisdiction of the chancellor. As early as 1327 mercantile cases were
assigned to chancery. In that year an English merchant addressed
a petition to parliament asking redress for the loss of ten sacks of wool
which a Florentine merchant had freighted for Florence three years
before but which, by reason of a quarrel between the Florentine and
members of another company, had been seized and sold in France.
The answer was that the petition should be given into chancery and
the merchants of the said company be called there and the reasons of
both sides being heard, justice should be done according to the law
used in such cases.[4] In 1343, a case concerning Spanish merchants
who claimed to have been attacked by the English while sailing to

[1] PRO K.R. Mem. 143, Brevia Retorn. Hil. The preceding entry on this roll is a similar
writ to Roger de Holm, clerk.

[2] *Ibid.*, 144, Brevia Retorn. Mich. d. It was issued *per thesaurarium et alios de consilio.*

[3] PRO Ancient Correspondence, vol. XLI, 9.

[4] *Rot. Parl.* ii, 437.

France, was brought before the chancellor and others of the council.[1] In 1353 merchants having complaints against sheriffs and other officials who refused to accept their oath for the value of merchandise sealed in barrels were ordered to seek justice in chancery.[2] Similar cases concerning the unjust seizure of goods during a truce, reprisals, or unfair demands for customs were often brought into chancery.[3]

In 1349, a definite step was taken toward granting separate jurisdiction to the chancellor. In a writ to the sheriffs of London, it was stated that 'the king wishes affairs concerning the common law of England and his special favour to be sued henceforth, those of the common law before the elect of Canterbury, the chancellor and those concerning the king's favour before the said chancellor or keeper of the privy seal, so that they may send the things which cannot be done without consulting the king together with their advices thereon to the king, so that after inspection he may signify his will to them, as he is so much occupied upon divers affairs touching him and the state of the realm.'[4] The attempt to relieve the pressure of legal business in the council was not wholly satisfactory as far as foreign merchants were concerned. In 1354, they petitioned that one of the council be assigned to hear quarrels and to answer them, for aliens dared not enter the councils, did not know when they were held and there was no one to whom they could declare their grievances except the treasurer and the chancellor who had so much great business that they had no time for small. No such commissioner, whose functions would have resembled those of the local justiciars of merchants, was appointed, although it was stated that the treasurer and chancellor, who would continue to hear complaints, would assign justices or other learned men for the purpose when they could not attend to the matter themselves.[5] There was a possibility that from dealing

[1] *Foedera*, ii, 2, p., 1929. Cf. *C.C.R. 1349–54*, pp. 80, 96, Case of merchants of Lübeck accused of plundering English ship heard and terminated in chancery (1349). *C.P.R. 1350–54*, p. 457, a case of seizure of goods during a truce was heard before the council and investigated by the local authorities who were ordered to send opposers to chancery (1353).

[2] *Rot. Parl.* ii, 251.

[3] *C.P.R. 1350–54*, p. 228; *ibid. 1361–64*, p. 447. *C.C.R. 1364–68*, p. 215.

[4] *C.C.R. 1346–49* ,p. 615. Cf. Sir H. C. Maxwell-Lyle, *Historical Notes on the Use of the Great Seal of England*, (London: H. M. Stationery office, 1926), p. 22.

[5] *Rot. Parl.* ii, 262. Cf. p. 91 above.

with such cases, the chancery might have developed into a court of
law merchant, and the tendency in this direction is seen in the statement in a fifteenth-century Year Book that 'aliens were not bound to
know the statutes of England and that they ought to sue . . . where
the matter would be determined according to the law of nature in the
chancery.'¹ The jealousy between the common law courts and the
courts of equity, however, in the fifteenth century led the former to
maintain their jurisdiction over aliens.²

The difficulty in dealing with cases involving aliens was also one
of the reasons for the development of a court of Admiralty.³ In the
Black Book of the Admiralty, it is asserted that the civil jurisdiction
of admirals began under Edward I, when it was ordained that 'any
contract made between merchant and merchant or merchant and
mariner beyond the seas or within the flood mark shall be tried before
the admiral and nowhere else.'⁴ But not until the middle of the fourteenth century, however, can the definite emergence of an admiralty
court be traced. Maritime cases could be brought before several
courts in the fourteenth century. They were heard in the King's
Bench, before justices of assize, or by the council or in chancery,
whence they were usually transferred to a commission of which the
admiral was a member, with the command to do justice 'according
to the law and custom of the realm and maritime law.'⁵ The inter-
working of the council, chancery, and commissions under an admiral
at this time is shown in a case that began in 1358. By a petition in
chancery in that year, it was shown that Saier Scoef, citizen of London, had loaded goods in Lescluse in a ship of a merchant of that
place. By the master of the ship he sent a letter to his wife telling the
nature and value of the goods. The letter was delivered but not the
goods. These, the master said, had been plundered by Norman pirates. He was ordered to appear in chancery, where he explained that

¹ Baldwin, *The King's Council*, p. 275.

² W. S. Holdsworth, 'The history of the law as to the status of British subjects and aliens.'
Revue de l'histoire du droit, III (1921), 205.

³ For a general account of the development of the court, see *Select Pleas of the Court of
Admiralty, 1390–1404* (R. G. Marsden, ed., *Selden Society* VI, 1892); T. L. Mears, 'The
History of Admiralty Jurisdiction, *Select Essays in Anglo-American Legal History*, II, 312–364.

⁴ (T. Twiss, ed., Rolls Series, 1871–76), I, 69.

⁵ *C.P.R. 1350–54*, pp. 389, 521; *ibid. 1374–77*, pp. 65, 217, 410.

the rest of the cargo had been saved only by delivering Scoef's goods to the pirates. Further petition was made to the king that justice be done in accordance with maritime law, for the master's discharge, and the recovery of the goods. The matter was referred to the admiral 'to whom cognizance of such accidents at sea belong and other skilled persons of the king's council.' This commission decided that Scoef's goods should be restored and since the ship had been unloaded, the sheriffs of London were ordered to seize and appraise the goods brought in the ship, to compel the other merchants owning the goods to contribute to the amount due to Scoef and to send a report to chancery.[1] The reference in this case to the powers of the admiral bears out the statement that in 1361 the council held that felonies, trespasses, and injuries done on the high seas should be tried by the admirals by maritime law and not according to common law.[2]

The origins of the court of Admiralty can be traced with some certainty to the period between 1340 and 1357. It was instituted principally in consequence 'of the difficulty which had been experienced in dealing with piracy and spoil cases made by and against foreign sovereigns.'[3] By 1357, there is mention of proceedings before the admirals,[4] in 1360, power to hold pleas was conferred upon them,[5] and by 1364, their court was recognized as a court of record.[6] A sharp decrease in the number of piracy cases brought before the King's Bench occurred after the middle of the century, and when we see the length of time a case might drag on there,[7] the reason for seeking some more expeditious means of obtaining justice is obvious. Throughout the period, however, maritime cases continued to be brought before the council, where they were usually transferred to a commission which included the admiral.[8] For example, in 1369, a

---

[1] *C.C.R. 1354–60*, p. 441.

[2] Mears, *op. cit.*, p. 329; *C.C.R. 1360–64*, p. 265; *Foedera*, iii, 2, p. 597.

[3] *Selden Soc.*, vi, p. xiv.

[4] *Ibid.*, p. xli.

[5] *Foedera*, iii, 1, p. 479.

[6] *Selden Soc.*, vi, p. xlv.

[7] A case of piracy which occurred in 1320 was still being heard in 1338. PRO Coram Rege Roll 295, m. 16; *ibid.* 312, m. 83d.

[8] *C.C.R. 1374–77*, p. 217; *C.P.R. 1374–77*, pp. 65, 410.

merchant of Vannes was arrested in Devon as an enemy. He appealed to the king and probably appeared before the council. The case was transferred to the admiral. It fell naturally within the jurisdiction of the admiral from the mouth of the Thames to the west but he was occupied with other matters. It was therefore sent to the other admiral who was ordered 'to deliver the merchant according to maritime law.' The admiral, Nicholas de Tamworth, associated with himself William de Wychingham, a judge of the Common Bench, Edmund de Chelreye, deputed to plead pleas before the king, and Robert Tresilian, learned in the law and the case was decided by jury in London.[1] The admiral's court was not yet a separate tribunal but there are signs of its emergence.

[1] *C.C.R. 1369–74*, pp. 58, 59.

VII

ALIENS IN THE EXCHEQUER

THE protection of the alien merchant's financial transactions was as essential for him as the safe-guarding of his life and merchandise. For aliens as well as natives the collection of debts was possible either by the process under a writ of debt or by the procedure defined in the Statute of Acton Burnell and the Statute of Merchants. Alien merchants could secure acknowledgments of indebtedness from their debtors, whether English or alien[1] before one of several authorities and had access to various courts to secure payment. According to the Statute of Merchants of 1285,[2] which amended the Statute of Acton Burnell of two years earlier,[3] recognizances of debt could be made before the mayors of boroughs or their clerks, and if the debt was not paid upon the specified date, the person of the debtor could be seized. He was then given three months to make payment. On further default, his lands and chattels were seized and delivered to his creditor, who held them until satisfied for his debt.[4] It was added in the statute of 1283 that 'if the creditor be a merchant stranger, he shall remain at the costs of the debtor for so long time as he tarrieth about the suit of his debt and until the moveable goods of the Debtor be sold or delivered to him.'[5] Later, according to Ordinance of the Staple of 1353, recognizances of debt could be made before the mayors of the staples.[6] It had also been provided in the earlier statutes that the writ of debt was not abated and 'the Chancellor, Barons of the Exchequer, Justices of the one Bench and of the other, and Justices Errant shall not be estopped to take recognizances

---

[1] E.g., Recognizance between Anthony Usus Maris and Francis Bache, (both of Genoa). *C.C.R. 1327–30*, p. 365.

[2] *Stat.* i, 53.

[3] *Ibid.*, p. 98.

[4] Holdsworth, *History of English Law*, iii, 131, 132.

[5] *Stat.* i, 54.

[6] *Stat.* i, 337. By a statute staple the debtor was not given the additional three months in which to pay.

of Debts of those who shall choose so to do before them; but the execution of Recognizances before them shall not be made according to the form aforesaid but according to the Law, Usage, and Manner heretofore used.'[1]

Recognizances of debt have a wider economic and financial importance,[2] but viewed in the light of the legal protection afforded to aliens, they are proof that an adequate machinery was provided for the collection of debts. Alien merchants appeared before all authorities making and receiving recognizances, suing and being sued for debt. The exchequer records are full of recognizances, writs commanding the appearance of debtors and writs ordering the sheriffs to make execution, as well as the appointments of attorneys to receive payment or to carry on the suit. The number of recognizances on the chancery rolls decreases toward the end of the reign. There are many cases of debt and account on the *De Banco* rolls,[3] in addition to the great number which were brought in the local courts. Why certain courts were chosen for acknowledging debts rather than others is a matter of conjecture. The greater power of the higher courts and the natural tendency of aliens to rely on royal support would perhaps account for the great number of their recognizances found on the exchequer and chancery rolls. Kunze's theory, that only the most prominent aliens came into the king's courts with their acknowledgments of debt,[4] seems scarcely tenable because of the number of seemingly obscure aliens who are found there. Usually no indication of why a certain case was brought in a certain court is given. It was doubtless largely a matter of convenience. Many of the debts acknowledged in this way were probably paid without recourse to legal proceedings. In some cases the creditors do not seem to have appeared on the day set for payment and thereby forfeited the money. On one occasion Richard de Bethon of London appeared before the barons of the exchequer with £50 due on that day to Wulfard de Gisel, Dynus Forcetti, and Peter Byni. After the money had been tested and weighed, the creditors were called but did not appear.

[1] *Stat.* i, 54.
[2] Postan, 'Credit in Mediaeval Trade,' *Economic History Review*, i (1928), pp. 234–61.
[3] See p. 78 above.
[4] Kunze, *Hanseakten aus England*, p. xxxi.

The money was therefore returned to de Bethon.[1] In a case in the King's Bench a creditor was fined for non-appearance to receive payment.

As the king's debtors or creditors alien merchants brought their suits in the exchequer. On the memoranda rolls of the king's remembrancer were recorded the details of the accounts particularly affecting the king's revenue, recognizances of debt, records of proceedings conducted by the treasurer and barons on the equity side of the exchequer and innumerable writs concerning the administration of the royal finance. They contain much material concerning aliens, who were frequently the farmers or assignees of all branches of the king's revenue, such as the customs, the subsidies, and the fines made in the courts; or who became involved in suits with officials who had to account at the exchequer: the collectors of customs and subsidies and those specially appointed to arrest the goods of aliens in time of war.

On the plea rolls of the Exchequer of Pleas are the records of the common law side of the exchequer administered by the treasurer and barons. Before its emergence as a distinct court, the exchequer had possessed or assumed a certain amount of common law jurisdiction which neither Magna Carta nor a series of statutes could remove from it. 'The barons of the Exchequer were invested with judicial power primarily over disputed matters which arose out of claims and counter claims relating to the king's revenue. Their experience in such matters led naturally to their being employed in the hearing of suits between subjects of common pleas, but neither did this create a Court of Common Pleas, for such pleas might be held elsewhere than in the Exchequer.'[2] This was still true in the reign of Edward III, as it was in that of Henry II. The privilege of bringing their suits into the exchequer was always granted to officials and their servants[3] but other suitors who did not come into that category were enabled to bring their cases also by the fictions by which the exchequer main-

[1] PRO Exch. Plea Roll 60, m. 17.

[2] R. L. Poole, *The Exchequer in the Twelfth Century*, (Oxford University Press, 1912), p. 179.

[3] Matthew Canaceon, merchant of Asti, imprisoned in Newgate for debts to various persons, amounting to over £100, was brought into the exchequer and then imprisoned in Fleet prison for a debt of £16 13s. 4d. to the valet of the chamberlain of the exchequer. PRO Exch. Plea Roll 91, m. 6d.

tained its common law jurisdiction. That some attempt was made to comply with the statutes which were designed to keep such cases out of the exchequer is shown in the following writ of 1336, addressed to the treasurer and barons:[1]

Cum secundum legem et consuetudinem regni nostri communia placita coram vobis ad scaccarium predictum placitari non debeant nisi placita illa nos aut aliquem ministrorum nostrorum eiusdem scaccarii specialiter tangenta, et iam ex insinuacione Prioris Takele, Nicholi de la Gore [and others named] accepimus quod Willelmus Wychard senior qui minister noster scaccarii predicti non est ut dicitur ipsos implacidet coram vobis in scaccario predicto de quadam transgressione eidem Willelmo per prefatos Priorem, Nicholam . . . apud Haitfeld illata ut dicitur contra legem et consuetudinem predictas vobis mandamus quod si ita est tunc placita illa coram vobis ulterius tenendo supersedeatis omnino et prefato Willelmo dicatis ex parte nostra quod breve nostrum de transgressione predicta ad communem legem versus predictos Priorem . . . sibi impetret si sibi viderit expedire.

One conclusion which might be drawn from the writ in the light of the following examples is that the parties to the suit did not possess sufficient influence to have the case brought into the exchequer, or that the king had not the slightest interest in the case. Early in the reign, the Peruzzi had won an action of trespass in the exchequer, when in 1338 they brought suit against a former sheriff of Kent for permitting their opponents, convicted in the exchequer, to escape.[2] A few aliens brought cases of account and receivership into the exchequer. In 1333, Anthony Bache of Genoa appointed attorneys to represent him in a suit against Nicholas Parker of Eltham concerning an account.[3] Some years later two Portuguese merchants were sued there by John Brutyn, cordwainer of London, and were allowed a jury *de medietate lingue*.[4] In 1357, the custodian of Fleet Prison sued for profits due to him from speculation undertaken for him by Matthew Noir, Florentine. He had given him £14 and received a letter obligatory for that amount and for the profits. The Florentine

---

[1] PRO K.R. Mem. 113, m. 42.
[2] PRO Exch. Plea Roll. 65, m. 19d; *ibid.* 66 m. 11.
[3] PRO Exch. Plea Roll 60, m. 36.
[4] *Ibid.* 67 m. 3. They finally paid the debt to Brutyn and 60*s.* fine to the king for trespass.

acknowledged the obligation and an auditor was appointed. The profits amounted to 13*s.* 4*d.* which Noir was unable to pay at the time. He was imprisoned for two years and finally paid the whole amount.[1]

The king's debts took precedence over all others and by his prerogative debtors were removed from Newgate to Fleet prison and cases from the lower courts to the exchequer. Such transfers are usually marked by a saving clause for the liberties of the city. At times, a greater tangle of jurisdiction resulted. Tidemann Smythous, merchant of Almain, having made a recognizance before the mayor of the staple at Hull of a debt of £47 owed to William fitz Emeric of that town and having failed to pay, was imprisoned in Newgate. Some months later his person and goods were attached for a debt of £47 13½*d.* for unpaid customs for which he had given a recognizance. He was brought from Newgate into the exchequer, whence he was sent to the Fleet prison until he should pay his debt to the king. While there, according to his own complaint, brought in the exchequer, he arranged with John Colyn, also of Hull, for the payment of the customs. Colyn was to pay the £47 13½*d.* within four years and received from Smythous a note for eleven marks signed by him and Lambard Lutyng, and £6 in part payment, but did nothing about paying the customs. Smythous brought suit against him in the exchequer. Colyn denied the charge and put himself upon the country. At this point the custodian of the prison appeared and claimed jurisdiction over all cases arising from contracts, pleas, or quarrels made or begun within the prison.[2] What the outcome of his claim was, we do not know. The record ends with the entry: 'Super quo quia curia vult plenius inde deliberare . . . datus est dies partibus predictis . . . in eodem statu quo nunc.' After the case had lasted almost two years the collectors of the customs certified that they had been paid and Smythous was released from Fleet prison and returned to Newgate.[3]

The king's debtors had two writs by which they might summon their debtors into the exchequer. Although the purpose of the two writs was the same: to enable those who were financially bound to the

---

[1] *Ibid.* 81, m. 1d; see also Appendix E for Matthew Noir.

[2] PRO Exch. Plea Roll 80, m. 1, 2, 26, 43.

[3] PRO K.R. Mem. 132, Brevia directa Hil.

king to collect their debts so that their obligations to the king might be met, there was a slight difference between a writ of aid and a writ of *quominus*. If the person in behalf of whom the writ was issued had been in the past and was likely in the future to be financially useful to the king, he would probably have received a writ of aid enabling him to sue his debtors in the exchequer. It was a graceful act on the part of the king, a reward for services past and future. On the memoranda roll of the king's remembrancer for the second year of Edward III's reign, is the following writ of aid in favor of the Bardi:[1]

Edward par la grace de dieu etc as Tresorer et Barouns de notre Eschekier salutz. Por ceo que noz chers marchandz de la compaignie de Bardi recevient plusures foitz noz deniers en divers lieux et auzint nous font sovent chevance des deniers grossement par noz besoignes espletter et tote foitz unt fait quant nous les avons voluz charger et eux ne paront suffire de nous servir en nos besoignes come ils unt fait cea en aroiere et viue mestoir nous seroit par lexploit dyceles si eux ne soient serviz des dettes que homme leur doit et devera en notre realme nous voillantz aeider a noz dit marchantz en ceste partie siavant come nous pooms de reson avoms grantez a eux de notre grace especiale quils puissent pleder et recouverir en notre dit Escheker totes les dettes que lour sont ou seront dues en notre realme solonc ce que lour feut grantiez en temps notre trescher seigneur et piere que deux assoill et vous nous mandoms que totez les foitz que les ditz marchandz voldrent suivre facez venir devant vous a notre dit Escheqer lor detours des dettes avantditz as ditz marchandz dy celes et apres lever mesmes celes dettes selonc les usages de notre Escheker en la manere avantdites. Donne souz notre prive seal a Nottingham le xi jour de Novembre lan de notre regne primer.

On later memoranda rolls and in the exchequer writs between 1332 and 1335, we find at least twenty orders to summon the debtors of the Bardi before the exchequer *per breve de privato sigillo de anno secundo*. As a rule it is not stated whether or not the Bardi held recognizances of these debts. The usual formula was that the debtor was summoned to answer for a certain sum *quos eis debet et iniuste detinet ut dicunt sicut rationabiliter monstrare poterunt quod inde respondere debet*. In the case of a debt of sixty shillings which John Patryk of Guilford owed and for which suit was brought in the ex-

---

[1] PRO K.R. Mem. 104, m. 23d.

chequer, concerning which there is a complete record on the plea rolls, it is stated that John is under obligations to the Bardi 'per scriptum suum.' The decision of the court was that the Bardi should recover the sixty shillings and also receive damages, which were put at one-half mark. Patryk was also fined for unjustly detaining the money.[1] In this way the creditor would have secured interest on his outstanding debts. Even under a writ of aid the collection of debts was a slow process. On 16 July, 1333, a writ was issued to the Bishop of Coventry and Lichfield to compel the appearance of Robert de Hoton, clerk, of his diocese before the barons of the exchequer because of a debt of £11 6s. 8d. due to the Bardi.[2] The order was repeated in the following January. Both writs were returned with the same endorsement: 'Ignoramus quis sit Robertus de Houton infrascriptus nisi per beneficium suum eccliasticum si quod habeat in nostra diocesa designetur.' The second writ bore the additional endorsement that he was parson of the church of Weryngton.[1] The debt was probably paid, because over a year later, 6 February, 1335, when a third writ was issued, he owed only forty shillings.[3]

The writ of *quominus* was probably, on the other hand, a means of securing speedy payment. The need of collecting the king's debts was immediate and urgent and to accomplish it the jurisdiction of the exchequer was extended to debtors of the king's debtors by the writ commanding B to pay a debt owed to A *quominus A Regi satisfacere possit*.[4] Several examples of the use of this process are found in the exchequer records of Edward III's reign, all involving Italian merchants and all in the latter part of the reign. In 1352,[5] and again in 1365,[6] the executors of the will of William de Acastre of York were summoned before the exchequer to pay sums owed to Anthony Provan and the society of the Malbaille, because Anthony 'minus sufficiens est' to pay his debts and those of the society to the king. In 1369, by examination of the chancery rolls Nicholas Sardouche of

[1] PRO Exch. Plea Roll 60, m. 11; PRO K.R. Writs 32.
[2] PRO K.R. Writs 33.
[3] PRO K.R. Writs 33.
[4] Holdsworth, *History of English Law* I, 240.
[5] PRO Exch. Plea Roll 77, m. 65d.
[6] *Ibid.* 86, m. 17.

Lucca was found to be in debt to the king. He was unable to pay because various merchants of London had not paid for merchandise purchased from him. The king therefore ordered the treasurer and barons:[1]

quod vocatis coram vobis dictis debitoribus ipsius Nicholi quorum nomina idem Nicholas vobis liberabit si inveneritis debita predicta per ipsos prefato Nicholo in forma predicta deberi tunc eosdem debitores ad debita illa prefato Nicholo solvendos sine dilacione compelli et distringi facietis.

The usual *quominus* phrase does not appear in the writ but the process is the same. Two years later, on the plea roll of the Exchequer of Pleas, there is the record of a case which illustrates how debtors to the third and fourth degree were attached to secure payment of the king's debt. The sheriffs of London were ordered to bring before the court in the octaves of Michaelmas, 1371, John Basset, mercer, of London to answer the king and Robert de Iklyngton concerning a debt of £144 which he owed to Alexander Flamme of Lucca, part of a debt which Flamme owed Robert de Iklyngton 'quominus idem Robertus Regi satisfacere valeat de debito quod Regi debit.' The parties came on the appointed day. Robert de Iklyngton testified that Flamme owed him £100, for which he had his letter obligatory bearing the name of John Basset. The latter disclaimed any responsibility for the debt of £100 and sought judgment in the matter. It was finally decided that Basset should be quit.[2] The other two cases were in 1374 and 1376. In 1374, a writ was issued to the sheriffs of London commanding them to have Thomas Gylors, merchant and vintner, before the barons of the exchequer at Westminster to answer for a debt of £165 5s. 3d. owed to Nicholas Russell, merchant of the new society of the Strozzi of Florence and John Credy, merchant of the old society of the Strozzi who owed the king £4,000. Gylors came and acknowledged that he owed the money, which was to be repaid at the will of the creditors. It was subsequently paid.[3] In 1376, the Prior of Bath was summoned to the exchequer to pay to the king £245 which he owed to Asselino Simonetti of Lucca, as part

[1] PRO K.R. Mem. 145, Brevia Directa Trin.
[2] PRO Exch. Plea Roll 91, m. 1.
[3] PRO K.R. Mem. 150, Brevia retorn. and irretorn. Mich.

payment of the sum which Simonetti and his associates owed to the king.[1]

The same expression and process was used in any case in which the payment of the king's debt was hindered by the action of another group of creditors.[2] Bartholomew Guidonis Castillon, the king's exchanger, was said to have been imprisoned in Newgate at the suit of his creditors, 'quominus idem Bartholomeus Regi de debito predicto [arrears of his farm for the exchange] iuxta prerogativam suam pre ceteris creditoribus . . . satisfacere possit.'[3] In 1354, Francis Spynola, of Genoa, a merchant of some importance because in the preceding year he had been permitted to sell red and white wine as well as sweet wine in spite of the custom of the city and the protest of the mayor to the contrary,[4] was deeply in debt to the king. He was also in debt to merchants of Lucca at whose suit he was imprisoned and was therefore less able to pay his debt to the king. By the king's prerogative, he was brought from Newgate to the exchequer, where his debtors announced that, not wishing to see him imprisoned longer, they had come to an agreement with him, so that he was now liable only for the king's debt.[5] It is more than probable that royal influence was largely responsible for the agreement.

The case of William Pouche, merchant of Florence, would normally have come before the exchequer, touching as it did the king's revenues, but the course of the case and the parties to it illustrate well the methods and persons employed in royal financial affairs and the position of alien merchants. One of Edward III's chief agents in the early part of his reign was Paul of Monte Florum, of the diocese of Fermo in Italy, the king's clerk. He is only one of a number of king's clerks who were active in the administration of the king's finances and he never rose to as high a position as most of his contemporaries. None of these, however, was so deeply involved in the great efforts made, at home and abroad, to raise the vast sums necessary for the French war. His career is more like that of an Italian banker.

[1] PRO K.R. Writs 60.
[2] Cf. general use of *subpoena* p. 99 above.
[3] PRO K.R. Mem. 140, Communia Hil.
[4] *Memorials of London* p. 270; *Cal. Letter Book G,* p. 5.
[5] PRO K.R. Mem. 130, Communia Pasch.; *ibid.* 131, Brevia directa Pasch.

He redeemed the royal crowns in 1335 and again in 1340.[1] He was one of the men appointed to dispose of the wool seized at Dordrecht in 1338,[2] and secured and lent to the king £10,000 to £12,000 for the furtherance of his secret affairs. The assignments and the benefices he received must have been inadequate repayment for his services, for in 1348 he was taken under the king's protection that the king might be satisfied before his other creditors.[3] The next year he was imprisoned in Fleet prison, from which he was released at intervals to answer charges brought against him.[4] During this period his case against William Pouche of Florence was heard in the exchequer.

Pouche must have been a merchant of some importance,[5] but most of our knowledge of him is taken from records of suits in which he was involved. In 1344, men were appointed 'to follow and arrest Gylemyn Pouche and Dolfyn Pouche, his brother, who are hiding themselves to evade payment of divers debts wherein they are held to the king and to bring them before the king and his council.'[6] This may have been a forerunner of the later affair which begins with a recognizance made in the exchequer 14 December, 1345 by William Pouche that he owed the king and Paul of Monte Florum £820 payable at the will of the creditors for the subsidy due on 540 sacks of wool which he had exported for the latter,[7] who had received an assignment of wool in payment for money expended in redeeming the crown. Within a month he had been imprisoned in the Tower and removed to Fleet prison, where he was to remain without mainprise until the debt was paid.[8] In 1346, he was pardoned for outlawry in Shropshire for non-appearance before the justices of the Bench to answer a charge of failing to render an account to Roger, son of Walter le Deghere of Ludlow, merchant.[9] In 1348, however, main-

---

[1] *Foedera*, ii, 2, pp. 909, 1186.

[2] *Rot. Parl.* ii, 114.

[3] *C.P.R. 1348–50*, pp. 21, 184. These letters were issued from 1351 to 1357.

[4] *C.C.R. 1349–54*, pp. 66, 85.

[5] On the Issue Roll for Eastern term 1342, he is called valet to Queen Philippa. PRO Issue Roll 325, 13 June.

[6] *C.P.R. 1343–45*, p. 289.

[7] PRO K.R. Mem. 122, Recogn. Mich.; Brevia Directa Hil.

[8] *Ibid.*, Brevia directa Hil.

[9] *C.P.R. 1345–48*, p. 197.

prise was allowed and for the next five years, days were set term after term for the appearance of the parties.[1] In 1351 and 1352 he was released to go abroad on special business for the king.[2] He also became involved in another suit which resembles a case of *quominus*. In July, 1348, he appeared in the exchequer and informed the court that a certain Pessh of Lucca, then imprisoned in Newgate, owed him £40. Pessh was immediately summoned before the exchequer, where it was found that he had been imprisoned for a debt of £50 to Kellius Sonasse.[3] He acknowledged the debt of £40 to Pouche, and by the king's prerogative, was removed to Fleet prison. In February, 1350, he petitioned for release, having secured possession of a letter of acquittance for the £40 dated 4 February, 1344, which he had not been able to produce earlier. The court ordered an inquisition in Canterbury, where the letter had been given, and Pessh was released on the mainprise of Henry Picard. Before the day set for his appearance Pessh died and Picard paid a fine of 6s. 8d. for his non-appearance.[4] The inquisition seems never to have been taken and days were being set for it until 1360.

The original case became more complicated. Pouche did not appear on one of the appointed days in November, 1352. Mainpernours had to be appointed for his mainpernours and after about a year and a half he was found, imprisoned in Newgate for debts to city merchants, John Stodeye and William Rahe, mercer. He was once more brought to the exchequer in May, 1353, and committed to Fleet prison. The original mainpernours made fine and the second group was discharged.[5] He apparently remained in prison, for in 1360 the following order was issued 'Upon petition made on behalf of William Pouche, shewing that for debts charged upon him by Paul of Monte Florum deceased he has been imprisoned in Flete Prison for eleven years and more and has endured extreme privation so that he has no means of living and that Master Paul at the point of death confessed

[1] PRO K.R. Mem. 126, Brevia directa Mich., Pasch.; *ibid.* 127, Brevia directa Hil.; *ibid.* 128, Brevia directa Hil.

[2] *C.P.R. 1350–54*, p. 30

[3] Probably Kellas Donas of Lucca.

[4] PRO Exch. Plea Roll 73, m. 63; *ibid.*79, m. 16; *ibid.* 80, m. 7; *ibid.* 82, m. 13. PRO K.R. Mem. 126, Brevia directa Mich.

[5] *Ibid.* 122, Communia Hil.; PRO K.R. Writs 39.

that he was bound to acquit William toward the king of the said debts, and caused acquittance to be made before a notary public and other true men: order to permit William to go at large, if he shall find mainpernors who will mainpern to have his body before the treasurer and barons at the exchequer upon notification from day to day and term to term to answer for debts which may be found due from him to the king.'[1] Before he was released, however, he was stabbed in the prison by John de Munden, also a prisoner for debt, during a quarrel which began at dinner on Sunday, 20 September, 1360. He died four days later.[2] The case is not exceptional except perhaps in its conclusion, but it is preserved in unusual detail and is typical of the suits which frequently brought alien merchants into the exchequer. That they appeared there, especially as plaintiffs, was due chiefly to the king's grace and the fictions by which the exchequer maintained its common law jurisdiction. By the exercise of his prerogative which could overreach the jurisdiction of the municipal courts and bring into the king's court the debtors of the king's debtors, the king could secure, in some cases, the payment of his debts, and could doubtless ask further support from the merchants thus favoured. To the alien, the collection of his debts in the king's court and in the king's name was an advantage. In general, however, it was probably easier for the alien merchant to collect debts from his ordinary creditors than from the king.

[1] *C.C.R. 1360–64*, p. 114.
[2] PRO Coram Rege Roll 401, m. 3 Rex.

VIII

CONCLUSION

THE difference in status between alien and native merchants seems to have been economic rather than legal. Disabilities existed for aliens in the matter of landholding and inheritance, but in the courts there were no bars against aliens. It might perhaps be wrong to stress the omissions in fourteenth-century letters of denization as compared with those of the next century; but the fact that there seemed to be no need to mention in them the courts in which aliens who were securing the rights of natives might sue, seems to be a confirmation of the conclusion drawn from an investigation of cases involving aliens in the ordinary courts. The government was willing and desirous[1] of having aliens sue and be sued in the usual courts, although some cases which might have come up in the common law courts were brought into the council because of the king's special interest.

England seems to have been unique, or at least, exceptional in not having special courts for merchants. In Naples, consuls of merchants had legal as well as commercial powers.[2] At Rome[3] and at Venice,[4] there were representatives for English subjects. The English merchants at the staple at Bruges had a master, an assembly, and important legal rights.[5] The appointment of a justiciar of merchants was one of the provisions of the *Carta Mercatoria*, but he was to act only when justice was not done by mayors and sheriffs, and in cases which could be settled by merchant law.[6] His jurisdiction was to

[1] In 1354, alien merchants tried to secure the appointment of a member of the council to hear their pleas, but their petition was refused. *Rot. Parl.* ii, 262.

[2] G. Yver, *Le Commerce et les Marchands dans l'Italie méridionale au XIIIe. et au XIVe. Siècle*, pp.197 ff.

[3] *C.P.R. 1370–74*, p. 279

[4] Rawlinson, 'The Flanders Galleys,' *Mariners' Mirror*, xii, 157.

[5] *Cartulaire de l'ancienne Estaple de Bruges*, i, 212.

[6] Gras, p. 262, c. 12. His functions would have been similar to those of the alderman of the Hanse.

117

supersede in no way the jurisdiction of the royal courts, and he was to be an intermediary between merchants and local officials, not between merchants and the crown.[1] The relations between alien merchants and the crown were direct.

Whether the merchants had any general organization through which they could make such bargains with the king as the *Carta Mercatoria*, or whether any particular group had representatives, to whom, for example, the sheriff of London could deliver a command such as was sent to the merchants of Lombardy commanding their presence before the council,[2] does not appear.[3] Very possibly they did not. When the king wished to consult with them, he probably summoned important merchants individually, as he did in 1353,[4] or the sheriff made general announcements by proclamation.[5] When a protest was to be made, concerning unjust collection of taxes or customs, for example, it was made by the individuals concerned, either by means of a petition or by suit brought in the courts. Alien merchants with the exceptions which we shall now consider, had no courts of their own, no general meeting places or gildhalls, no consuls or representatives.

The German Hanse and the woad merchants are, up to a certain point, the exceptions. The Hanse developed early what was in many respects a normal type of commercial organization for the period and retained it throughout its career. They had in London their own gildhall, their alderman, their court. In early days, the alderman was usually a citizen of London, often one of their number who had received the freedom of the city. From the middle of the fourteenth century there were two aldermen, one German and the other English. This was probably due to the fact that about this time a German who became a citizen lost his membership in the Hanse.[6] The

---

[1] Such an official was, however, not appointed.

[2] *Cal. Letter Book G*, p. 91

[3] Stubbs, II, 552, says that before 1303 the customs were 'regulated only by separate arrangement with the several bodies of foreign traders, each of which had its agency at the great ports.'

[4] *C.C.R. 1349–54*, p. 605.

[5] *C.C.R. 1354–60*, p. 662. The fact that the Hansards alone protested against the cloth custom of 1347 seems to indicate that the alien merchants acted independently in matters of this sort.

English alderman, who might be the Mayor of London, acted as intermediary between the city authorities and the Hanse and looked after its interests. The German alderman, who was presented to the city authorities on his election by the members of the Hanse from the governing committee of twelve, was the actual head of the Hanse.[1] He was responsible to both the city and the Hanse,[2] and he had certain important judicial powers, which he had possessed as early as 1282 and probably earlier.[3] His powers were defined as follows in a *quo warranto* inquiry of 1321:

qui quidem aldremannus dicte societatis curiam suam tenebit in domo que vocatur Gilda Aula Aldermannorum in Civitate predicta de omnibus placitis convencionum, debitorum et contractuum que moveri contigerit inter mercatores de hansa predicta; et si quis de eadem hansa per aliquem implacitetur coram Majore seu Vice comitibus Londoniensibus de aliquo placito convencionis, debiti seu contractus personalis, quod idem Aldermannus de societate predicta petet inde Curiam suam et ea optinebit et inde faciet justiciam in Aula Alemannorum predicta.[4]

He administered the law in the Morgensprache, heard cases between members of the Hanse arising from the causes mentioned above, and also cases between Hansards and Englishmen when the former were defendants. Only when a creditor could not collect his debt in the alderman's court was he free to have recourse to the city or higher courts.[5]

The other merchants which possessed privileges as old as those of the Hanse were the woad merchants of Amiens, Nesle, and Corbie. The privileges granted in 1237 had been granted to the merchants of the three towns, but Nesle and Corbie had come to hold a much inferior position.[6] By the agreement of 1237 they secured, in return for

---

[6] K. Engel, 'Die Organization der deutsch-hansischen Kaufleute in England in xiv. and xv. Jahrhundert bis zum Utrechter Frieden von 1474.' *Hansische Geschichtsblätter*, xix (1913), 499.

[1] *Ibid.* xx (1914), 176.

[2] *Ibid.* xix (1913), 508.

[3] *Liber Albus*, pp. 485 ff.

[4] *Placita de quo warranto temporibus Edwardi I, II, III.* (Record Commission, London, 1818), p. 455.

[5] Lappenberg, *Urkundliche Geschichte des Hansischen Stahlhofes*. p. 34

[6] The privileges were confirmed in 1334 to the merchants of Amiens alone, because the

an annual payment of fifty marks, the right to store their goods in their own storehouses, to have their own hostels, and their assembly and a proctor, and to sell to aliens as well as to citizens. Only when members of their own group failed to do justice to one another did the sheriff intervene.[1]

In both these cases, however, the agreement by which these privileges were secured were made with the authorities of London, not with the king. The Hanseatic composition of 1282,[2] although made under the supervision and sealed with the seal of the exchequer, was the settlement of a local dispute which arose out of the fact that the Hansards had neglected the repair of Bishopsgate which they had previously undertaken in return for privileges.[3] The terms of the settlement and of the findings of the *quo warranto* inquiry of 1321 show that the jurisdiction of the alderman's court was over such commercial causes as would have been heard in the mayor's court. He apparently had no jurisdiction over cases actionable in the king's courts. The same seems to be true of the woad merchants. The alderman of the Hanse was a consular agent between the Hanse and the city, not between the Hanse and the king, and there is apparently no mention of his acting in the latter capacity. As far as the relations between the central government and alien merchants were concerned, they were direct. The government recognized organizations such as the Hanse, and such attorneys as individuals or groups might choose to appoint[4] for a particular purpose, but it created no legal or administrative system or office through which relations with alien merchants were maintained.

The economic disabilities of aliens were principally certain restrictions on trading within the country, and the higher customs which they paid, but those customs, with the exception of the cloth custom of 1347, had been defined in the *Carta Mercatoria*, with the

---

merchants of the other two towns did not send deputations. Later the farm is being paid by the merchants of Amiens, but in the name of all three towns. *Liber Albus*, pp. 426–28; *Cal. Letter Book G*, p. 30; *Cal. Letter Book H*, pp. 425, 429, 446.

[1] *Liber Albus*, pp. 418 ff.
[2] *Liber Albus*, pp. 485 ff.
[3] Lappenberg, *op. cit.* pt. 2, p. 14.
[4] *C.P.R. 1364–67*, p. 63; PRO Chanc. Misc., file 30,8/4.

consent of alien merchants. Additional subsidies were imposed from time to time, but these were regarded as emergency war measures, and were collected from aliens and natives at the same rate.[1] Aliens could, by securing letters of denization, pay customs at the lower rate, but they then had to pay the taxes, the tenths and fifteenths which were not collected from aliens.

Conclusions concerning a limited period like this will be more useful when put in their proper place among the conclusions concerning earlier and later periods. But it seems evident that alien merchants in England between 1350 and 1377 could usually count on a friendly attitude on the part of the government, which sometimes overcame the opposition of the towns and gave aliens equal trading privileges with natives. The government demanded higher customs from them than from English merchants and occasionally sought to increase its customs revenue by establishing a monopoly for alien merchants in the exportation or importation of some one commodity. Yet it gave them equal rights with natives to sue in the king's courts and the privilege of removing economic disabilities by securing letters of denization and by assuming the obligations of native-born merchants.

[1] This is not true of other periods.

APPENDIX A

THE FINAL SETTLEMENT BETWEEN RICHARD II AND THE BARDI

The original documents relating to the final settlement between Richard II and the Bardi are among the K.R. Accounts, Various (Foreign Merchants),[1] in the index to which they are described as 'Documents relating to money transactions with the Bardi, 13 Edward III to 14 Richard II.' They are a file of seven documents. The first six are those surrendered

Fourteenth-Century Notarial Mark (see p. 123).

by Walter de Bardi at the time of the settlement and the seventh is the document drawn up at his request at that time. They are:

1 Quitclaim of Walter de Bardi to Richard II, 24 October, 1391.
2 Letter of Attorney of Peter de Bardi, 8 September, 1384.
3 Letter patent of 28 June, 1339.
4 Letter patent of 7 November, 1348.
5 Letter patent of 4 August, 1339.
6 Letter patent of 20 April, 1345.
7 *Publicum instrumentum* 13 November, 1391.

[1] PRO K.R. Accounts, Various, Foreign Merchants, 127/38 (1–7).

All, together with the writ of 8 November, 1391, in which Richard II promised to pay 3000 marks, are enrolled on the K.R. memoranda roll for 1391–92.[1] The four letters patent have been printed in the calendars of patent rolls.

An interesting feature of three of the letters patent (Nos. 3, 4, and 6) is that the amount of the debt acknowledged in the letter is written on the tongue for the seal in Arabic numerals in a contemporary hand.[2] Through slits in the upper left-hand corner of the letter of 20 April, 1345, is run a narrow strip of parchment, with the directions: *A Tresorer et Chamberlains de notre Eschequier*. On the *publicum instrumentum* of 13 November, 1391 is an interesting example of a fourteenth-century notarial mark (reproduced on the opposite page), that of John Russel, clerk of Lincoln. Such marks are rare in English mediaeval archives. Notaries were appointed by the Emperor or the Pope and 'had only a limited popularity in England.'[3]

The following transcript has been made from the enrolment on the memoranda roll. Punctuation and paragraphing have been introduced for convenience, and *u* has been changed to *v* in accordance with modern usage. The same practice has been followed in other transcripts in this appendix.

Angl. De relaxacione et remissione Regi et aliis factis per Gautronum de Bardes mercatorem societatis de Bardes et attornatum mercatorum eiusdem societatis de Florencia.

Dominus Rex[4] mandavit hic breve suum de privato sigillo suo quod est inter communia de hoc termino in hec verba-Richard par la grace de dieu Roy dengleterre et de France et Seignur dirlande as Tresorer Barons et Chamberleins de notre Eschequer saluz. Come notre bien ame Gautron de Bardes marchant de la compaignie de Bardes et attorne des marchantz de la dite compaignie de Florence eit par ses lettres remys relesse quitclamee et pardonee pur et en noun de lui et de touz les marchantz de la dite compaignie et de chescun persone dycelle compaignie a notre aiel le Roy qe dieux assoill et a nous et a noz heirs et executours et a certeins seignurs especifiez en les dites lettres du dit Gautron et a leur heirs et executours toutes accions quereles et demandes et qeconqes sommes de deniers as ditz

[1] PRO K.R. Mem. 168, Communia Hil.

[2] For the early use of Arabic numerals, see C. Johnson and C. H. Jenkinson, *English Court Hand* (Oxford University Press, 1915), I, 73 ff; G. F. Hill, 'The Early Use of Arabic Numerals in Europe,' *Archaeologia* LXII (1910), 137 ff.

[3] H. Jenkinson, *The Later Court Hands in England* (Cambridge: Cambridge University Press, 1927), p. 31. For examples of marks of this period, see *ibid*. Plate 1, one of 1390 and another of 1400, taken from The Common Paper; also *British Numismatic Journal*, 1st series, X (London, 1913), 106, the mark of Richard de Snowehulle, clerk of Worcester about 1330.

[4] PRO K.R. Mem. 168, Communia Hil.

marchantz ou a aucun de eux ou a leur heirs ou executours duz par notre dit aiel ou par nous ou par aucun des seignurs avantditz et ad le dit Gautron par celle cause nous baillez diverses lettres patentes seallees des sealx de notre dit aiel et des ditz seignurs fesantes mencion de pluseurs grandes sommes de deniers par eux duz as marchantz susditz pur estre cancellees en la Receite de notre Eschequer et a y demorer entre autres noz remembraces en descharge de nous et de lalme de notre dit ayel et des ditz seignurs et de noz heirs et executours par consideracion de queles choses nous avons grantez au dit Gautron trois mille marcs a avoir de notre tresor a qui nous volons qe vous avantditz Tresorer et Chamberleins facez avoir de mesmes les trois mille marcs prest paiment ou suffissant assignement selonc leffect de notre grant susdit. Et avons outre par mesme le cause pardonez au dit Gautron sept centz et vynt et cynk livres quatre soldz et oyt deniers queles il receust nadgairs de nous dapprest pur sustenir leschange deinz notre cite de Londres dont il est Gardein et aussi cent et trente et cynk marcs de lor a nous appartenant par encheson de notre sennrage en loffice de mesme notre eschange par lui receues puis le dys et noefisme iour de Januer lan de notre regne unzisme les queles sept centz vynt et cynk livres quatre soldz et oyt deniers coergent sur lui en demande en notre dit Eschequer par noun de Walter Barde meistre de notre monoie deins notre Tour de Londres et Gardein de notre Eschange deinz notre citee de Londres et par les susdites causes avons aussi pardonez sibien au dit Gautron come a les susditz marchantz de la dite compaignie et a chescun de eux et a leur heirs executours et attornez toutes les sommes de deniers et autres choses de nous receues en value de deniers en qeconque lieu qil soit par eux ou aucun de eux ou currantz sur eux ou aucun de eux en demande par qeconque cause a notre Escheqer susdit. Par quoi selonc leffect de notre dit pardon nous volons que vous avantdites Tresorer et Barons deschargez et facez estre quites envers nous a mesme notre Escheqer sibien le dit Gautron de les sept centz vynt et cynk livres quatre soldz et oyt deniers et cent et trent et cynk marcs avantdites come mesme celui Gautron et les dites marchantz de mesme la compaignie et chescun de eux et lour heirs executors et attornez de toutes les dites sommes de deniers et autres choses de nous receues en value de deniers par eux ou aucun de eux ou par lour attornez ou currantz sur eux ou aucun de eux en demande a notre dit Escheqer par qeconque cause ou encheson qe ce soit. Donne souz notre prive seal a Westmester le viii iour de Novembre lan de notre[1] quinzisme.

Et super hoc venit hic modo in crastino sancti Hillarii predictus Gal-

---

[1] *Regne* is omitted in the enrolment.

terus in propria persona sua. Et exhibuit curie quoddam instrumentum puplicum cuius tenor sequitur in hec verba: In[1] dei nomine amen per presens publicum instrumentum cunctis appareat evidenter quod anno domini millesimo CCC^{mo} nonogesimo primo secundum cursum et computacionem ecclesie Anglicane Indiccione xv^{ma} pontificati sanctissimi in Christo patris et domini nostri domini Bonifacii divina providencia pape noni anno secundo mense Novembris die xiii in magna aula palacii Regii apud Westmonasterium in Cancellaria domini nostri Regis presentibus tunc ibidem Reverendis in Christo patribus et dominis dominis Thoma dei gratia Eboracense Archiepiscipo Anglie Primato et apostolice sedis legato Cancellario Anglie et Johanne eadem gratia Episcipo Sarisberiense Thesaurario Anglie necnon venerabilis viris magistro Edmundo Stafford custode privati sigilli et domino Johanne Burton custode rotulorum et aliis pluribus tam magistris dicte Cancellarie quam aliis in multitudine copiosa. In mei eciam notarii publici et testium subscriptorum presencia personaliter constitutus Galterus de Bardes mercator et socius societatis de Bardes ac attornatus seu procurator mercatorum dicte societatis de Florencia ut asseruit duas litteras patentes unam videlicet sigillo Petri de Bardes de Florencia cum cera rubea pendenti alteram vero sigillo suo proprio cum cera rubea pendenti munitas[2] exhibuit, quas quidem litteras vidi palpavi et diligenter inspexi ac eas ad rogatum speciale dicti Galteri de verbo ad verbum in hoc presenti instrumento inserui et transcripsi. Quarum quidem litterarum tenores secuntur et sunt tales:

Sachent[3] touz gentz par ycestes moy Piers de Bardes de Florence compaignon et attorne de la compaignie de Bardes de Florence sibien en noun de moy mesmes come de la dite compaignie avoir assigne et establie Gautron de Bardes Angel de Bardes Thomas et Barthelmeu de Bardes de Florence mes attornez generales iointement et severalment a demander recouverir et receivre touz maneres dettes et deniers ou a la dite compaignie de Bardes en aucun manere duez soit il de notre seignur le Roy Richard qore est ou des executours de noble Roy Edward son ayel qi dieu assoill ou de qeconque autre persone deinz la Roiaume dengleterre donant et grauntant as ditz attornez et a chescun de eux par soy plein poair defaire les

---

[1] The original document is PRO K.R. Accounts, Various, Foreign Merchants, 127/38 (7).

[2] The seals are no longer on the documents.

[3] The original document is PRO K.R. Accounts, *ut supra*, 127/38 (2). It is endorsed as follows: 'Irrotulatur in quodam instrumento irrotulato in memorandis scaccarii videlicet inter recorda de termino sancti Hillarii anno quintodecimo Regis Ricardi secundi ex parte Rememoratoris Regis in quodam videlicet processu tangente Galterum Bardes attornatum de societate Bardorum.'

chose susditz et de les resceites acquitances faire et generalment toutes autres choses en ycestes compouir et parfaire siavant come iestei illoeqes present en ma propre persone a avoir pur ferme et estable quanqe les avant-ditz attornez feront iointement et severalment es choses susditz. En tes-moignance de quele chose a yceste mon present escrit iay mys mon seal. Donne a Londres le viii iour de September lan du grace M^l CCC oeptave quart et lan du regne le Roy Richard susdit puis le conquest oeptisme.

A touz[1] ceux qe cestes lettres verront ou oront Gautron de Bardes marchant de la compaignie de Bardes et attorne des marchantz de la dite compaignie de Florence saluz en dieu Savoir vous face qe par certeins causes parlees et accordees parentre le grand conseil de notre souverain tresexcel-lent et tresredoute seignur notre seignur le Roy Richard le second puis le conquest de son comandement dune part et moy avant (dit)[2] Gautron dautre part touchantz les salute et descharge de lalme du tresnoble et tres-gracious Roy Edward le tierz qe dieux pardonit aiel a notre souverain seignur le Roy Richard susdit et de ses heirs et executours et des almes de Johan iadys Ercevesque de Cantirbirs primat de toute Engleterre Henry iadys Evesque de Nicole et Richard iadys Evesque de Duresme Henry iadys conte de Derby William conte de Norhampton William ore conte de Sal-resbirs et Robert iadys conte de Souffolk et de leurs heirs et executours et pur le bien profit et quite de touz les marchantz qestient et sont de la dite compaignie et de leur heirs et executours ay remys quiteclame et relesse et par ycestes mes lettres remitte quitclame et relesse pur et en noun de moy et de touz les marchantz de la dite compaignie a notre dit seignur le Roy Richard et au dit tresnoble Roy Edward et a leur heirs et executours et as ditz Johan Henry Richard Henry William William et Robert et a leur heirs et executours et a chescun de eux toutes maneres dactions quereles et de-mandes et ay aussi pardonez pur et en noun come dessus toutes sommes de deniers a moy ou as ditz marchantz de la dite compaignie ou a acun de nous en quelconque manere ou par quelconqe cause ou encheson duez par le dit tresnoble Roy Edward ses heirs et executours et les ditz Johan Henry Richard Henry William William et Robert et leur heirs et executours ou par aucun de eux issint qe les ditz marchantz et moy et noz heirs executours et attornez soiens par ycestes forsbarrez et excluses a touz iours de touz maneres accions quereles et demandes avoir poursuir ou user envers le dit Roy Edward notre dit seignur le Roy Richard qorest les ditz seignurs ou

---

[1] The original document is PRO K.R. Accounts, *ut supra*, 127/38 (1). It is endorsed like the preceding document (see p. 125, n. 1 above), and also as follows: Irrotulatur in dorso clausi cancellarii Regis infrascripti mense Novembris anno infrascripto.

[2] *Dit* is omitted in the enrolment.

aucun de eux ou envers leur heirs et executours par quelconque cause ou
encheson que ce soit du comencement du mounde tanque au iour present.
En tesmoignance de quele chose a ycestes iay mys mon seal. Escrit a
Londres le xxiiii iour doctobre lan du regne de notre dit seignur le Roy
Richard quinzisme.

Post quarum quidem litterarum exhibicionem prefatus Galterus
publice fatebatur se alias pure libere sponte et absolute relaxasse et
quietumclamasse omnes omnimodas acciones prout in predictis litteris
eiusdem Galteri sigillo sigillatis plenius continetur. Et iterum et exhabun-
danti ex certa sua scientia ut dixit easdem acciones quascumque quietum-
clamavit et relaxavit ac remisit quietumclamat relaxat et remittit nomine
suo proprio et nomine omnium mercatorum dicte societatis prefato domino
nostro Ricardo Regi moderno et prefato recolende memorie Edwardo
quondam Regi Anglie et ipsorum et utriusque eorum heredibus et executoribus Johanni quondam archiepiscipo Cantuariensi Henrico quondam
Lincolnensi et Ricardo quondam Dunolnensi Episcipis Henrico quondam
comiti de Derby Willelmo quondam comiti Norhamptonie Willelmo quondam Comiti Saresbiriensi moderno et Roberto quondam comiti de Souffolcia
et eorum heredibus et executoribus et cuilibet ipsorum omni modo et forma
quibus melius potuit et potest remisit eciam et remittit specialiter et expresse nominibus quibus supra quascumque pecuniarum summas sibi aut
mercatoribus dicte societatis aut eorum alicui per dominos predictos aut
eorum aliquem heredes et executores ipsorum aut eorum aliquem qualiter-
cumque seu ex quacumque causa debitas et solempni stipulatione inter-
posita pactum fecit de ulterius non petendo exhabundantique omnibus et
singulis accionibus querelis et demandis que sibi vel dictis mercatoribus
prefate societatis contra prefatos dominos Edwardum quondam Regem et
dominum Ricardum nunc Regem et alios dominos quoscumque supradictos
ac quemlibet eorum illorumque heredes et executores competebant vel
competere poterunt in futurum ratione aliquorum contractuum convencionum seu obligacionum cuiuscumque fuerint nature seu condicionis inter
dictas partes initorum seu factorum ab inicio mundi usque in diem confec-
tionis presencium ac omni comodo et effectu earundem palam et expresse
ac per pactum solempne interveniens renunciavit. Ita quod prefati mercatores et predictus Galterus et ipsorum et cuiuslibet eorum heredes executores et attornati sint exnunc ab omnibus accionibus querelis et demandis et
prosecutione earundem decetero ex quacumque causa seu ratione versus
prefatos Edwardum quondam Regem et dominum Ricardum nunc Regem
predictos et alios dominos quoscumque predictos et quemlibet eorum
illorumque heredes et executores movendo seu faciendo exnunc imper-

petuum totaliter exclusi. Insuperque ad maiorem firmitatem et robur dictarum remissionis relaxacionis et renunciationis accionum predictarum ac in signum finalis quitacionis et plene liberacionis idem Galterus quatuor litteras obligatorias magno sigillo bone memorie domini Edwardi quondam Regis Anglie communitas per eundem dominum Regem tam sibi quam prefatis mercatoribus societatis antedicte factas quas tunc ad manus habebat in cancellaria restituit liberavit ac custodi rotulorum realiter tradidit cancellandas et petiit cancellari. Super quibus omnibus et singulis prefatus Galterus nomine suo proprio et nomine procuratorio dicte societatis requisivit me notarium publicum quod conficerem publicum instrumentum sive instrumenta. Acta sunt hec omnia et singula prout suprascribuntur et recitantur sub anno indictione pontificato mense die et loco predictis presentibus discretis viris dominis Thoma Middleton precentore ecclesie cathedralis Cicestrensis Johanne Ravensere canonico Lincolnense et aliis multis testibus ad premissa vocatis specialiter et rogatis. Et ego Johannes Russel clericus Lincolnensis diocese publicus auctoritate apostolica et Imperiali notarius premissis omnibus et singulis dum sic ut premittitur sub anno indictione pontificato mense die et loco in principio presentis publici instrumenti insertis per prefatum Galterum agerentur et fierent personaliter interfui unacum testibus antedictis eaque sic fieri vidi et audivi scripsi puplicavi et in hanc publicam formam redegi manu propria me hic scribendo et signum meum consuetum apponendo in testimonio premissorum specialiter rogatus.[1]

Et exhibuit eciam dictus Galterus quatuor litteras patentes sub sigillo domini Edwardi nuper Regis Anglie avi Regis huius quarum tenores sequuntur unius videlicet in hec verba:

There follow (1) the letter obligatory, dated at Westminster, April 20, 1345, which is printed in the Calendar of Patent Rolls, 1343–45, pp. 467–469, with the following endorsement:[2] Memorandum quod mercatores de societate Bardorum onerantur ad scaccarium compotorum in Rotulo 19 in

---

[1] The enrolment does not contain the final sentence of the original document, which is as follows: 'Constat michi de rasura superius per me facta in sexta et septima lineis computando a pede instrumenti quam feci proprium corrigendo errorem et illam volo omni suspicione carere ego notarius antedictus.' The erasures come after *obligatorias, Regis,* and *Anglie* (lines 4 and 5 above). The original is endorsed as n. 2 below, with the omission of the words in italics and the addition of *infrascriptum* before *Galterum.*

[2] The original document is PRO K.R. Accounts, *ut supra,* 127/38 (6). It has the additional endorsement: 'Irrotulatur in memorandis scaccari videlicet inter Recorda de termino sancti Hillarii anno quintodecimo Regis Ricardi secundi in quodam *videlicet* processu tangente Galterum Bardes *attornatum de societate de Bardorum* ex parte Rememoratoris Regis.' In the endorsement given above the Roman numerals have been changed to Arabic numerals.

Item London̄ de 2595li. 18s. 2d. de prestito eis facto ad Receptam scaccarii diversis annis et eciam de 139li. 16s. 6½d. de precio 23 saccorum 7 petrarum 12¾ librarum lane recepte de assessoribus lanarum in comitatu Kancie necnon de 117li. 19s. 4d. de precio 10 saccorum 12 petrarum 13¼ librarum lane recepte de collectoribus lanarum in comitatu Herefordie et de 1 sacco 9 petris 3½ libris lane de incremento proveniente de 70 saccis 12 petris 13¾ libris lane per ipsos recepte de collectoribus predictis. De quibus quidem 2595li. 18s. 2d. et de lanis predictis fit mencio in hiis litteris patentibus et allocantur per superplusagium eisdem mercatoribus debitum in Rotulo 17 in Item. Res. London̄. Item receperunt inde 150li. ad Receptam scaccarii ut patet in pelle 16 die Octobris anno 22 virtute cuiusdam brevis de magno sigillo inter mandatis de eodem termino. Item receperunt inde ad dictam Receptam per diversas vices et in diversis prestitis super debito infrascripto in subsidio expensarum suarum morandi London̄ videlicet inter 10 diem Aprilis anno 20 et 15 diem Julii anno 29 utroque die computato in 51 particulis 3177li. 8s. 5d. Item receperunt inde ad Receptam scaccarii inter quintum diem Julii anno 31 et 16 diem marcii anno 33 per diversas vices in 21 particulis 1155li. 18s. Item receperunt inde ad Receptam scaccarii inter 9 diem Julii anno 33 et quintum diem Decembris anno 38 per diversas vices in 18 particulis 1738li. 3d. Item receperunt tertio Julii anno 39 462li. Item Petrus de Bardi et Walterus de Bardi mercatores de societate infrascripte receperunt 16 die Augusti anno 46 de exitibus custumarum et subsidii Regis in portu London̄ quinque milia marcarum in partem solucionis debiti infrascripti ut patet per litteras suas acquietancie datas London̄ 16 die mensis Augusti anno 46 que quidem littera remanet penes Thesaurarium et camerarios in Recepta scaccarii dicto anno 46 ut patet in Rotulis Recepte eodem die London̄ irrotulata in memorandis de anno 39 Regis Edwardi tertii inter Recorda de termino sancti Michaelis ex parte Rememoratoris Thesaurarii Rotulo 34. Item iidem Petrus et Walterus receperunt 13 Julii anno 47 dicti Regis Edwardi tertii de exitibus custumarum et subsidii Regis in portu London̄ tria milia li. in partem solucionis debitorum suorum ut patet per litteras suas acquietancie remanentes in hanaperio de hoc termino Pasche dicto anno 47 et in Rotulis Recepte die et anno supradictis. Item iidem Petrus et Walterus receperunt 23 die Augusti anno 48 dicti Regis Edwardi tertii de exitibus custumarum et subsidii Regis in diversis portubus Anglie 5853li. 15s. 8d. ut patet in Rotulis de Recepta eisdem die et anno et ut patet per litteras suas acquietancie remanentes in hanaperio de termino Pasche anno 48. Item iidem Petrus et Walterus receperunt 31 (*sic*) die Februarii anno 49 dicti Regis Edwardi tertii per manus Ricardi comitis Arundell 1000li. ut patet per litteras acquietancie remanentes in hanaperio de termino sancti Michaelis anno 49 et ut patet in Rotulo de termino sancti Michaelis supradicto. Item iidem Petrus et Walterus receperunt 27 die Junii anno septimo Regis Ricardi secundi per manus proprias 800 marcas ut patet per litteras suas acquietancie remanentes in hanaperio de termino Pasche dicto anno 7. Item idem Walterus recepit quarto die Marcii anno 8 Regis Ricardi secundi 777li. 15s. 5d. Item iidem Petrus et Walterus receperunt 13 die Decembris anno nono predicti Regis Ricardi secundi per manus predicti Walteri 800li. Item primo die Maii anno 9 Regis Ricardi predicti iidem Walterus et Petrus receperunt 911li. in partem solucionis summe infrascripte. Item 8 die Junii eodem anno nono 500 marcas. Vacate quia restitute fuerunt eo quod Galterus de Bardes mercator de societate Bardorum et attornatus mercatorum eiusdem societatis in Florencia 24 Octobris anno regni Ricardi secundi quintodecimo per scriptum suum in Rotulis cancellarie eiusdem domini Regis de anno predicto irrotulatum remisit relaxavit et quietum clamavit pro se et in nomine mercatorum predictorum prefato domino Rege et Willelmo comiti Sarisberiensi heredibus et executoribus suis ac heredibus et executoribus domini Edwardi nuper Regis Anglie avi dicti domini Regis, Johannis quondam archiepiscopi Cantuariensis, Henrici quondam Episcopi Lincolnensis et Ricardi quondam episcopi Dunolnensis, Henrici quondam comitis Derbie Willelmi quondam comitis Northamptonie et Roberti quondam comitis Suffolcie et cuiuslibet eorum omnimodas acciones querelas et demandas quas ipsi vel mercatores predicti versus eundem dominum Regem et alios predictos ratione quarumcumque summarum denariorum per ipsos prefato Galtero et aliis de societate predicta debitarum. Et ideo iste littere cancellantur et dampnantur.

(2) The letter patent dated at Vilvorde, June 28, 1339, which is printed in the Calendar of Patent Rolls, 1338–40, p. 388.

(3) The letter patent of protection dated at Brussels, August 4, 1339, which is printed in the Calendar of Patent Rolls, 1338–40, p. 391.[1]

(4) The letter patent dated at Westminster, November 7, 1348, which is printed in the Calendar of Patent Rolls, 1348–50, p. 11.[2]

Exhibuit eciam curie predictus Galterus duas litteras patentes quarum una

---

[1] Four seals in red wax remain attached to the document: the seals of the Bishop of Lincoln, the Bishop of Durham, the Earl of Derby, and the Earl of Northampton.

[2] A fragment of a seal in brown wax, with a figure of the King remains. All the letters have the same endorsement as 1, from *Vacate quia* to the end, and p. 128, n. 2. Letter 4 has in addition the following endorsement: 'Irrotulatur in memorandis de anno xxxix Regis Edwardi tertii inter Recorda de termino sancti Michaelis ex parte Rememoratis Thesaurarii. The originals of letters 2, 3, 4, are PRO K.R. Accounts, 127/38 (3, 5, and 4).

sigillatur sigillo Petri de Bardes et altera sigillo predicti Galteri que quidem littere superius irrotulantur in instrumento predicto.

Et scrutatis rotulis quo ad debita de quibus fit mencio superius in brevi compertum est in rotulo exannuali in Londoñ inter debita extracta de Rotulo quinquagesimo primo Regis Edwardi tertii quod 1092li. 19s. 5d. exiguntur ad opus Regis de mercatoribus de societate Bardorum videlicet 166li. 13s. 4d. de prestito ad Receptam scaccarii 17 die Julii anno 37 per manus Petri de Barde et Nicholi Marini in persolucionem 250 marcarum sibi liberatarum de termino Pasche proximo futuro de illis 500 marcis annuatim quas Rex eisdem mercatoribus nuper concessit in auxilium sustentacionis sue in partem[1] debitorum suorum ad scaccarium percipiendas, 40li. de prestito ad dictam Receptam 9 die Septembris eodem anno per manus Nicholi Marini super eo quod eis aretro est de dictis 500 marcis per annum, 166li. 13s. 4d. de consimili prestito ad dictam Receptam quinto die Decembris anno 38 per manus Philippi de Barde super eo quod eis arestro est de dictis 500 marcis annuatim; 100li. de prestito ad dictam Receptam nono die Decembris anno 35 per manus Philippi de Bardi super annuo certo predicto; 86li. 6s. 1d. de prestito ad dictam Receptam sexto die Marcii eodem anno per manus Philippi Barde super eo quod eis aretro est de annuo certo predicto; 166li. 13s. 4d. 10 die Julii eodem anno per manus dicti Philippi super eo quod eis aretro est de annuo certo predicto; 166li. 13s. 4d. de prestito 20 die Junii anno 36 super eodem certo et 200li. de prestito 8 die Augusti eodem anno super eodem certo suo. Et quod 6853li. 15s. 8d. exiguntur ad opus dicti Regis de predictis Petro de Barde et Waltero de Barde mercatoribus de societate predicta videlicet 5853li. 15s. 8d. de prestito ad Receptam scaccarii 23 die Augusti anno 48 per manus Ricardi Lyons et Johannis Pyel in allocacione eis facta infra summam 20,000li. super debitis in quibus Rex eisdem mercatoribus tenetur et 1000li. de prestito ad dictam Receptam 31 die Januarii anno 49 in denariis eis liberatis per manus Ricardi comitis Arundell super debitis in quibus Rex eis tenetur. Et quod 18,000li. exiguntur ad opus Regis de Radulpho de Barde chevaler Gerardo Bonenseignie et Dynno Forset mercatoribus de societate predicta et sociis suis in quibus obligarunt se teneri Regi solvendis in festo sancti Martini anno vicesimo. Et quod 9940li. exiguntur ad opus Regis de predictis mercatoribus de predicta societate Bardorum videlicet 7003li. de prestito sibi facto 19 die Januarii anno 19 incipiente resolvendo ad festum Pasche proximum sequentem et 2930li. de consimili prestito 20 die Januarii eodem anno. Et quod 56li. 13s. 4d. exiguntur similiter ad opus Regis de predictis

[1] *Solucionis* is omitted.

mercatoribus de societate Bardorum videlicet 10li. de prestito super 1000li. quas nuper assumpserunt Regi mutuare 26li. 13s. 4d. de prestito super diversis pecuniarum summis in quibus Rex eis tenetur et 20li. de consimili prestito super eisdem summis. Compertum est eciam in magno Rotulo de anno 13 Regis huius in Res. Londoñ. quod 1333li. 6s. 8d. sunt exiguntur ad opus Regis de Petro de Barde et Waltero de Barde mercatoribus de societate Bardorum et attornatis eiusdem societatis videlicet 533li. 6s. 8d. de prestito eis facto ad Receptam scaccarii 27 die Junii anno 7 in denariis eis liberatis per manus eorundem super debitis in quibus dominus Rex Edwardus avus Regis huius eisdem mercatoribus tenebatur ut patet per litteras acquietancie ipsorum Petri et Walteri nomine predicte societatis factas remanentes in hanaperio de termino Pasche anno 7 ut patet per litteras Regis predictas patentes predicti avi quas dicti Petrus et Walterus inde penes se habent indorsatas de summa predicta que quidem allocatio facta est eisdem pro eo quod ipsi mutuarunt ad opus domini Regis nunc 1200 marcas pro guerris suis sustentandis 800li. de prestito eis facto ibidem 13 die Decembris anno 9 in denariis eis liberatis per manus eiusdem Walteri per assignationem eis super quintadecima factam super debitis in quibus dominus Edwardus Rex avus Regis huius eisdem mercatoribus certis de causis tenebatur ut patet per litteras patentes predicti avi quas dicti Petrus et Walterus penes se habent indorsatas de summa predicta que quidem allocatio facta est eisdem pro eo quod ipsi pro rescussu ville de Gaunt duo milia librarum ad instanciam et supplicationem domini Regis et consilii sui mutuarunt. Et quod 2022li. 4s. 5d. exiguntur similiter ad opus Regis de predicto Waltero Barde Lumbardo attornato mercatorum de predicta societate Bardorum videlicet 777li. 15s. 7d. de prestito sibi facto ad Receptam scaccarii 4 die Marcii anno 8 in denariis eidem societati liberatis per manus eiusdem Walteri super debitis in quibus dominus Edwardus avus Regis huius dictis mercatoribus tenebatur ut patet per litteras acquietancie Petri de Barde et dicti Walteri nomine dicte societatis factas remanentes in hanaperio et per litteras patentes predicti Regis avi quas dictus Walterus inde penes se habet indorsatas de summa predicta. 911li. 2s. 2d. de prestito sibi facto ibidem primo die Maii anno nono in denariis eidem societati liberatis per manus eiusdem Walteri super debitis in quibus idem Rex Edwardus certis de causis tenebatur et 333li. 6s. 8d. de prestito sibi facto ibidem 8 die Junii anno 9 in denariis eidem societati liberatis per manus eiusdem Walteri super debitis in quibus Rex Edwardus avus Regis huius tenebatur ut patet per litteras acquietancie ipsius Walteri nomine dicte societatis factas remanentes in hanaperio termino Pasche anno nono ut patet per litteras patentes predicti Regis Edwardi avi quas dictus Walterus inde penes se habet indorsatas de summa predicta.

There follows then some accounting with Walter de Bardi as master of the mint: for 723li. 4s. 8d. received for expenses, and 135 marks for the seigneurage of the mint. The enrolment then continues:

Cognoscendo insuper idem Galtronus pro maiore securitate et acquietancione domini Regis et avi sui et aliorum dominorum superius specificatorum necnon heredium et executorum eorum in premissis quod ipse est unus de dicta societate Bardorum et attornatus mercatorum eiusdem societatis de Florencia et pro magistro eiusdem societatis reputatur et eciam expresse fatebatur et cognovit coram eisdem Baronibus quod satisfactum est ei et aliis mercatoribus de societate predicta de omnibus denariorum summis in predictis litteris Regis Edwardi avi Regis huius patentibus contentis petens sibi et aliis mercatoribus predictis fieri in premissis iuxta tenorem brevis regii supradicti quod curia, etc.

Super quibus habita deliberacione per Barones consideratum est quod tam predictus Galtronus de predictis 725li. 4s. 8d. ab eo exactis de prestitis quam ipse et alii mercatores supradicti de societate predicta de omnibus aliis summis supradictis ab eis ut premittitur exactis exonerentur et quieti existant pretextu premissorum. Et quod dominus Rex nunc ac predictus dominus Edwardus nuper Rex anglie avus suus heredes et executores sui necnon predicti domini in predictis litteris dicti Galtroni specificati heredes et executores sui tam de omnibus et singulis denariorum summis in predictis quatuor litteris patentibus sigillo predicti avi Regis huius specificatis quam de omnibus aliis denariorum summis prefato Gautrono aut prefatis mercatoribus de predicta societate de Barde de Florencia vel alicui eorum ex quacumque causa per ipsum dominum Regem nunc aut prefatum avum suum seu prefatos dominos heredes seu executores suos debitis necnon de omnibus accionibus querelis et demandis quas predictus Gauterus aut prefati mercatores de societate predicta versus predictum dominum Regem aut prefatum Edwardum avum suum seu prefatos dominos heredes vel executores suos a principio mundi usque predictum 24 diem Octobris anno quintodecimo predicti Regis nunc exonerentur et quieti existant pretextu relaxationis cognicionis predicti Gautroni et aliorum premissorum. Et memorandum quod supradicte due littere patentes una videlicet sub sigillo supradicti Petri de Bardes et alia sub sigillo predicti Galtroni ac predictum instrumentum puplicum necnon predicte quatuor littere patentes sub sigillo predicti Edwardi avi Regis huius liberantur ad Receptam huius scaccarii ibidem custodienda et Johannes Innocent clericus Thesaurarii Anglie ea ibidem recepit.[1]

[1] There follows some further accounting with Walter de Bardi concerning the mint. In the margin opposite the last paragraph is written: *In Rotulo 14 in Res. London. et in Rotulo 15 Item London.*

APPENDIX B

PROTECTION *CUM CLAUSULA NOLUMUS* FOR THE HANSE OF ALMAIN[1]

Rex universis vicecomitibus, maioribus, ballivis, ministris et omnibus aliis fidelibus suis necnon collectoribus muragii, pontagii et pavagii tam infra libertates quam extra ad quos etc. Sciatis quod cum celebris memorie dominus Edwardus quondam Rex Anglie avus noster inter ceteras libertates quas per cartam suam quam confirmavimus[2] concessit mercatoribus de Alemannia et aliis mercatoribus extraneis et alienigenis pro quibusdam prestationibus et custumis per ipsos mercatores de rebus et mercimoniis suis eidem avo nostro et heredibus solvendis concessisset eisdem quod ipsi salvo et secure sub tuitione et protectione nostra in regnum nostrum Anglie et ubicumque infra potestatem nostram alibi veniant cum mercandisis suis quibuscumque de muragio, pontagio et pavagio liberi et quieti et quod nulla prisa vel arrestacio seu dilacio occasione prise de mercimoniis et mercandisis seu aliis bonis suis per nos vel per alium seu alios pro aliqua necessitate vel casu contra voluntatem ipsorum mercatorum fieret aut fieri permitteretur nisi statim soluto precio pro quo ipsi mercatores aliis huiusmodi mercandisa vendere possint vel eis alias satisfacto ita quod reputent se contentos et quod super mercimonia et mercandisas seu bona ipsorum per nos vel ministros nostros nulla appreciatio seu estimatio imponeretur et quod in omnibus generibus placitorum salvo casu criminis pro quo infligenda sit pena mortis ubi mercator implacitatus fuerit vel alium implacitaverit cuiuscumque conditionis idem implacitatus extiterit extraneus vel privatus in nundinis civitatibus villis sive burgis ubi fuerit sufficiens copia mercatorum predictorum et inquisitio fieri debeat si medietas inquisitionis de eisdem mercatoribus et medietas altera de aliis probis et legalis hominibus loci illius ubi placitum illud erit ac bone memorie dominus Edwardus nuper Rex Anglie progenior noster per cartam suam quam similiter[3] per aliam cartam nostram confirmavimus concesserit pro se et heredibus suis prefatis mercatoribus Alemannie illis videlicet qui habent domum in civitate Londonie qui Gildhalla Teuthonicorum vulgariter nuncupatur quod ipsi et eorum successores universi et singuli domum predictam habitur in omnibus hiis libertatibus et liberis

[1] PRO Patent Roll 212, m. 38. Cf. *C.P.R. 1343–45*, p. 320.

[2] *Carta Mercatoria* of 1303. Confirmed by Edward III in 1328. *Foedera*, ii, 2, pp. 747–48.

[3] In 1317 Edward II confirmed the charters of Henry III and Edward I, which were confirmed by Edward III in 1327. *Cal. Letter Book E*, p. 220.

consuetudinibus quibus ipsi usi fuerunt et gavisi manutenerentur imperpetuum et servarentur et quod ipsos mercatores extra huiusmodi libertates et
consuetudines non traheret nec quantum in ipso fuit aliqualiter trahi per-
mitteret et quod predicti mercatores Alemannie et eorum successores predictam domum habituri imperpetuum infra regnum et potestatem nostra
has haberent libertates videlicet quod ipsi aut eorum bona vel mercimonia
infra idem regnum et potestatem pro aliquo debito de quo fideiussores aut
principales debitores non extiterint nec pro aliqua transgressione facta seu
facienda per alios quam per ipsos non arestarentur nec gravarentur prout
in cartis et confirmationibus predictis plenius continetur. Nos prefatos
mercatores Alemannie cum rebus et mercimoniis suis infra regnum et
potestatem nostram predictam venientes ne ipsi vel eorum aliquis super
libertatibus eis sic concessis molestentur indebite seu graventur favore
benivolo prosequi volentes suscepimus ipsos et eorum quemlibet ac homines
et servientes suos necnon naves et alias res et mercandisas suas proprias
quascumque in protectionem et defensionem nostram specialem necnon in
salvum et securum conductum nostram districte inhibentes ne quis eis in
personis navibus aut aliis rebus seu bonis suis veniendo ad regnum nostrum
causa mercandisandi dampnun inferat aut gravamen nec quicquam de eis
contra voluntatem suam capiat seu ipsos super libertatibus suis eis sic
concessis indebite perturbare presumat contra tenores cartarum et con-
firmacionum predictarum, ita tamen quod custumas et subsidia nobis in
regno nostro Anglie debita inde solvant ut debebunt. Et ideo vobis mandamus quod ipsos mercatores et eorum quemlibet ac homines et servientes
suos naves ac alias res et bona sua veniendo in regnum nostrum cum mercandisis suis sicut predictum est manuteneatis protegatis et defendatis,
nos inferentes eis vel inferri permittentes iniuriam molestiam, dampnum,
impedimentum aliquod seu gravamen et si quid eis forisfactum fuerit id eis
sine dilatione faciatis emendari. Nolumus enim quod de navibus vel aliis
rebus bonis seu mercandisis predictis quicquam capiatur ad opus nostrum
aut alterius cuiuscumque contra voluntatem ipsorum mercatorum absque
satisfactione debita eis inde facienda. In cuius etc Teste Rege apud Westmonasterium viii die Julii. (1344).[1]

[1] The letter of protection is for the merchants of the Hanse of Almain, confirming to them
the privileges of the general *Carta Mercatoria* and of their own particular charters; not as the,
Calendar of Patent Rolls says 'for merchants of Almain as well as for the merchants of the
same having a house in London.' *C.P.R. ut supra.*

APPENDIX C

TABLE OF IMPORTS AND EXPORTS, 1350-1377

1. Introduction to the Customs Accounts

The twelve rolls of customs accounts for the reign of Edward III[1] among the records of the lord treasurer's remembrancer do not represent a chronological series, nor do they seem to have been made up with more than an approximate regard for subject-matter.[2] They are, moreover, the records of goods imported and exported and of the customs levied on the same only for those periods when the money was collected by the customers and when it was paid into the exchequer. During the periods when the customs or any part of them were farmed, the accounting was done, if at all, without details, on the pipe rolls. If, as was done during John Malewayn's receivership in 1350–51, a record is put on the customs rolls, only the total of the customs and subsidy received in each port is given.[3] The wine custom paid by aliens, and for part of the period, the cloth custom were collected by the king's butler. The detailed records of the wine custom are among the butlerage accounts and those of the cloth custom are among the king's remembrancer's accounts.[4] There is apparently no enrollment of the wine custom.[5] Until 1353, while the cloth custom was being collected by the butler, only the sum of the yearly totals for all ports was entered on the enrolled accounts.[6] After 1353, the cloth custom was collected by the customers and the returns were enrolled in the usual manner.

There are unaccountable variations in the method of enrollment, but in general the *antiqua custuma;* the *nova custuma* on wool, cloth and merchandise; the subsidies on wool and on general merchandise; the cloth custom of 1347 and the subsidy on cloth exposed for sale within the country were each entered on separate rolls until about 1369. It is, perhaps, more convenient than accurate to speak of customs rolls in the fourteenth century

---

[1] PRO L.T.R. Enrolled Customs Accounts, 4–14, 30. They will be referred to hereafter in this section as Rolls 4–14, 30.

[2] Cf. Introduction to tables, G. Schanz, *Englische Handelspolitik gegen Ende des Mittelalters* (Leipzig, 1881), II, 1–5.

[3] Roll 8, m. 41.

[4] PRO K.R. Accounts, Various, 80/1–22 (Butlerage); *ibid.*, 457/20–23 (Wool).

[5] There is, however, among the loose membranes of Roll 30, one (8875) which contains what seems to be an enrollment, carelessly done, of the wine custom from 12 February, 1338, to Mich. 1354. Similar membranes may be sewed into other rolls but none appear in the rolls for this period.

[6] Roll 7, m. 9.

for the sewing together of the membranes on which the accounts for each kind of custom were recorded was not necessarily contemporaneous with the writing of them. Some were never sewed together.[1] Their present form, however, makes the term roll appropriate. In each entry on all rolls, the amount of the commodity imported or exported, usually for a year from Michaelmas to Michaelmas, is given, with the amount of the customs due and the rate at which they were paid. Only when there is a difference in the rates, is it stated whether the goods were taken by English or by alien merchants. On the *antiqua custuma* roll, the tronage, when it was paid into the exchequer, and the payments for the cockets are recorded. On that roll, also, were recorded the payments out of the customs, the exemptions from payment,[2] the totals of the *nova customa*, the wool subsidies and the cloth custom,[3] the allowances made to the collectors for expenses, and the general balancing of the account. After 1369, the *antiqua custuma*, the *nova custuma* on wool, and the wool subsidy were entered on the *antiqua custuma* roll as a lump sum and called custom and subsidy.[4] The *nova custuma* roll continued to record the petty custom on general merchandise and wax, while the subsidy roll contained such subsidies on general merchandise as were not farmed. The change in the manner of enrolment was made eleven years earlier in the accounts for London, where the customs and subsidy on wool are combined from 18 January, 1358,[5] after the *nova custuma* on wool and hides had been recorded as a separate account from the 1303 custom on cloth and general merchandise from Michaelmas 1354.[6] In the accounts for Yarmouth the grouping begins at Michaelmas 1368.[7] It had been done earlier for the period from 11 February, 1363, to Michaelmas 1364,[8] but for the next four years there was a reversion to earlier methods. The same grouping was made in the entry for Chichester for Michaelmas, 1363 to 28 November following.[9] In the returns for Ipswich, the subsidy is recorded only on the *antiqua custuma* roll, as a separate item, from Michaelmas, 1368, until 26 June, 1369, when the accounts stop because Ipswich was not one of the staple ports at that time.

[1] Roll 30.

[2] These were occasionally recorded on the other rolls as well.

[3] This was not done in 1350–51 when the customs were farmed. The returns for the subsidies are entered on the roll of subsidies only.

[4] Roll 8.

[5] Roll 8, m. 59d.

[6] Roll 9, m. 33.

[7] Roll 8, m. 54.

[8] *Loc. cit.*

[9] *Ibid.*, m. 49d.

When the accounts begin again, 3 December, 1370, the three payments are combined.[1]

On the *antiqua* and *nova custuma* rolls, the returns for each port are enrolled consecutively and, on the whole, chronologically for long periods. The subsidies and the cloth custom are much less systematically recorded, for there are seldom more than two consecutive entries for any port and there is no attempt to follow an orderly sequence or to put the returns for each port on a separate membrane. One sort of custom is occasionally entered on the roll of another sort[2] and all the rolls are made up in a rather haphazard fashion. Duplicate enrolments, fragments of which remain,[3] were apparently made at this period. In all the rolls there are errors in addition, in the rates given, or amount of money or goods, as when the custom on general merchandise is said to be 4*d.* in the pound.[4] In most cases the errors can be corrected from other rolls or by testing the amount given for the customs with the amount of merchandise.

Originally the enrolled accounts could have been checked and supplemented by the customs accounts among the records of the king's remembrancer,[5] which are the detailed returns made by the collectors and controllers[6] of customs in the several ports. These, although far from uniform, usually give, under the date of the customing, the name of the ship with, frequently, the name of its master and its home port, an itemized account of the shipments with their weight or value, the name of the merchant who

---

[1] *Ibid.*, m. 52.

[2] E.g., London: petty custom, 12 July–Mich. 1361 on Roll 7, m. 9d. Hull: all customs, Mich. 1369–70 on Roll 8, m. 57, cloth custom, Mich. 1370–74 on Roll 9, m. 29d. Newcastle: cloth custom, Mich.–24 Dec. 1372 on Roll 8, m. 65. Bristol: cloth custom, Mich. 1370–20 Jan. 1371 on Roll 8, m. 48d. cloth custom, Mich. 1371–72 on Roll 8, m. 48d.

Note: Roll 7 is the roll of the cloth custom. Roll 8 is the *antiqua custuma* roll. Roll 9 is the *nova custuma* roll. See pp. 161, 140 below.

[3] Rolls, 11, 12, 13, 30.

[4] Roll 8, m. 57. It is obviously a slip when twelve pipes of wool are said to have been exported. Roll 8, m. 56. The other rolls have *petra*. On Roll 9, m. 24 there is an entry of customs paid on 37 quintall 8½ *corium*. In the same roll (m. 24) the 61 quintalls of wax said to have been exported were probably imported.

[5] The K.R. accounts also include cockets, accounts of the seizures of uncustomed goods or of the enforcement of orders to prohibit exportation, and general memoranda on all matters connected with the collection and administration of the customs. Additional information concerning the levying of customs and subsidies, licenses to export, exemptions from the payment of customs is given in the memoranda of the exchequer, and in the records of chancery and parliament.

[6] The controllers were appointed on condition that they 'write the rolls with their own hands, stay there (in the port) continually and execute the office in person and not by a substitute.' *C.P.R. 1364–67*, p. 123.

is shipping them and the amount of customs or subsidy paid. If there is any difference in the rate of customs, it is stated whether the merchant is English or alien, but there unfortunately the differentiation stops. There is in most cases no indication of the nationality of the alien, except when the Hansards were paying a different cloth custom. It is rare otherwise to find it stated that a merchant who exported wool was from Barcelona or that one who imported cloth or sugar was from Lucca.

A greater defect in the K.R. Accounts for this period is their scarcity. It is, perhaps, the leanest period for these records for all customs except the wine custom where the returns are exceptionally numerous. We are, therefore, forced to rely chiefly upon the enrolled accounts and to deal, to a great extent in generalities, which, however, shed considerable light on the share which aliens had in importation and exportation.

The tables have been made from the figures as they stand in the customs accounts. That these may not be wholly accurate records of shipments is possible. In 1350, orders were issued concerning the weighing of wool 'to avoid frauds and that better answer may be made to the king for the customs.'[1] That customs collectors were negligent is shown in the statement of a Fleming who was sued for non-payment of customs on herrings. He said that when he came into port he searched long in various places for the collector and, not finding him, sold his fish uncustomed to avoid losing them by spoiling.[2] No account has been taken of goods smuggled in or out of the country. From the scattered suits arising out of smuggling and from occasional accounts of the searchers in the ports it would be impossible to make even an estimate of the goods on which customs were not paid. The amount of smuggled goods must be regarded as a constant, which, although it would increase the gross totals, would not affect the ratio between alien and native shipments.

In the following tables for all commodities the figures are for years which extend from Michaelmas to Michaelmas unless it is otherwise stated.

2. RECORDS OF THE EXPORTATION OF WOOL

The most accurate record of the *antiqua custuma* on wool and hides for the latter half of the reign of Edward III is in roll 8 of the L.T.R. enrolled accounts. It contains some earlier accounts, the record of John Malewayn's receivership and, for our purpose, the accounts of the wool custom from Michaelmas, 1351, to approximately 1376, from which time the accounts

[1] *C.C.R. 1349–54*, p. 228. See also ordinances of the council regarding the collection of wool customs printed by Baldwin. *The King's Council*, p. 486.

[2] PRO K.R. Mem. 140, Communia Trin.

are continued on roll 14 which goes on into the reign of Henry IV. Roll 11, consisting of 5 membranes, contains duplicate accounts for five ports for short periods:

London	9 April, 1361–Michaelmas, 1366
Berwick	20 June, 1357–Michaelmas, 1366
Chichester	4 November, 1351–Michaelmas, 1366
New Castle	4 November, 1351–Michaelmas, 1364
Hull	4 November, 1351–Michaelmas, 1358

The account for London begins and ends abruptly in the middle of an entry. The preceding part and the continuation are among the loose membranes of roll 30 (8853, 8868), which contains duplicate accounts for various customs and subsidies for scattered periods from 1338 to 1381. Roll 11 is obviously made up of a few of these membranes sewed together probably at a date later than the fourteenth century.

The *nova custuma* on wool is recorded on roll 9 until 1369 and the subsidies are on roll 5 until the same date, after which time the combined customs and subsidy are entered on roll 8. There is a duplicate account of the subsidies of 1350–51 on roll 12.

In the tables of wool exported, the amount given for 1350 was actually taken from February to June, the period during which the subsidies were collected. Complete annual returns are not available until the farming of the wool customs came to an end at Michaelmas in 1351. From 1350 to 1351, and again from 1356 to 1362, it is impossible to separate alien shipments from those of English merchants. For the first year the figures are taken from the returns for the subsidy which was the same for all merchants. During the second period English merchants were paying alien rates and no distinction is made between their shipments and those of aliens. For the other years English shipments are obtained by subtracting the amount taken by aliens as given on roll 9 from the total given on roll 8. After 1369, alien and native shipments are recorded separately on roll 8.[1]

For the sake of uniformity the quantities of wool are given in terms of sacks and cloves, although sarplars and stones are occasionally used in the rolls.[2] The table of weights for wool is as follows:

1 clove	=	7	pounds		
1 stone	=	14	pounds	= 2 cloves	
1 sack	= 364		pounds	= 26 stones	= 52 cloves[3]
1 sarplar	=	1½	sacks.[4]		

[1] Cf. p. 137 above.

No wool was exported from English ports during the following periods:

Michaelmas, 1351– 4 November, 1351 (31 Oct. for Southampton)
Michaelmas, 1362–18 February, 1363 (11 Feb. for Yarmouth)
31 January, 1365– 2 February, 1365.

Periods when no wool was taken from a particular port are given with the tables for that port. Wool taken to the staple at Calais from 1372 to 1376 has been indicated by C. placed after the number of sacks or wool fells. A distinction was made in the returns because a tax of 19*d.* per sack was paid on wool taken elsewhere.[1]

----

[2] Stones are given in the tables for Hull because they are used throughout the period in the rolls. For other ports *stone* was used for the following periods: Boston, until Mich. 1365; Yarmouth, until Mich. 1365; Chichester, until Mich. 1351; Southampton, until Mich. 1352.

[3] *Rot. Parl.* ii, 133, 240; *Stat.* i, 321. At an earlier period, the stone was 13 pounds and there were 28 stones to the sack. E. Varenbergh, *Histoire des Relations Diplomatiques entre le Comté de Flandre et l'Angleterre au Moyen Age* (Brussels, 1874), p. 152. On the Coram Rege Roll for Trin. 1350, (360, m. 29d.) there is a case of merchants being prosecuted for having had 28 stones to the sack and 14 pounds to the stone, when formerly they were accustomed to take only 13 pounds to the stone.

[1] PRO K.R. Mem. 145, Communia Pasch.; Parliamentary and Council Proceedings, File 7, No. 24 (printed by Baldwin, *The King's Council, p. 486*); *Cal. Plea and Mem. Rolls, London,* I, 212.

[1] See p. 27 above.

NEWCASTLE

	WOOL						WOOLFELLS		
	Native		Alien		Total		Native	Alien	Total
	sacks	cl.	sacks	cl.	sacks	cl.	fells	fells	fells
1350					297	14			
1350–51					920½	18			42,060
1351–52	99				99		5,124		5,124[1]
1352–53			85	50	85	50		4,090	4,090
1353–54			887	12	887	12		44,008	44,008
1354–55			555		555			27,279	27,279
1355–56			256	3	256	3		26,774	26,774
1356–57					682	15			53,448
1357–58					401	12			23,748[2]
1358–59					229	12			16,194
1359–60					761	3			19,324
1360–61					680	17			18,556[3]
1361–62					1,167	25			18,483[4]
1362–63	1,246	46			1,246	46	26,881		26,881
1363–64	564	10½			564	10½	73,183	1,020	74,203
1364–65	347½	28	16	23	363½	51	41,999	16,272	58,271
1365–66	709½	6			709½	6	41,478		41,478
1366–67	559½	16			559½	16	35,909		35,909[5]
1367–68	445	15			445	15	23,362		23,362[6]
1368–69	346½	50½	25	20	372½	18½	9,851		9,851
1369–70			20		20			5,441	5,441
1370–71	297	20			297	20	18,603		18,603
1371–72					none		3,250	1,109	4,359
1372–73	197	7			197	7	18,812	260	19,072[7]
1373–74	390½	8			390½	8	17,766	526	18,292
1374–75	111½	10C.			111½	10C.	3,603C.		3,603C.[8]
	337½	1	1	5	338½	6	37,668		37,668
	449	11	1	5	450	16	41,271		41,271
1375–76	48	4			48	4	2,300C.		2,300C.
							6,415		6,415
June							8,715		8,715
1376–77	136½	16C.			136½	16C.	2,463C.		2,463C.

NEWCASTLE

[1] 4 sacks 28 cloves were allowed to the merchants for the weight of the cords, canvas, and corners used in packing the wool, according to a writ of November, 1351, ordering 4 cloves per sarplar to be allowed until the following Michaelmas. Roll 8, m. 53, 68. *C.C.R. 1349–54*, pp. 228, 248, 250. 2 cloves were allowed for 2 cords and a staff, and 2 cloves for the canvas and corners. *C.C.R. 1349–54*, p. 335.

[2] Allowance was made to the collectors for 1 mark of the customs and subsidy on 223 sacks 19 cloves beyond the total given above exported by the burgesses of Berwick on Tweed, who had been granted permission to export 300 sacks 'in relevatione status sui.' Roll 8, m. 63.

[3] In Roll 5, m. 18d, the account is said to extend only to 24 April but it is evident that it is meant to cover the entire year because it is said that the collectors for the following period account 'a quo festo,' which obviously refers to Michaelmas, 1361.

[4] Roll 9, m. 40 has 18,482 fells.

[5] Roll 5, m. 21d has no date for this entry except 'ab eodem festo Sancti Michelis proximum sequentem'; the year and 'ad idem festum' being omitted after *Michelis*. It is evident from comparison with the other rolls that the account is for this year.

[6] All the customs rolls extend the period covered by this account to 15 December, 1368, but begin the following entry at Michaelmas, 1368. Roll 8, m. 64; Roll 9, m. 40d; Roll 5, m. 22, 22d; Roll 7, m. 13, 13d.

[7] 60 sacks of wool and fells were taken to Calais. Roll 8, m. 65.

[8] This period extends to 23 November, 1375. The wool exported by aliens was taken by John Faytt. Roll 8, m. 65.

No wool was exported during the following periods: Michaelmas, 1352–14 August, 1353; Michaelmas, 1364–2 October, 1364; 5 August, 1369–Michaelmas, 1369; Michaelmas, 1371–Michaelmas, 1372; See also p. 141 above.

KINGSTON UPON HULL

| | WOOL | | | | | | WOOLFELLS | | |
| | Native | | Alien | | Total | | Native | Alien | Total |
	sacks	st.	sacks	st.	sacks	st.	fells	fells	fells
1350					1,032½	11			1,222
1350–51					6,004	16			41,371
1351–52	4,453	23	256	10	4,710	7	43,456	156	43,612[1]
1352–53			2,011	18	2,011	18		8,602	8,602[2]
1353–54			6,334	11	6,334	11		52,695	52,695[3]
1354–55			5,441	7¾	5,441	7¾		49,836	49,836[3]
1355–56			5,873	1½	5,873	1½		44,399	44,399[3]
1356–57					8,185	7½			58,604
1357–58					5,891	12¾			46,563
1358–59					5,404	7¾			47,418
1359–60					5,897	16¾			67,620
1360–61					4,301	12½			46,677
1361–62					6,443	12½			58,819[4]
1362–63	4,487	25½	439	13	4,927	12½	77,359	2,163	79,522

KINGSTON UPON HULL (*Continued*)

	WOOL						WOOLFELLS		
	Native		Alien		Total		Native	Alien	Total
	sacks	st.	sacks	st.	sacks	st.	fells	fells	fells
1363–64	3,067	5¾	464	15	3,531	20¾	81,722	4,752	86,474[5]
1364–65	4,583	½	409	9	4,992	9½	60,372	19,913	80,285[6]
1365–66	4,683	10¼	107	25½	4,791	9¾	55,772	3,767	59,539[6]
1366–67	2,803	16¾	42	12¾	2,846	3½	27,913	3,573	31,486
1367–68	3,096	6¼	12	16½	3,108	22¾	9,506	874	10,380[7]
1368–69	1,763	15½	127	2	1,890	17½	7,851	288	8,139
1369–70			2,964	1¾	2,964	1¾		3,951	3,951[8]
1370–71	3,261	20½	754	25½	4,016	20	9,877	643	10,520
1371–72	1,504	18½C.	22	2C.	1,526	20½C.	2,678C.	2,235C.	4,913C.[9]
					3,100	1½			6,536
					4,626	22			11,449
1372–73	2,980	½C.	40	13½C.	3,020	14C.	496C.		496C.
	1,726	20½	756	8½	2,483	3	11,836	11,767	23,603
	4,706	21	796	22	5,503	17	12,332	11,767	24,099
1373–74	1,521	24½C.			1,521	24½C.			
	2,603	23½	493	19	3,097	16½	31,532	32,836	64,368
	4,125	22	493	19	4,619	15	31,532	32,836	64,368
1374–75	3,531	12½C.			3,531	12½C.	966C.		966C.
	876	23½	163	13	1,040	10½	36,590	22,523	59,113
	4,408	10	163	13	4,571	23	37,556	22,523	60,079
1375–76	2,903	4C.	1	2C.	2,904	6C.	3,494C.	6,544C.	10,038C.[10]
	206	9½	27	10	233	19½	5,301	6,495	11,796
	3,109	12½	28	12	2,137	26½	8,795	13,039	21,834
June 1376–77	1,247	3C.	102	23C.	1,350	C.	202C.		202C.
	1,209	12	25	22	1,235	8	6,604	4,082	10,888
	2,456	15	128	19	2,585	8	6,806	4,082	11,090

BOSTON

| | WOOL | | | | | | WOOLFELLS | | |
| | Native | | Alien | | Total | | Native | Alien | Total |
	sacks	cl.	sacks	cl.	sacks	cl.	fells	fells	fells
1350					370	4			
1350–51					5,415	14			5,454
1351–52	2,166		448	6	2,616	6	3,000	30	3,030[1]
1352–53			3,428	42	3,428	42		2,105	2,105
1353–54			7,381	18	7,381	18		12,496	12,496
1354–55			6,024	49	6,024	49		5,704	5,704[2]
1355–56			3,996	29	3,996	29		5,535	5,535
1356–57			6,859	49½	6,859	49½		10,525	10,525[3]
1357–58					5,080	42½			7,434
1358–59					5,040	38			7,587[4]
1359–60					6,364½	12			14,295
1360–61					5,398	3½			9,256[5]
1361–62					9,095	25½			16,083
1362–63	1,481	22	1,971	40	3,453	36	35,776	8,398	44,174
1363–64	2,184	18	1,620	32	3,804	50	18,263	3,418	21,681[6]
1364–65	3,243	15	2,517	11½	5,730	26½	3,712	10,845	14,557[7]
1365–66	4,070	½	1,559	36	5,629	36½	11,248	6,113	17,361
1366–67	3,419	44	1,744	25½	5,264	17½	10,987	5,457	16,444
1367–68	3,974	4½	956	2	4,930	6½	8,426	1,154	9,580
1368–69	2,538	35	4,715	20½	7,254	3½	2,737	39	2,776
1369–70			3,208	7½	3,208	7½		864	864
1370–71	4,180½		1,824	32	6,004½	32	4,943	47	4,990
1371–72	172	36C.			172	36C.			———[8]
					4,111	29½			
					4,284	13½			500
1372–73	2,726		4,616	6	7,342	6	1,431	6,793	8,224[9]
1373–74	2,459	36	2,738	46	5,198	30	154	10,508	10,662
1374–75	841	6C.			841	6C.	414C.		414C.
	2,458	14	4,135	46	6,594	8	2,837	11,360	14,197
	3,299	20	4,135	46	7,434	14	3,251	11,360	14,611
1375–76	2,635	40C.	407	C.	3,042	40C.	1,449C.	1,658C.	3,107C.[10]
	786	32	1,829	43	2,616	23	2,583	13,826	16,409
	3,422	20	2,236	43	5,659	11	4,032	15,484	19,516
June									
1376–77	2,940	28	335	34	3,276	10	1,991		1,991

KINGSTON UPON HULL

[1] 191 sacks 36 cloves were allowed in weighing. Cf. p. 143, n. 1 above.

[2] Roll 5, m. 16 has 28 stones.

[3] This wool is called *grossa lana*. Roll 8, m. 55.

[4] Roll 8, m. 56 has 12 *pipe*, but the other rolls have 12 *petre*.

[5] Roll 5, m. 19d has 25 *petra* in the total amount exported.

[6] This period extends to 10 October.

[7] Roll 8, m. 57 has 3108 sarplars but from the amount of customs paid it must be sacks.

[8] On Roll 8, m. 57 there are two consecutive entries for this year. The first states that there were no exports or imports for the year. The second gives not only the wool and fells as given in the table but cloth and general merchandise as well. The customs and subsidy are accounted for together at this time, and there are, therefore, no entries on the other rolls by which to check Roll 8. The collectors accounting were not the same in the two entries.

[9] The wool not taken to Calais was exported by aliens and native merchants, both paying the same customs. Their shipments are not, therefore, accounted for separately. Cf. p. 27, n. 9.

[10] The alien shipments not taken to Calais were exported by Albert van Putt, Roll 8, m. 57. He was a Hansard from Dortmund, variously called Albrecht del Putte, Albert de Puteo and Albrecht atte Putte. Kunze, *Hanseakten aus England*, p. 148.

No wool was exported during the following periods: Michaelmas, 1356–18 October, 1356; Michaelmas, 1364–2 October, 1364; 10 October, 1366–28 October, 1366. Michaelmas, 1372–4 November, 1372. See also p. 141 above.

BOSTON

[1] It is stated that allowance is made for canvas and cords but the amount of wool allowed is not given. Cf. p. 143, n. 1. above.

[2] The number of stones, which have here been changed to cloves, given in Roll 8, m. 42d. is 23½, but according to the amount of customs paid, it should be 24½ as in Rolls 9 and 5.

[3] 371 sacks 24½ cloves of wool and 2760 wool fells, included in this total were Scotch wool on which 13*s*. 4*d*. per sack was paid as customs and subsidy. Roll 8, m. 42d.

[4] One sack was Scotch wool.

[5] Roll 5, m. 18d has 10,256 fells but the amount of customs paid is for the smaller quantity.

[6] This period extends to 2 October. No customs were accounted for on 30 out of 66 sarplars of wool of Francis de Carledon, Godfrey Lemyng, John Hars, aliens; on 12 out of 20 sarplars of John Wilton; on 5 sarplars of Wynad de Edremyghouse; or on 6 sarplars of Herman Rudene lost while sailing out of port. Roll 8, m. 43d.

[7] This period extends to 20 October.

[8] 4111 sacks 29½ cloves and 500 fells were exported by aliens and native merchants, both paying 53*s*. 4*d*. per sack. The wool was probably taken to ports other than Calais, and native merchants were paying higher customs for that privilege.

[9] Of this wool, 6,683 sacks and 6,693 fells must have been taken elsewhere than to Calais because 19*d*. per sack which was collected on all wool not taken to the staple was paid on that quantity of wool. Roll 8, m. 44d.

[10] The alien shipments not taken to Calais were taken by Thomas Besse. Roll 8, m. 44d. Cf. p. 151, n. 11 below.

No wool was exported during the following periods: Michaelmas, 1356–18 October, 1356. See also p. 141 above.

IPSWICH

	WOOL						WOOLFELLS		
	Native		Alien		Total		Native	Alien	Total
	sacks	cl.	sacks	cl.	sacks	cl.	fells	fells	fells
1350					88½	23			none
1350–51					1,364	6			20,557
1351–52	947½	22	22	46	970½	16	41,020	3,223	44,243[1]
1352–53					none				none[2]
1365	63½	45½	18½	20	83	13½	5,021	1,282	6,303[3]
1365–66	366½	2½	27	3	393½	5½	5,426	324	5,750
1366–67	865½	25½	3½	3	869	28½	18,388	349	18,737
1367–68	477	14			477	14	18,703		18,703
1368–69	195½				195½		2,942		2,942[4]
1370–71[5]	183	12	10	7½	193	19½	979	5,723	6,702
1371–72	94½	17C.	8	4½	94½	17C.	1,396C.	2,279C.	3,675C.
					8	4½			
					112½	21½			
1372–73	119	24½C.			119	24½C.		724C.	724C.
	11	9			11	9			
	130	33½			130	32½			
1373–74	64	1C.			64	1C.	1,520C.		1,520C.
	37	1			37	1			
	101	2			101	2			
1374–75	325½	45C.			325½	45C.	1,772C.		1,772C.
1375–76	101½	20C.			101½	20C.	480C.	3,947C.	4,427C.
1376–77[6]	81½	7			81½	7			none

[1] 32½ sacks 4 cloves were allowed in weighing. Cf. p. 143, n. 1 above.

[2] Export stopped 24 October, 1353 because of the establishment of home staples. Ipswich was not a staple port at this time. Roll 5, m. 17. Cf. p. 26 above.

[3] Ipswich was made a staple port when home staples were established in 1365. Shipment of wool began 25 May. The period extends to 28 October. Cf. p. 26 above.

[4] The port was again closed for the export of wool 26 June, 1369, when the foreign staple was given up and several changes made in the home staples. Cf. p. 27 above.

[5] Ipswich was made a staple port again in 1370 and shipments were made after 3 December. Cf. p. 27 above.

[6] The period extends to Michaelmas, 1377.

LYNN

	WOOL						WOOLFELLS		
	Native		Alien		Total		Native fells	Alien fells	Total fells
	sacks	cl.	sacks	cl.	sacks	cl.			
1350					202	2			2,170
1350–51					1,285	20			21,464
1351–52	511½	40	23	18	535½	6	20,614	4,418	25,032[1]
1352–53					none				none[2]
1373–75	470½	10C.	68¾	1C.	539½	11C.	7,222C.	17,291C.	24,513C.[3]
1376–77	198½	13			198½	13	179		179[4]

[1] 22½ sacks 2 cloves were allowed in weighing. Cf. p. 143, n. 1 above.

[2] The port was closed for the exportation of wool with the establishment of home staples. Cf. p. 26 above.

[3] Lynn became a staple port in November, 1373. Cf. p. 28 above. The wool and fells exported by aliens were taken by Francis Maryol. Roll 14, m. 27.

[4] This period extends to 31 October. No wool was exported Michaelmas, 1375–75. See also p. 141 above.

[1] 65 sacks 4 cloves were allowed in weighing. Cf. p. 143, n. 1 above.

[2] Roll 8, m. 53 has 39 *petre*, but the amount of customs given is correct for 29 *petre*, as in the other rolls.

[3] Roll 9, m. 28d. has 1,542 sacks 17 cloves.

[4] During this year the customers were ordered to take their scales to Ipswich to weigh such wool as Walter de Bardi might export from that port. *C.C.R. 1369–74*, p. 121.

[5] Native merchants were paying the same customs as aliens at this time for the privilege of taking wool to other ports than Calais.

[6] This period extends to 27 November. 23½ sacks 8½ cloves of the wool exported by aliens were taken by John Cambre, Roll 8, m. 54.

[7] This period extends to 1 February.

No wool was exported during the following periods: Michaelmas, 1357–4 November, 1357; 10 November, 1374–4 February, 1375. See also p. 141 above.

YARMOUTH

	Wool						Woolfells		
	Native		Alien		Total		Native	Alien	Total
	sacks	cl.	sacks	cl.	sacks	cl.	fells	fells	fells
1350					172				
1350–51					836	34			
1351–52	1,427	46	16	18	1,444	12	20,636	12,613	33,249[1]
1352–53			535	44	535	44		24,394	24,394
1353–54			2,762	37	2,762	37		137,564	137,564
1354–55			1,700	6	1,700	6		60,665	60,665[2]
1355–56			482	18½	482	18½		46,204	46,204
1356–57					904	17			53,853
1357–58					1,240	31½			91,154
1358–59					1,076	45½			80,026
1359–60					1,194	47			61,625
1360–61					1,158	14½			25,389
1361–62					1,552	17			39,300
1362–63	634	43½	81	39	716	30½	23,823	45,582	69,405[3]
1363–64	1,280	39	142	44	1,423	31	24,598	34,999	59,597
1364–65	611	26	150	9	761	35	7,828	28,419	36,247
1365–66	776	42	155	10½	932	½	25,446	21,256	46,702
1366–67	1,001½	7½	7	7½	1,008½	15	40,773	30,044	70,817
1367–68	488	½	1	48	489	48½	16,540	17,244	33,784
1368–69	119	17½	118	36	238	1½	10,725	11,305	22,030
1369–70			274	36	274	36		35,912	35,912[4]
1370–71	99	21	325	12	424	33	3,102	36,865	39,967
1371–72					340	39			26,722[5]
1372–73	311	13	68	41½	380	2½	7,686	8,720	16,406
1373–74	247	14	127	3½	374	17½	878	21,901	22,779
1374–75	276¾	35	140½	42½	418¼	25½	4,567	3,453	8,020[6]
1375–76	262½	4	15½	20	278	24		18,185	18,185
1376–78	123½	3	267½	7	391	10		37,284	37,284[7]

LONDON

	Wool						Woolfells		
	Native		Alien		Total		Native	Alien	Total
	sacks	cl.	sacks	cl.	sacks	cl.	fells	fells	fells
1350					1,178				8,545
1350–51					15,336	7			122,332
1351–52	7,393	50	1,216		8,609	50	93,286	1,745	95,031[1]
1352–53			8,072	23	8,072	23		39,215	39,215[2]
1353–54			22,795	½	22,795	½		188,839	188,839[3]
1354–55			14,672	24	14,672	24		127,503	127,503

LONDON (*Continued*)

	Wool						Woolfells		
	Native sacks	cl.	Alien sacks	cl.	Total sacks	cl.	Native fells	Alien fells	Total fells
1355–56			15,427	29	15,427	29		119,875	119,875
1356–57					18,802	5			131,851[4]
1357–58					18,201	20			138,832
1358–59					15,078½	51½			171,648
1359–60					15,892	22			188,498
1360–61					12,227	34			107,465
1361–62					21,526½	23			177,050[5]
1362–63	9,826½	12	4,086½	4	13,913	16	88,424	45,892	134,316
1363–64	1,334½	20	4,206	19½	5,540½	39½	133,132	64,206	197,338
1364–65	10,026	16	6,458	41	16,485	5	88,789	89,050	177,839[6]
1365–66	11,392½	20½	4,236	14	15,628½	34½	129,326	40,583	169,909[7]
1366–67	10,003½	21½	4,295	5½	14,298½	27	156,754	66,204	222,958
1367–68	7,255½	25½	3,467½	7	10,723	32½	115,986	15,627	131,613
1368–69	6,245½	16	8,013½	11½	14,259	27½	81,445	32,014	113,459
1369–70			9,501½		9,501½			112,341	112,341[8]
1370–71	10,222½	10	3,516½	25	13,739	35	179,569	22,284	201,853
1371–72	3,092	9C.	126	9½C.	3,218	18½C.	15,600C.	8,620C.	24,220C.[8]
			5,599	1½	9,237	22½		43,586	104,474
					12,455	41			128,694
1372–73	4,601½	13C.			4,601½	13C.	42,283C.		42,283C.
	959	8½	4,967	24½	5,926	33	40,563	35,888	76,451
	5,560½	21½	4,967	24½	10,527½	46	82,846	35,888	118,734
1373–74	4,060½	4½C.	87	10½C.	4,147½	15C.	988C.		988C.
	1,127	1½	5,047	1½	6,174	3	48,535	26,621	75,156
	5,187½	6	5,134	12	10,321½	18	49,523	26,621	76,144[9]
1374–75	6,445¼	6C.	402	5½C.	6,847½	11½C.	8,766C.		8,766C.
	667	31	4,140	21	4,808		63,104	45,362	108,466
	7,112½	47	4,542	26½	11,655½	11½	71,870	45,362	117,232[10]
Oct. 1375–76	5,598	12C.	1,532½	19½C.	7,130½	31½C.	26,784C.	4,545C.	31,329C.
	121½	5½	2,094	19½	2,215½	25	46,485	27,617	74,102
	5,719½	17½	3,626½	39	9,347	4½	73,269	32,162	105,431[11]
Oct. Aug. 1376–77	4,364½	1½C.	1,208½	3½C.	5,573	5C.	74,697C.	1,501C.	76,198C.
	58	7			58	7	6,000		6,000
	4,422½	8½	1,208½	3½	5,631	12	80,697	1,501	82,198[12]

LONDON

[1] 447 sacks 28 cloves were allowed in weighing. Cf. p. 143, n. 1 above.

[2] Roll 9, m. 33 has 8,075 sacks 1 clove with the correct amount of customs for that quantity of wool. The *nova custuma* for this period is not entered on Roll 8 as is usual. The number of sacks given in the account of the subsidy agrees with that in the table, Roll 5, m. 16d.

[3] Roll 9, m. 33 has 20,103 sacks 32½ cloves, but the amount of customs is for the larger quantity of wool.

[4] About 10,000 sacks of wool and wool fells may have been exported in this year by Peter Provan and Hugh Provan of Turin. They were to be allowed 20s. on wool and 40s. on every last of hides exported by them and their associates because they had lent money to the king. In this year they were allowed £10,395 9s. 6d. and were quit of that amount on the pipe roll. Roll 8, m. 59; Pipe Roll 202, Item Lond.

[5] Export stopped at Michaelmas, 1362, and was not resumed until 9 February, 1363.

[6] The wool exported by aliens from Michaelmas, 1363 is given by H. Hall, *The Customs Revenue of England* (London, 1885), II, 214, table 7. The figures given by Hall for this year are actually those for the period between 2 February and 17 May only. The exports for the rest of the year were as follows:

	Native	Aliens
Mich.–31 January	4,070½ sacks	1,415 sacks 2½ cloves
	38,129 fells	9,978 fells
17 May–Mich.	5,955½ sacks 16 cloves	3,195 sacks 23 cloves
	50,660 fells	26,498 fells

[7] The particulars of the account for this year are found in PRO K.R. Customs 70/18. The alien shipments were made by 129 merchants.

[8] No figures are given by Hall for this period. It is merely stated that aliens alone were exporting. The same statement is made for the year 1371–2, when native merchants were also exporting. The 3,638 sacks, 21 cl. and 60,888 fells included in the totals were taken to Holland and Zeeland by divers merchants who paid at the rate aliens paid. They were probably natives who paid the higher rate for privilege of not taking the wool to Calais. The other three entries give the amounts taken by aliens and natives to Calais and by aliens elsewhere.

[9] The amounts given by Hall are incomplete. For Michaelmas–11 January only the wool not taken to Calais is given; the shipments from 11 January to 26 February are said to have been exported from 26 February to Michaelmas.

[10] The amounts of wool given by Hall as having been exported from Michaelmas to 26 July, and from then to 15 November are actually those exported 26 February to Michaelmas, and from then to 26 July.

[11] The entry for this year makes the period begin at Michaelmas although the preceding entry carried the preceding period to 15 November. The amount given by Hall for this year is the wool taken elsewhere than to Calais 26 July to 15 November, 1375. The alien shipments not taken to Calais were made by Thomas Besse. Roll 8, m. 62d. Cf. p. 146, n. 10 above.

[12] The amount given by Hall as taken by aliens 16 October to 21 June is actually that taken by natives Mich. 1375 to 6 October, 1376 elsewhere than to Calais, and the amount given for 22 June to 24 August is the amount for this whole period.

SANDWICH

	Wool						Woolfells		
	Native		Alien		Total		Native fells	Alien fells	Total fells
	sacks	cl.	sacks	cl.	sacks	cl.			
1350					12				150
1350–51					213	34			2,972
1351–52	153	31	16	11	169	42	4,798	668	5,466[1]
1352–53					none		132		132[2]
1353–54			307	51	307	51	34	12,875	12,909[3]
1354–55			349	36	349	36	188	9,888	10,176[3]
1355–56			78	21	78	21		10,651	10,651
1356–57					232	12	43		6,911[3]
1357–58					138	41			7,161
1358–59					72	3			5,473
1359–60					169	45			6,961
1360–61					246	9			6,396
1361–62					290	22			11,226
1362–63	370	18			370	18	9,527		9,527
1363–64	301	44½			301	44½	11,786	2,255	14,041[4]
1364–65	292	10½	43	51	336	9½	3,331	6,799	10,130
1365–66	369	32	4	11	373	43	10,238	150	10,388
1366–67	425	15½			425	15½	8,592	1,307	9,899
1367–68	107	18½			107	18½	9,164	703	9,872[5]

[1] 9 sacks 24 cloves were allowed in weighing. Cf. p. 143, n. 1. above.

[2] The fells were *ovium vivarum* on which the custom rates were the same as on other fells. Roll 8, m. 68.

[3] The fells taken by native merchants were *ovium vivarum*. *Loc. cit.*

[4] In addition to these, native merchants took 194 live sheep. *Ibid.*, m. 68d.

[5] The staple was moved to Queenborough. Cf. p. 27 above.

QUEENBOROUGH

| | Wool | | | | | | Woolfells | | |
| | Native | | Alien | | Total | | Native | Alien | Total |
	sacks	cl.	sacks	cl.	sacks	cl.	fells	fells	fells
July									
1368–68	75	12½			75	12½	165		165
1368–69					136	15			5,441
1369–70			148½	10½	148½	10½			none
1370–71	244½	13½			244½	13½	6,153		6,153
1371–72	116	11½C.			116	11½C.			
					140	5½			
					256	17			none[1]
1372–73	225	7C.			225	7C.	366C.		366C.
1373–74	114	41C.			114	41C.		1,360C.	1,360C.
1374–75	159½	14C.			159½	14C.	502C.		502C.[2]
1375–76	119	7C.			119	7C.	95C.		95C.[3]
1376–77	86½	10	23½	2	110	12	224	123	347[4]

[1] 140 sacks 5½ cloves were taken by alien and native merchants, both paying at the same rate, to ports other than Calais. Roll 8, m. 69.

[2] This period ends 12 August.

[3] This period begins 8 September.

[4] This period ends 22 June.

No wool was exported during the following periods: Michaelmas, 1369–15 January, 1370; Michaelmas, 1371–8 February, 1372; 3 May, 1373–4 December, 1373. See also p. 141 above.

CHICHESTER

	WOOL						WOOLFELLS		
	Native		Alien		Total		Native	Alien	Total
	sacks	cl.	sacks	cl.	sacks	cl.	fells	fells	fells
1350					$77\frac{1}{2}$				
1350–51					$498\frac{1}{2}$	6			4,195[1]
1351–52	386	28			386	28	16,033		16,033[2]
1352–53					none				none
1353–54			374	34	374	34		3,548	3,548
1354–55			473	28	473	28		3,602	3,602
1355–56			12	49	12	49		158	158[3]
1356–57					242	17			5,470
1357–58					662	4			8,710
1358–59					278	47			6,847
1359–60					383	47			6,499[4]
1360–61					438	1			5,556
1361–62					524	22			8,166
1362–63	1,078	38			1,078	38	13,104	228	13,332
1363–64	$217\frac{1}{2}$	47	30	46	$248\frac{1}{2}$	41	5,332	1,372	6,704
1364–65	593	20			593	20	6,577		6,577
1365–66	870	$49\frac{1}{2}$	$30\frac{1}{2}$	20	$901\frac{1}{2}$	$17\frac{1}{2}$	5,375	500	5,875[5]
1366–67	675	$30\frac{1}{2}$			675	$30\frac{1}{2}$	2,582	1,850	4,432
1367–68	$505\frac{1}{2}$	$8\frac{1}{2}$	1	7	$506\frac{1}{2}$	$15\frac{1}{2}$	12,280	1,500	13,780[6]
1368–69	581	51	3	48	585	47	4,762	708	5,470
1369–70			389	21	389	21		780	780
1370–71	$578\frac{1}{2}$	23			$578\frac{1}{2}$	23	2,057		2,057
1371–72	360				360		2,585		2,585
1372–73	449	15			449	15		2,400	2,400[7]
1373–74	700	23			700	23	6,388		6,388
1374–75	223	41C.			223	41C.	1,960C.		1,960C.
	405	26			405	26	3,394		3,394
	629	15			629	15	5,354		5,354
1375–76	$372\frac{1}{2}$	24C.			$372\frac{1}{2}$	24	2,410C.		2,410C.
	$77\frac{1}{2}$	1	$1\frac{1}{2}$	4	79	$5\frac{1}{2}$	958		958
	450	25	$1\frac{1}{2}$	4	$451\frac{1}{2}$	$29\frac{1}{2}$	3,368		3,368
1376–77	316	5			316	5	4,042		4,042

MELCOMBE

	WOOL						WOOLFELLS		
	Native		Alien		Total		Native	Alien	Total
	sacks	cl.	sacks	cl.	sacks	cl.	fells	fells	fells
1350					151	1			
1350–51					571	24			1,700[1]
June									
1365–66	275½	17	6½	7	282	24	2,874	114	2,988[2]
1366–67	335	45½	99	24	435	17½			none[3]
1367–68	268½	10½	30	2½	298½	13			"
1368–69	154¼	21	182¾		337	21			"
March									
1371–73	84				84				"
1373–74					none				"[4]
1374–75	475½	20½			475½	20½			"
1375–76	196½	5½			196½	5½			"
1376–77	343½	12			343½	12			"

[1] Until Michaelmas, 1351 the wool exported from Weymouth is included in the accounts for Melcombe.

[2] From the opening of Melcombe as a staple port 27 June, 1365 until the following Michaelmas 12 sacks 24½ cloves of wool were exported; 8½ sacks 2½ cloves by native merchants and 3½ sacks 22 cloves by aliens. The remainder was taken in the following year. Roll 14, m. 52; Roll 9, m. 5d.

[3] According to Roll 14, m. 52, all the wool was taken by native merchants, but 99 sacks 24 cloves are accounted for on Roll 9, m. 5d. as alien shipments.

[4] This period extends to 24 December.

No wool was exported during the following periods: Michaelmas, 1366–14 December, 1366; Michaelmas, 1373–24 December, 1374.

EXETER

	WOOL						WOOLFELLS		
	Native		Alien		Total		Native	Alien	Total
	sacks	cl.	sacks	cl.	sacks	cl.	fells	fells	fells
1353–54			301	21	301	21[1]			
1354–55			333½	15	333½	15		120	120
1355–56					none				none
1356–57					29	23			"2
1357–58					346	46			240
1358–59			110½	8	110½	8		3,750	3,750
1359–60	91½	2			91½	2	325		325
1360–61					61½	25			720
1361–62	34				34		230		230
1362–63	18	12			18	12	31		31
1363–64	51½	18			51½	18	263		263[3]

[1] Between 24 September, 1350 and 14 September, 1351, 10 sacks were exported from Cornish ports: Looe, Fowey, Lostwithiel, Padstowe. Roll 5, m. 14d. Export from Exeter began with the establishment of the staple 30 July, 1353.

[2] This wool was exported 12 August, 1357. Roll 8, m. 51.

[3] The account continues to the end of the reign but no wool was exported.

No wool was exported during the following periods: Michaelmas, 1359–23 January, 1360; Michaelmas, 1361–16 November, 1361; Michaelmas, 1364–end of reign. See also p. 141 above.

BRISTOL

	Wool						Woolfells		
	Native sacks	cl.	Alien sacks	cl.	Total sacks	cl.	Native fells	Alien fells	Total fells
1350–51					109				300
1351–52	375	44			375	44	2,240		2,240[1]
1352–53			30		30				none[2]
1353–54			28½	4	28½	4			"
1354–55			86	6	86	6			"[3]
1355–56					none				"
1356–57					53	4			"[4]
1357–58					none				"
1358–59	130				130				"
1359–60					204½	2			314
1360–61					308	4			none
1361–62					73	20			1,200
1362–63	145½	4			145½	4	300		300
1363–64					none		5,800		5,800
1364–70					"				none
1370–71					"		5,000		5,000
1371–74					"				none[5]
1374–75			245½	20	245½	20			"
1375–76			2½	10	2½	10			"

[1] 20 sacks 14 cloves were allowed in weighing. Cf. p. 143, n. 1 above.

[2] This wool was exported 18 February by Peter Gillian, a Spanish merchant. Roll 8, m. 48.

[3] This wool was exported 14 September, 1355, Roll 8, m. 48.

[4] This wool was exported 12 September, 1357. *Ibid.*, m. 48.

[5] This period extends to 24 December.

No wool was exported during the following periods: Michaelmas, 1353–10 December, 1353; Michaelmas, 1354–4 November, 1354; Michaelmas, 1355–25 April, 1357; Michaelmas, 1361–1 February, 1362; 28 May, 1362–Michaelmas, 1362; Michaelmas, 1363–24 December, 1374 (except a few fells). See also p. 141 above.

TOTAL ANNUAL EXPORT OF WOOL AND WOOLFELLS[1]

	Wool	Fells[2]	Total	Native Wool	Native Fells	Native Total	Alien Wool	Alien Fells	Alien Total
1350	4,182	40	4,222						
1350–51	34,696	1,000	35,696						
1351–52	22,722	1,086	23,808						
1352–53	16,379	301	16,680						
1353–54	42,851	1,650	44,501						
1354–55	31,855	1,026	32,881						
1355–56	26,670	883	27,553						
1356–57	36,954	1,089	38,043						
1357–58	32,809	1,123	33,932						
1358–59	28,410	1,161	29,571						
1359–60	31,972	1,254	33,226						
1360–61	25,272	755	26,027						
1361–62	41,244	1,123	42,367						
1362–63	27,628	1,294	28,922	20,882	950	21,832	6,746	344	7,090
1363–64	17,220	1,598	18,818	10,688	1,226	11,914	6,532	372	6,904
1364–65	31,818	1,369	33,187	21,859	774	22,633	9,959	595	10,554
1365–66	31,270	1,249	32,519	25,075	997	26,072	6,195	252	6,447
1366–67	28,294	1,475	29,769	21,776	1,099	22,875	6,518	376	6,894
1367–68	22,588	921	22,509	17,818	796	18,614	4,770	125	4,895
1368–69	27,108	754	27,862	12,955	567	13,522	14,153	187	14,340
1369–70	16,835	697	17,532						
1370–71	26,757	1,233	27,990	19,597	956	20,553	7,160	277	7,437
1371–72	24,488	741	25,229						
1372–73	25,549	843	26,392	14,657	565	15,222	10,892	278	11,170
1373–74	22,431	891	23,322	13,619	465	14,084	8,812	426	9,238
1374–75	26,796	1,127	27,923	17,497	710	18,207	9,299	417	9,716
1375–76	19,211	760	19,971	13,299	415	13,714	5,912	345	6,257

[1] These tables are compiled from the preceding returns for the ports. The total annual export does not appear on the customs rolls.

[2] The number of fells exported is here expressed in terms of sacks. According to the customs rates, until 1368 one sack was equivalent to 300 fells; after 1368 one sack was equivalent to 240 fells. See p. 41, n. 4 above.

3. RECORDS OF THE IMPORTATION AND EXPORTATION OF WOOLLEN CLOTH

The accounts for the custom of 1347 on English woollens and worsteds exported up to August, 1353, are among the K.R. Accounts, Various (Wool).[1] The yearly totals are recorded on roll 7. For the rest of the period the accounts are recorded in the usual manner on roll 7 and the totals for each port entered also on roll 8, where the general accounting for all customs was done. Occasionally accounts for a year or two are entered on one of the other rolls. London, as usual, followed a somewhat different method. After 1361 the cloth custom was recorded on roll 9, with the petty custom.[2] The 1303 custom on cloth imported and exported was enrolled on roll 9.

The tables for the exportation of English cloth are made from roll 7 and checked when possible from roll 9. Fractional parts of cloths occasionally given in ells have been given in the tables as fourths. The figures for the exportation and the importation of woollens are necessarily incomplete and not always distinguishable one from the other. The customs of important ports were farmed and the shipments of Hansards, especially after 1361, are usually included with the imported cloth because the customs were the same for both, just as their worsteds are inextricably buried in the mass of general merchandise.

---

[1] PRO K.R. Accounts, Various, Wool, 457/20–23. The butler's accounts run until 3 August, 1353, but the accounts on the customs roll for the following period begin 30 July.

[2] See p. 48, n. 6 above.

NEWCASTLE

| | Exported | | | | Imported[2] | Exported | |
| | WOOLLEN CLOTH UNDYED | | | | WOOLLEN CLOTHS | BED CLOTHS | |
	Eng.	Alien	Hans.	Total		Eng.	Alien
1356–57[1]		2		2	77		
1357–58	12	3		15	6		
1358–59	9	31		40	2½		
1359–60	19½			19½			
1360–61	11¾			11¾	12¼		
1361–62	4	9¾		13¾	9		
1362–63		1¾		1¾			
1363–64	2	4½		6½			
1364–65	23½	40¼		63¾			
1365–66	35¼	45½		80¾			
1366–67	30	11¼		41¼			
1367–68							
1368–69			2¾	2¾		3 (double)	
1369–70	96	54		150			
1370–71	17	48¾		65¾		2 (single)	
1371–72	39	100		139	28		
1372–Dec.		10½		10½			
June June						4 (single)	2 (double)
1376–77	49¾	19¾		69½			

[1] There was no cloth exported before this date, except 23 undyed cloths taken between 4 November, 1351 and Michaelmas, 1352. Since there is no record of these in the butler's accounts of English cloth exported, they were probably cloths of foreign manufacture re-exported. They were carried by Peter de Beuland. Roll 9, m. 40.

[2] Cloth was imported before 1356 as follows:

1352–53	6
1353–54	72
1354–55	61½ (1 was scarlet)
1355–56	13

KINGSTON UPON HULL

Woollen Cloth

	Exported										Imported
	Undyed			½ Dyed			Dyed				
	Eng.	Alien	Hans.	Eng.	Aln.	Hans.	Eng.	Aln.	Hans.	Total	
1350–51		8½								8½	
1351–52		2½								2½	13¼[1]
1352–53											—[2]
1353–54	62	100¼								162¼	—[3]
1354–55	23	55¼		1¼						79½	—[4]
1355–56	292¼	61					1½			354¾	132½
1356–57	297½	143¾					1			442¼	153¾
1357–58	139¼	134¼								273½	35
1358–59	131½	260								391¼	40
1359–60	218	227¼					¼[5]			445½	15½
1360–61	566		135½[6]				2	1		701½	—[7]
1361–62	96¾	28¾	61½	1			9	4		201	73½
1362–63	323¼	18¾	107				4¼			453¼	
1363–64	326	16¾	169¼				2¾			514¾	37
1364–65	1,111½	181¾	349¾	3¼			8¾			1,655	7[8]
1365–66	1,136¾	173	302½	1			1½			1,612¾	—[8]
1366–67	1,233¾	123½	70¼	2½			1½			1,431¼	4½
1367–68	1,064¼	180	151				1			1,396¼	
1368–69	1,067½	259½	103½							1,430½	
1369–70	1,485½	51¼	187½							1,724¼	19½[9]
1370–71	1,275	92¾	194½							1,562¼	
1371–72	1,127	80½	126¾							1,334¼	
1372–Dec.	83½	15¼	77¾							176½	
June Aug. 1376–77	1,326	100¾	141½							1,568¼	

[1] ½ blanket cloth was also exported. Roll 9, m. 29. It is not mentioned in the butler's accounts.

[2] According to Roll 9, m. 29, 96 undyed cloths were exported by aliens, who paid 12*d.* per cloth. In the butler's accounts for Mich. 1352 to July there are no cloths for Hull and in roll 7, m. 7 where the account is continued from July until the following Michaelmas there are 52. The 96 cloths may include these and others of foreign manufacture.

[3] Roll 9 m. 29 has 281½ undyed cloths and ¼ scarlet exported in this year. The customs paid was 12*d.* per cloth on the undyed cloth.

[4] Roll 9, m. 29 has 419½ undyed cloths exported in this year.

[5] This appears only on Roll 9, m. 29. The customs rate was 2*s.* 4*d.* It is not stated by whom it was exported.

[6] Roll 9, m. 29 has 35½.

[7] Two of the cloths imported were dyed cloths.

[8] This period extends to 10 October.

[9] The imported cloth was brought by Hansards. The returns for this year are entered on Roll 8, m. 57.

KINGSTON UPON HULL

	Exported					
	WORSTEDS		BED CLOTHS			
			Single		Double	
	Eng.	Alien	Eng.	Alien	Eng.	Alien
July						
1353–54				7		
1354–55						
1355–56	1½					
1356–57						
1357–58						
1358–59			1		9	6[1]
1359–60						2[1]
1360–61					4	4
1361–62						1[1]
1362–63			11	6	2	
1363–64			25	3	23	6
1364–65			30	11	1	—[2]
1365–66			26	25	3	—[2]
1366–67			53	18		
1367–68			23	8		
1368–69			16	5		
1369–70			61	1		
				8[3]		
1370–71			31	3		
1371–72				25	27	
				8[3]		
1372–Dec.			3	5		
Dec. Aug.						
1376–77				25		

[1] These were bed cloths of York.
[2] This period extends to 10 October.
[3] These were taken by Hansards.

BOSTON
WOOLLEN CLOTH

	Exported								Imported			
	Undyed			½ Dyed		Dyed			Undyed	½ Dyed	Dyed	Total
	Eng.	Aln.	Hans.	Eng.	Aln.	Eng.	Aln.	Total				
1351–52									151½		3	154½
1352–53									105½			105½
1353–54	189	84¼						273¼	1,090½[1]			1,090½
1354–55	103½	27¼						130¾	144		1	145
1355–56	79	21½						100½	308	1½	1	310½
1356–57	298½	461½						760	858	2		360
1357–58	438	560¾						998¾	96¾			96¾
1358–59	528¾	462						990¾	1,088		3	1,091
1359–60	472½	549½		1		½		1,023½	339			339
1360–61	604	195½	79½					879	85¾			85¾
1361–62	474½	98[2]	145					717½	618	7	5	630
1362–63	42½	69½	846¾		4½			963¼	484¼		7¼	491½
1363–64	505¾	175	1,783¼[3]					2,464				
1364–65	674	281½	1,756¾	¼ (Hans)				2,712½	790	7	3[4]	800
1365–66	728½	69½	1,974½[5]	¼			1					
1366–67	1,031½	61	1,197¼[6]			1½		2,291¼	118			118
1367–68	1,139	47				1			2,008½[7]			
1368–69	1,455¼	64½							928½[7]			
1369–70	2,308	121½							1,073½[7]			
1370–71	1,691	84¼							1,646¼[7]			
1371–72	1,541¼	129	1,625[8]					3,295				
1372–Dec.	79¾	5¾	75½[9]	½				161½				

[1] Of these, 770¼ are said to include both imported and exported cloth. Roll 9, m. 23.

[2] These are said to have been exported by English merchants but the custom paid was 21*d*. Roll 7, m. 10.

[3] According to Roll 9, m. 23d. cloths were both exported and imported by Hansards. The periods extends to 2 October.

[4] The period extends to 20 October.

[5] Roll 7, m. 12. Hansard cloth is both imported and exported.

[6] 14¾ cloths (undyed) are said to have been exported by English merchants in addition to the above quantity, paying 12*d*. customs. Roll 7, m. 12d.

[7] These cloths are said to have been imported and exported by aliens and English, paying 12*d*. Roll 7, m. 13.

[8] On 41 cloths English merchants paid 12*d*. Roll 7, m. 14.

[9] On 68¾ cloths English merchants seem to have paid 12*d*. Roll 7, m. 14.

BOSTON

	Exported						
	WORSTEDS			**BED CLOTHS**			
				Single		Double	
	English	Alien	Total	English	Alien	English	Alien
1350–51				20			
1351–52							
1352–53							
1353–54							
1354–55		111½	111½				
1355–56	100		100				
1356–57	9	70	79				
1357–58	80½		80½	3			
1358–59	6	58	64				
1359–60		12[1]	12				
1360–61	76½	13	89½	3			
1361–62	56		56	4			
1362–63		6	6	12[2]			
1363–64	410	9	419	1[3]			
1364–65	738	232	970	14	11[5]		
1365–66	553	160	713	4[4]		3	
1366–67		269	269	24			
1367–68				11	18		
1368–69				10			
1369–70	2		2	6	1		
1370–71	320		320	14	3		
1371–72	872½	2	874½	1	1		
1372–Dec.	45		45				

[1] These are omitted in the tables of cloth exported as given in *E.H.R.* xxxix (1924) p. 34.

[2] English merchants also exported one tester (worsted). There was no cloth exported until 18 February, 1363.

[3] This period extends to 2 October.

[4] These are said to have been double cloths, but the custom paid on them was 5*d*. Roll 7, m. 12.

[5] This period extends to 20 October.

YARMOUTH

	Exported							Imported
	WOOLLEN CLOTH			WORSTEDS		BED CLOTHS		WOOLLEN CLOTH
		Undyed					Single	
	Eng.	Alien	Total	Eng.	Alien	Eng.	Alien	
1350–51	$9\frac{1}{2}$		$9\frac{1}{2}$	2,972				8
1351–52	2		2	2,901	40			27
1352–53[1]	22		22	2,370				$88\frac{1}{2}$
1353–54	15	$3\frac{1}{2}$[2]	$18\frac{1}{2}$	5,919				80[5]
1354–55	$12\frac{1}{2}$		$12\frac{1}{2}$	5,606				26[6]
1355–56	$134\frac{1}{2}$	4	$138\frac{1}{2}$	3,312				491
1356–57	$619\frac{1}{4}$	$34\frac{3}{4}$	654	9,056				$136\frac{3}{4}$
1357–58	898	$61\frac{1}{2}$	$959\frac{1}{2}$	24,184		$6\frac{1}{2}$		$114\frac{1}{2}$
1358–59	$770\frac{1}{4}$	$31\frac{3}{4}$	802	16,703	1	$4\frac{1}{2}$		$59\frac{1}{2}$
1359–60	$538\frac{3}{4}$	53	$591\frac{1}{4}$	15,662		1[3]		22
1360–61	$433\frac{1}{2}$	61	$494\frac{1}{2}$	9,643	62	$11\frac{1}{2}$[3]	2	$137\frac{1}{4}$[7]
1361–62[4]	$618\frac{1}{2}$	47	$665\frac{1}{2}$	13,762	15	$2\frac{1}{2}$		

[1] This period extends only to 30 July, 1353.

[2] Aliens also exported 12 ells of narrow cloth. Roll 7, m. 7d.

[3] English merchants also exported 1 double bed cloth.

[4] The cloth custom was farmed 22 July, 1362 to George Felrigg and William Elys. Roll 7, m. 10d; *C.F.R. 1356–69*, pp. 241, 292.

[5] Two were partly dyed cloth.

[6] One was scarlet cloth.

[7] Two cloths were partly dyed and one was scarlet.

LONDON
Woollen Cloth

	Exported									Imported			
	Undyed			½ Dyed		Dyed				Dyed	Undyed		Total
	Eng.	Alien	Hans.	Eng.	Aln.	Eng.	Aln.	Hans.	Total				
1350–51	29	48							77				
1351–52	3½	40½							44	16	1,899[8]		1,916
1352–53		39							39	48	4,670		4,718
1353–54	110½	342½							453	77½	4,968½		5,046
1354–55	54	288							342	45	2,557½	6 long	2,608½
1355–56	241½	475¼							716¾	29	3,621¾	57 long	3,707¾
1356–57	490½	527¾							1,028¼	17	3,739½	81 long	3,837½
1357–58	450½	869							1,319½	10	2,728[10]		2,766
1358–59	763¾	443½	283½[11]				1¼		1,492	8¾	3,073½		3,082¼
1359–60	433	528¾	587[2]						1,548	1	2,252½		2,253½
1360–61	526	505½		14	2		1		1,048	21	2,230		2,251
1361–62	481	581¼	43½			1¼	¾	1	1,108¾		2,208[9]		2,208
1362–63	609½	791¼	135		1	10½	5½		1,552¾	80½	3,030½		3,111
1363–64	687	1,216¼	91½[3]			7	3½		2,005¼	23½	1,982½		2,006
1364–65	772½	920	178[4]			22½	16½		1,909½	20½	2,064		2,084½
1365–66	690½	1,135¾	77[5]	1		¾	12		1,917	12½	2,159¾		2,172¼
1366–67	1,350¾	1,761½	70[6]	¼		14½	1¼		3,198¼	11½	2,993		3,004½
1367–68	1,231¾	1,461½	46	¼		13¼	2½		2,755¼	½	1,496½[11]		1,497
1368–69	1,013¼	1,300¼	153	3½	½	25¼	2½		2,498¼		562[11]		562
1369–70	1,697¾	1,234½	241			8			3,181¼		1,363		1,363
1370–71	1,866½	1,464¼	162½		1½	2½	5		3,502¼	1½	950		951½
1371–72	952¾	1,031	281			3½	½		2,268¾		875		875
1372–Dec.	135	353	31½[7]							6	470		476

LONDON (*Continued*)

WOOLLEN CLOTH

	Exported									Imported		
	Undyed			½ Dyed		Dyed				Dyed	Undyed	Total
	Eng.	Alien	Hans.	Eng.	Aln.	Eng.	Aln.	Hans.	Total			
1375	657	542	101¼	1½	4	1¼	1		1,308		447½ [12]	447½
1375–76	1,274½	1,639	119½	1	1	5½	17½	1	2,058		1,076¼ [13]	
1376–77	845¼	1,161½	245		¾	1¼	4¾				530¾	

[1] These are omitted in the tables of cloth exported, as given in *E.H.R.* xxxix (1924), p. 34.

[2] Cloth taken by Hansards, but with 323 narrow cloths omitted, is given as alien cloth. *Loc. cit.*

[3] In addition to English cloth, aliens also exported 19¼ cloths made in Flanders. Roll 9, m. 34.

[4] Aliens also exported 12 Flemish cloths. Roll 9, m. 34.

[5] Aliens also exported 12 Flemish cloths. Roll 9, m. 34d.

[6] Aliens also exported 3 Flemish cloths. Roll 9, m. 34d.

[7] This includes cloth made in England exported by Hansards, and cloth made in Flanders exported by aliens, on both of which the custom was 12d. Roll 9, m. 35.

[8] From 1351 to 1361 and 1376 to 1377 the figures in this table give the total amount of cloth imported and exported on which 12d. was paid. Although the amount imported might be obtained approximately by subtracting the amount of English cloth exported by aliens, the result would still include re-exported cloth and possibly some taken by Hansards. The total for imported cloth 1350–51 includes 1 half-dyed cloth.

[9] 34¾ of these cloths were imported by Flemings. Roll 9, m. 33d.

[10] 28 additional cloths were imported free of duty by a merchant of the society of the Malbaille for the use of the Cardinal of Perigord. Roll 9, m. 33; *C.C.R. 1354–60*, p. 473.

[11] The imported cloth was made in Flanders. Roll 9, m. 34d.

[12] This period extends from 25 March to 1 October.

[13] The cloth carried by Hansards and the cloth in the table of imported cloth was both imported and exported, no distinction being made on the customs roll. Roll 9, m. 35d.

LONDON

	Exported						
	WORSTEDS			BED CLOTHS			
				Single		Double	
	Eng.	Alien	Total	Eng.	Alien	Eng.	Alien
1350–51	150	60	210		13		
1351–52	360	342	702				
1352–53	250	1,351¹	1,601				
1353–54	867	3,430	4,297				
1354–55	1,083	948	2,031		8		
1355–56	828	1,368	2,196		17		½
1356–57	491	2,223	2,714	2½	30		2
1357–58	384	1,718	2,102	5	52½		2
1358–59	3,326	1,971 / 1,171²	6,468	2	29½		13
1359–60	3,852	779 / 2,709²	7,340	3	38½		3
1360–61	2,127	1,251	3,378	10	26½		4
1361–62	2,409	2,231	4,640	5½	22	2	27
1362–63	1,645	1,514	3,159	2	71	4	28
1363–64	951	3,396	4,347	7	39	13	26
1364–65	22	3,066	3,088	4	51	4	40
1365–66	668	1,709	2,377	24	67	15	21
1366–67	2,530	2,045	4,575	49	79	19	14
1367–68	95	1,879	1,974	54	82	5	100
1368–69	271	2,451	2,722	92	76	7	72
1369–70	541	2,661	3,202	11	85	7	51
1370–71	469	4,601	5,070	30	55	14	29
1371–72	1,265	1,398	2,663	40	28	6	13
1372–Dec.	173	753	926	9	3	4	13
1375	20	522	542³	1	23 / 1⁴		22
1375–76	45	1,071	1,116	11	28	12	26
1376–77		1,194½	1,194½	6	40	2	28

¹ This period extends to 30 July, 1353.
² These worsteds were exported by Hansards, Roll 7, m. 9, 9d.
³ This period extends from 25 March to 1 October.
⁴ This was exported by Tydemann Wyse, a Hansard. Roll 9, m. 35.

SANDWICH

WOOLLEN CLOTH

	Exported			Imported
	Undyed			
	Eng.	Alien	Total	
1351–52	3	19	22	
1352–53		19	19	
1353–54	21½	58¼	79¾	55[1]
1354–55	38	52½	90½	19½
1355–56	69	81	150	19
1356–57	78½	104½	183	9
1357–58	203½	78½	282	742[2]
1358–59	25½	26½	52	23
1359–60	49	25½	74½	10
1360–61	12	9	21	
1361–62	12	14	26	
1362–63	46	7	53	
1363–64	4½	21	25½	
1364–65	55½	31	86½	8
1365–66	22¾	31	53¾	
1366–67	76½	21¼	97¾	
1367–68	16¾	85	101¾	

[1] Seven scarlet and two half-dyed cloths were also imported.
[2] One scarlet cloth was imported.

QUEENBOROUGH
WOOLLEN CLOTH

	Exported		
	Undyed		
	Eng.	Alien	Total
July 1368–69	15¼	7¾	23¼
1370–71	17		17
1371–72	17		17

CHICHESTER
WOOLLEN CLOTH

	Exported		
	Undyed		
	Eng.	Alien	Total
July			
1353–54	$\frac{1}{2}$	$15\frac{1}{4}$[1]	$15\frac{3}{4}$
1354–55		40[2]	40
1355–56	$33\frac{1}{2}$	$\frac{1}{2}$	34
1356–57	$37\frac{3}{4}$	$15\frac{1}{2}$	$53\frac{1}{4}$
1357–58	$94\frac{3}{4}$	$10\frac{1}{4}$	105
1358–59	$54\frac{1}{2}$		$54\frac{1}{2}$
1359–60	109		109
1360–61	$51\frac{1}{2}$	$15\frac{1}{4}$	66
1361–62			
1362–63	25	1	26
1363–64	$13\frac{1}{4}$		$13\frac{1}{4}$[3]
1364–65		$6\frac{1}{4}$	$6\frac{1}{4}$
1365–66	47	$31\frac{3}{4}$	$78\frac{3}{4}$
1366–67	81	$25\frac{1}{2}$	$106\frac{1}{2}$
1367–68	$13\frac{1}{4}$	$\frac{3}{4}$	14
1368–69		$1\frac{1}{2}$	$1\frac{1}{2}$

[1] $2\frac{3}{4}$ undyed cloths were also exported, paying 12*d.* customs.

[2] This cloth was exported by both English and alien merchants. The 12*d.* custom was paid on $2\frac{1}{2}$ cloths. Roll 9, m. 25.

[3] This was probably partly dyed cloth. The rate is 21*d.* and it is said to be *diversi coloris.* Roll 7, m. 11.

LYNN   **IPSWICH**
WOOLLEN CLOTH   WOOLLEN CLOTH

	Exported			Im-ported		Exported			Im-ported
	Eng.	Alien	Total			Eng.	Alien	Total	
1350–51	30	3	33		1350–51	59½		59½	
1351–52	14	2½	16½	51	1351–52	76½		76½	42
1352–53				223½	1352–53	80	23	103	

PLYMOUTH   **WEYMOUTH**
WOOLLEN CLOTH   WOOLLEN CLOTH
Exported   Exported

	Eng.	Eng.	Alien	Total
July 1352–53	15	25	41½	66½

SOUTHAMPTON

	Exported									Imported
	Woollen Cloth			Worsteds		Bed Cloths				Woollen Cloth
	Undyed					Single		Double		
	Eng.	Alien	Total	Eng.	Alien	Eng.	Alien	Eng.	Alien	
1350–51	10		10							
1351–52	137	22	159							
1352–53	57	51[1]	108							
1353–54	688½	96¾	785¼							54½
1354–55	462½	40¼	502¾							40¼
1355–56	1,260	184	1,444							
1356–57	3,419¾	348½	3,768							
1357–58	2,005¾	232¾	2,238							
1358–59	260	112	372							
1359–60	2,954¼	106¼	3,060½							
1360–61	1,132½	32[2]	1,164½							32
1361–62	946½	203½	1,150							
1362–63	1,385¼	81¼	1,466½							81¼
1363–64	626	159¼	945¼							
		160	(Hans)							
1364–65	880	267[3]	1,150							
1365–66	607¾	228½[4]	839¼							
1366–67	669½	80½	750			7				
1367–68	268½	43½[5]	313½			21				
1368–69	459¾	316½	876			7				
1369–70	1,796¾	264[6]	2,210¼		283				1	
1370–72	1,175	831½[7]	2,150		89		6		2	
1372–Dec.	162¾	24[8]	187¾							
June June										
1376–77	514	73¼	587¼							

[1] This period extends only to 30 July, 1353.

[2] English merchants also exported 30 ells of dyed cloth.

[3] English merchants also exported 3 scarlet cloths.

[4] English merchants also exported 2 scarlet cloths.

[5] English merchants also exported 1½ scarlet cloths.

[6] English merchants exported 150½ long cloths paying 17½*d.* customs. Alien merchants exported 8 long cloths, paying 2*s.* 2¼*d.* customs.

[7] There was also exported: by English: 88 undyed cloths, paying 17½*d.* customs; 2¾ long cloths, paying 2*s.* 11*d.* customs; 1 scarlet cloth, paying 2*s.* 11*d.* customs; 1 long cloth, paying 2*s.* 2½*d.* customs; 12 ells of half dyed cloth, paying 2*s.* 2½*d.* customs. By aliens: 46 long cloths undyed, paying 2*s.* 2¼*d.* customs; 4¾ scarlet cloths, paying 2*s.* 2¾*d.* customs.

[8] English merchants also exported 1 long cloth paying 17½*d.* customs.

	EXETER					MELCOMBE		
	WOOLLEN CLOTH					WOOLLEN CLOTH		
	Exported					Exported		
	Undyed		Dyed			Undyed		
	Eng.	Alien	Eng.	Alien	Total	Eng.	Alien	Total
1351–52	188				188[7]			
1353–54	626½[1]				626½			
1354–55	471¼	30½			501¾			
1355–56	842	30			872			
1356–57	812¼[11]				812¼			
1357–58	868	13½			881½			
1358–59					—[8]			
1359–60	1,486¾	12			1,498¾			
1360–61	779¼	4	1		784			
1361–62	533½				533½			
1362–63	1,016½				1,016			
1363–64	593¼	9			602¼			
1364–65	1,212½				1,212½	482½	19½	502
1365–66	846¼	52¼[12]			898½	324½	36½	361
1366–67	1,304	17½[13]			1,321½	482½	11¼	493¾
1367–68	826½	63½[4]			890	447½	17½	465
1368–69	847½	34½[5]			882	176	140	316
1369–70	2,123¼	42¼[16]	1		2,166½			
1370–Dec. 1372	736½	11½	1		749	800¼	39[9]	839¼
June Dec. 1376–77	863¾	3½	1		868¼	388½	22[10]	410½

[1] These have been omitted in the table of cloth exported, as given in *E.H.R.* XXXIX (1924) p. 34.

[2] This period extends to 25 January, 1367.

[3] This period extends to 25 January, 1368.

[4] This period extends to 14 April, 1369.

[5] This period extends to 25 April, 1370.

[6] This period extends to 12 November, 1371.

[7] The following cloth was exported from Dartmouth by English merchants: 1350–51, 54½; 1352–53, 53.

[8] The accounts for this year seem to be omitted on all rolls, except Roll 8, where only the amount received from the cloth custom, £78. 4s. 2½d., is given.

[9] This cloth was exported between 28 March, 1371 and Mich. 1372.

[10] This cloth was exported between June, 1376 and Mich. 1377.

BRISTOL
Woollen Cloth

| | Exported | | |
| | Undyed | | |
	Eng.	Alien	Total
1350–51	447½		447½
1351–52	804	30	834
1352–53	324	38½[11]	362½
1353–54	1,491½	19	1,510½
1354–55	1,065½	9[2]	1,077½
1355–56	1,609	24	1,633
1356–57	2,627½		2,627
1357–58	2,800	129	2,929
1358–59	2,517		2,517
1359–60	3,475½	78	3,553½
1360–61	4,363½	36	4,399½
1361–62	5,737½	253½	5,991
1362–63	6,918		6,918
1363–64	2,742		2,742
1364–65	5,396	11	5,407
1365–66	4,160½	36½	4,197
1366–67	7,532½	168	7,700½
1367–68	3,781	44½	3,825½
1368–69	5,352	611	5,963
1369–70	3,963	103½[3]	4,067½
1370–71	2,895	232[4]	3,128
1371–72	1,805½	56½	1,862
1372–Dec. June Mich.	650	109	759
1376–77	2,210	162½	2,372½

[1] This period extends only to 30 June, 1353.

[2] Two dyed cloths were exported by English merchants and by aliens who also took 3 single bed cloths. 77 cloths were imported this year.

[3] One dyed cloth was exported by English merchants.

[4] One dyed cloth was exported by English merchants.

TOTAL ANNUAL EXPORT OF WOOLLEN CLOTH AND WORSTEDS

	WOOLLEN CLOTH			WORSTEDS		
	Native	Alien	Total	Native	Alien	Total
1350–51	640	60	700	3,122	60	3,182
1351–52	1,128	117	1,245	3,261	382	3,643
1352–53	577	212	789	2,620	1,351	3,971
1353–54	3,206	719	3,925	6,786	3,430	10,216
1354–55	2,232	545	2,777	6,689	1,059½	7,748½
1355–56	4,563	881	5,444	4,241	1,368	5,609
1356–57	8,693	1,638	10,331	9,556	2,293	11,849
1357–58	7,913	2,093	10,006	24,648	1,718	26,366
1358–59	5,060	1,652	6,712	20,035	3,201	23,236
1359–60	9,758	2,167	11,925	19,514	3,500	23,014
1360–61	8,481	1,072	9,553[1]	11,846	1,326	13,172[1]
1361–62	8,915	1,492	10,407	16,227	2,246	18,473

[1] After this year, the totals do not include the cloth exported by Hansards, who were paying at the same rate on imported and exported cloth, and only the petty custom on worsteds.

4. RECORDS OF THE IMPORTATION OF WINE

The butler's accounts for the wine custom collected from aliens, which are the most complete customs records of the period[1] are among the K.R. Accounts, Various (Butlerage). For this period they extend, with a few gaps, from Michaelmas, 1349 to Michaelmas, 1372. They give the returns by ports, the date of importation of each shipment, the name of the ship, its master and the importer, the amount of wine and of the customs paid.[2] The returns are given in tuns and pipes,[3] sometimes quite irrationally, as 20 tuns 5 pipes. In such cases it has been changed in the tables to 22½ tuns, 2 pipes being equal to 1 tun.

The wine custom does not seem usually to have been enrolled. One of the membranes of customs roll 30 (8875) contains the enrolment of the accounts from 12 February, 1338, to Michaelmas, 1354. It is carelessly copied and seems to be unique. The subsidies collected from both alien and English merchants were enrolled on roll 5. The returns for the subsidy of 1371–72 are among the butler's accounts.[4]

[1] PRO K.R. Accounts Various 80/1–22.

[2] It is not usually specified what kind of wine was brought. There are occasional references to Rhenish wine and *vinum de vernachia* (vernage, a strong, sweet white wine of Italy, *N.E.D.*) and to Gascon wine. There is also a list of ports into which no wine was brought.

[3] Cf. p. 179 n. 3, 4 below for slight variations.

[4] PRO K.R. Accounts Various, 80/22.

WINE IMPORTED BY ALIEN MERCHANTS

	1349–50[1]	1350–51	1351–52	1352–53	1353–54	1354–55	1355–56
Ipswich..............	65½[2]	29	22½	31½	53	29	31
Yarmouth...........	82½	26½	38	59	128		
Lynn...............	29½[3]	3	10				18½
Hull................	10[4]	145½		43½	131	181½	300
Bristol..............	185	43	154½	130	149	302	140
Weymouth..........	80			94			100
Southampton........	257½	103	150	592	219[10]	321	200
Sandwich	561	951	336	737½[8]	664		
London.............	544½[15]	766[6]	326½[7]	924½	793½	614½	592
Dartmouth..........		102					
Exmouth............			13½				
Bridgewater.........				34[9]			
Topsham...........					216	84	
Boston.............					36	297½	400
Newcastle..........							18[11]
Winchelsea.........							
	1,815½[5]	2,169[6]	1,051[7]	2,646	2,389½	1,829½	1,799½

[1] The lists are made from the butlerage accounts. PRO K.R. Accounts Various 80/1–22. The accounts for 1349–54 are enrolled on Roll 30 (8,875).

[2] Roll 30 (8,875) has 61½ tuns and the correct amount of customs for that quantity of wine.

[3] 15 tuns were Rhenish wine.

[4] This was Rhenish wine imported by Tidemann Smythous, Hansard.

[5] 384 tuns are not included in the total given in the account (1,431½) because the customs on them were paid to Guillelmus du Casse and his associates, merchants of Gascony in part payment of the king's debt to them for wine bought for his use.

[6] 455½ tuns not included in total (1,713½). Cf. n. 5.

[7] 152½ tuns not included in total (898½). Cf. n. 5. Only the customs on 63 tuns were assigned to the Gascon merchants. The customs on the remaining 89½ tuns are said to be due from the returns.

[8] Roll 30 (8,875) has 727½ and £73 15s. customs.

[9] Roll 30 (8,875) has 33 and 68s. customs.

[10] Roll 30 (8,875) has 220 and £21 18s. customs.

[11] This wine is not included in the total given in the butler's account (1,781½) for all of which the butler does not answer because the custom has been given to John Brocas. The butler answers only for the 18 tons taken to Newcastle.

WINE IMPORTED BY ALIEN MERCHANTS

	1357–58	1358–59	1359–60	1360–61	1361–62	1363–64	1364–65
Ipswich	21						
Yarmouth	54½	141½	11½	33	47½		51½
Lynn					54		5½
Hull	155			174	449	39	69½
Bristol	106			40	147	337	5
Weymouth	98½	23		54		40	
Southampton	63	207	190	286½	269	200½	258
Sandwich	521	324	421½	183½	371	160	291
London	911½	845½	967½	666½	1,158½	618½	472½
Dartmouth							
Exmouth					47		
Bridgewater							
Boston	121½	99	218½		225½	98	191
Newcastle							
Winchelsea					87½		
	2,052	1,640	1,809	1,437½	2,856	1,493	1,454

WINE IMPORTED BY ALIEN MERCHANTS

	1366–67	1367–68	1370–71	1371–72[1]
Ipswich		40	159	74½
Yarmouth	9	23	13½[4]	—[2]
Lynn	3½	63	3½[4]	7
Hull		1,322		
Bristol	39½			62½[3]
Weymouth		79½		4
Southampton	186½	80	256½	31
Sandwich	73½	210	221½	229
London	414	269	135½	784½
Dartmouth	51	40	24	
Boston	15½	36½	4[4]	10½[5]
Winchelsea	358	205		
	1,150½	1,178	817½	1,202½

[1] These figures are taken from the account for the subsidy on wine collected from All Saints, 1371 to All Saints, 1372. PRO K.R. Accounts Various 80/22.

[2] Yarmouth and Lynn are accounted for together. *Ibid.* 80/22.

[3] In addition to this 14 bottles of vernage were imported by aliens, paying 1*s.* per bottle. *Ibid.* 80/22.

[4] This was Rhenish wine, on which amounts varying from 2*s.* upwards per tun was paid, probably because the size of the tuns varied, for the pipes are said to be *magne et parve.* The custom paid was as follows: Yarmouth 27 pipes 30*s.*; Lynn 7 pipes 10*s.*; Boston 8 pipes 10*s.*; *Ibid.* 80/20.

[5] It was not specified whether this wine, which was Rhenish wine, was imported by native merchants or aliens. On 9 tuns 25*s.* customs were paid. Cf. n. 4 above.

WINE IMPORTED BY ENGLISH AND ALIEN MERCHANTS

	28 Feb.–28 June, 1350[1]	24 Sept. 1350– Mich., 1351[6]	1371–72[12]
Ipswich...................	10	202	169
Yarmouth.................	15	200½	
Lynn.....................	95	217[7]	253[13]
Hull.....................	337	798	464
Bristol...................	151	1,265½	985½
Weymouth................		278[8]	261
Southampton.............	177½	644½	264
Sandwich.................	148[2]	2,139[9]	400
London...................	2,025½[3]	1,941[10]	2,570½
Dartmouth...............		571	113½
Exeter...................	2½		458½[14]
Boston...................	70	249½	10½
Newcastle................	28½	11¼	
Winchelsea...............	106	96½	48
Plymouth................	25[4]	343	
Cornwall.................		49[11]	
Ravenscar...............	2½[5]		
	3,194½	9,005½	5,998

[1] Returns for 1s. subsidy. Roll 5, m. 13d; Roll 12, m. 6d.
[2] 120 tuns were the king's wine and free of customs.
[3] 233½ tuns were free of customs.
[4] Roll 5 gives this as the wine imported during a year from 24 February, 1350 but the subsidy stopped 28 June.
[5] This was Rhenish wine.
[6] Returns for 40d. subsidy. Roll 5, m. 13d, 14; Roll 12, m. 1, 6d.
[7] This was Gascon wine.
[8] This was brought to Weymouth and Melcombe.
[9] 1,088½ tuns were free of customs.
[10] 118½ tuns were free of customs.
[11] Taken to Fowey, Looe, Polruen, Lostwithiel, Padstowe.
[12] Returns for 2s. subsidy. PRO K.R. Accounts Various 80/22.
[13] This includes wine taken to Yarmouth.
[14] This includes wine taken to Plymouth and Fowey.

APPENDIX D

A SHIPPING AGREEMENT MADE IN 1357[1]

Hec sunt conventiones facte ac concordate inter Johannem dictum breedporte anglicum opidanum in London marcatorem ex una parte necnon Hughonem Zagher nautam opidanum Dordracengem ex parte altera. Primo videlicet quod antedictus Johannes navem prenominati Hughonis conduxit cum ea dei omnipotentis adiutoris ad velificandum cum onere suo versus portum dictum Hulle, ibidemque deonerandem navem jamdictam infra Hulle et Ravensoer ad placitum Johannis prefati. Insuper idem Johannes ibi tardare potest per tres septimanas pro factum suum faciendo necnon navem antedictam onerando sed si post terminum illum ibi tardaverint ex tunc jamdictus Johannes dabit prenominato naute omnes suas expensas in navi durando donec de loco jamdicto perrexint. Et nauta habebit de Johanne pro suo integro naulo quinque libras cum quatuordecim solidis grossorum monete flandrie de quibus habebit loco dicto Hulle viginti quatuor solidos grossorum, residuam vero partem dabit si Johannes predictus infra sex dies postquam forum in Hollandia appropinquaverunt. Ulterius conventio est quod postquam iterum cum suo onere redierint in mare immediate ibi ponent suam ancoram et Johannes jamdictus habebit electionem peregendo versus bricle vel oudewater vel Dordrecht et unicumque illarum civitatum eligit ibidem cum navi et onere venient per velantem ibidemque Johannes antedictus navem deonerabit incontinenti infra sex dies postquam ibi appropinquaverint partem nauli sui prout dictum est fideli soluendo. In cuius rei testimonio presentibus sigilla nostra alternatim apposuimus. Datum Dordraci feria secunda post Valentini festum anno domini millesimo tricesimo quinquagesimo septimo,

Endorsed—Indentura super quibusdam convencionibus factis inter Johannem Bredport de London et Hugonem Zagher de Dordreht.

[1] W.A.M. 9273. The fragment of a green seal remains. Cf. Kunze, *Hanseakten aus England*, p. 141: receipt for payment of £70 14*d.* for freight for salt brought from France to Bristol, and all costs, with mutual remission of all actions. PRO L.T.R. Mem. 137, Communia Hil.: agreement between English merchant and an alien to whom he sold 1600 cheeses worth £15 16*s.* 6*d.* The latter was to take them to Flanders at his own risk and if any were lost at sea, the alien was to bear the loss. In Bruges, he would receive money called *Goddessilver* and a sum in part payment called *Ernes*. He could not sell the cheeses to anyone else.

APPENDIX E

A LIST OF CASES IN THE KING'S BENCH TO WHICH ALIEN MERCHANTS WERE PARTIES, 1350–1377

In the following lists the references given are to the Coram Rege Rolls, unless it is stated that they are to the Controlment Rolls. The dates and the references are to the first records of the cases found. The terms Hilary, Easter, Trinity, and Michaelmas are indicated by the letters H, E, T, M. In most instances the cases went on from term to term to no definite conclusion.

In cases marked †, juries *de medietate lingue* were summoned. In cases marked ‡ aliens were apparently not included in the juries. In most cases, however, there is no mention of a jury of any kind.

The cases are arranged first by according to the form of action and then by counties.

Aliens are indicated thus: *

County	Plaintiff	Defendant	Subject	Date	Reference
London	Beatrice, wife of Thomas de Oldesheles	*Jacob de[1] Navere, Lombard; John James-servant de Navere, sr.; John James-servant de Navere, jr.; Andreas James-servant de Navere	Death of Thomas de Oldesheles	M.1359	397 m.14d.
London	William[2] Knight	John Bassyng-bourn de Messenden; John Taillour de Chesham	Death of *a Fleming and theft	M.1360	401 m.26d. Rex.

[1] Defendant quit, Appelor fined for bringing false charge. PRO Coram Rege Roll 401, m. 1d. Rex. A Jacobus de Navarre was citizen of London in 1360. *Ibid.* 401, m. 51d.

[2] William Knight was an approver.

County	Plaintiff	Defendant	Subject	Date	Reference
London	Rex[1]	John atte More	Death of *Nicholas Sardouche	M.1371	443 m.33 Rex
London	Rex[2]	*Donatus de Florence	Homicides and felonies	H.1351	362 m.4d. Rex
Essex	Rex[3]	Henry Tendring of Welcomstowe	*Death of alien merchant	M.1364	416 m.36 Rex
Lincoln	Rex[4]	*Galfridus Webster de Brabant	Death of *Reginald Webster of Brabant	M.1375	459 m.34 Rex
Middlesex	Richard[5] of Hackeneye	William de Kirkeby; *Hermann Munyter; Juliana wife of John de Hardyngham	Death of Nigel of Hackeneye	E.1353	371 m.31d. Rex
Norfolk	Rex	Thomas[6] Potter de Estrudham	Death of *John de Gisdam, alien	M.1352	369 m.26d. Rex
Norfolk	Rex	Simon Baker de Berton	Death of *Constantius son of Peter of Holand, alien	M.1364	416 m.36 Rex
London	Katharine Porter	*Venturus[7] de Alisander, Lombard	Rape	M.1372	447 m.72

[1] Cf. p. 14 above.

[2] Donatus de Florence was one of four who had been imprisoned a long time in the Tower and who petitioned for an investigation.

[3] The defendant was quit.

[4] Cf. p. 80 above.

[5] Cf. p. 20 above.

[6] The defendant was pardoned. *C.P.R. 1350–54*, p. 171.

[7] In 1371, he had been imprisoned in Newgate for debts to Thomas Serland of Lucca and Zenobius Martyn of Florence and was being sued in the exchequer for a debt to the king's butler. PRO Exch. Plea Roll 91, n. 21.

County	Plaintiff	Defendant	Subject	Date	Reference
Middlesex	Johanna[1] Bassyngbourn	*John Maryn, Lombard	Rape	H.1377	464 m.60d.
London	John Pender, Brewer	Ralph de Norfolk, vintner; *Simon Fotekyn, Fleming	Mayhem	E.1354	375 m.62
London	†Lawrence Sherman, Fleming	*Peter Mone, Fleming; John *de Mone, Fleming	Mayhem	H.1362	405 m.17
London	†John Pyttok	*John Selekyttere, Fleming; John van Poperyng	Mayhem	E.1367	426 m.63
York	Rex	Henry de Burton iuxta Ripon and others	Theft from —Bartholomew de Estland	M.1362	Controlment Roll 20, m.50d.
Suffolk	Rex	*Peter Fleming of Seland	Divers Felonies	E.1353	371 m.42d. Rex
London	John Flecchere de Hertefeld	*John Lazaret, Lombard	Abduction	H.1358	390 m.66d.
London	†Richard Brond	*John Dyne, Lombard;	Abduction	M.1369	435 m.51d.
London	*John Clerk, Fleming	*John Fynger, Fleming	Abduction	M.1370	439 m.66
London	William Warwyk, skinner	*Dynus Sandwich of London, Lombard; *John Maryon[2]	Abduction	T.1371	442 m.38d.
London	‡Thomas Hardyng	*John Combere, Fleming	Abduction	E.1375	457 m.52d.

[1] The defendent was quit. Appellor was imprisoned and made fine, 1 Richard II.
[2] Cf. Bassingbourn v. Maryn (rape); Maryn v. Wyleves (Trespass to chattels).

County	Plaintiff	Defendant	Subject	Date	Reference
London	*†Benedict Zacherie	*Francis Bache; Norman Francisman Bache	Abduction	H.1367	425 m.42
London	*Francis Bache	*Benedict Zacherie	Trespass	E.1368	430 m.29d.
London	Robert de Thwang	*Venturus Alisander of Florence	Trespass	T.1367	427 m.45d.
London	John Blounde, parson of church of Erpyngham	*Albert Pouchemaker of Almain	Trespass	M.1351	365 m.30d.
London	*Anthony Bache	Henry de Ware, ismonger	Trespass	M.1354	377 m.101d.
London	William Thomas of Chipping Norton	*Peter Burson, Lombard and merchant; Eustace Maners	Trespass (false imprisonment)	M.1354	377 m.19
London	‡John Tyghlay, chaplain	*Cyprianus le Smyth, Fleming	Trespass (false imprisonment)	T.1355	380 m.17
London	*Matthew Noire of Florence	*Michael Gerard of Florence	Trespass	E.1360	399 m.11
London	Thomas Martyn	*Peter Wys, Fleming	Trespass to chattels	E.1362	406 m.12
London	*William atte Forthe of Flanders	John Marshall of Wisbech; Adam Clement of Evemeth	Trespass to chattels	H.1363	409 m.33
London	†Godfrey de Lymonia (Prior of Hospital of St. Anthony)	*Nicholas[1] Nigrebon	Trespass (assault)	M.1363	412 m.23

[1] He made fine for 10s. PRO Coram Rege Roll 421, Fines.

County	Plaintiff	Defendant	Subject	Date	Reference
London	*†Nicholas Nigrebon of Venice	Godfrey de[1] Lymonia	Trespass (assault)	M.1364	416 m.25
London	*†John Maryn, Lombard	Henry Wylwes	Trespass (to chattels)	T.1375	458 m.21
Bucks	*Anthony Citroun	Robert Cornvylle of Great Marlowe	Trespass	E.1352	367 m.28
Bucks	*Benedict de Lucca	Robert de Morton of Mussenden; John Smyth of Mussenden	Trespass (assault and contempt)	E.1375	457 m.9d.
Devon	Robert de Possebury; Adam de Fulford	Men of Looe, Plymouth and *Hankinus de Estland	Trespass	T.1353	372 m.43d.
Hertford	*Benedict de Lucca	John Sandrys de Erdele; William Sandrys de Erdele	Trespass	M.1375	459 m.2d.
Lincoln	*Hildebrand Suderman; *Tidemann Daleman, merchants of Almain	*Ditmar Clipping; *John Spicenagel, merchants of Almain; John Cromhous	Trespass (to chattels)	M.1350	361 m.82
Lincoln	†Isabella Thousandpound	Hankin de Louthe of Boston; *Lamkyn Borkyn; *Berthold de Munster, merchants of Almain	Trespass (to chattels)	M.1355	381 m.81d.
Lincoln	Hankin de Louthe; *Lamkyn Borkyn; *Berthold de Munster	Isabella Thousandpound	Trespass	E.1356	383 m.55

[1] He made fine for 20s. PRO Coram Rege Roll 413, Fines.

County	Plaintiff	Defendant	Subject	Date	Reference
Lincoln	Rex	Numerous persons and vils and *Hildebrand Bereswerd, Esterling	Trespass (and contempt)	H.1350	358 m.4 Rex
Middlesex	John Pendale	*Bartholomew[1] Myne, Lombard	Trespass	T.1371	442 m.37d.
Norfolk	William, son of Nicholas de Worstede	*Hermann de Cologne, webster and others	Trespass	M.1363	412 m.87d.
Norfolk	Rex and *Salaman de Almain, goldsmith	Gerard de Gaunt, senior; Gerard de Gaunt, junior; Robert de Stokes of Norwich	Trespass (and contempt)	M.1354	377 m.39
Northants	*Tidemann of Limberg	John de Marssh of Grafton	Trespass	H.1351	362 m.62d.
Northants	*Lambert Bamesse of Ipre, Fleming	Peter Henriesman de Thorp, sorntere	Trespass	T.1355	380 m.4
Somerset	Isabella de Olneye	Walter de Milton; *Otto Hildebrandservant Suderman	Trespass	M.1350	361 m.24d.
Somerset	Ralph, bishop of Bath and Wells	Alan de Lodere; John Bovedich; Walter de Milton; *Otto Suderman	Trespass	M.1357	389 m.51
Somerset	*Conrad Afflen of Almain	*John Suderman	Trespass	H.1356	382 m.25

[1] He was citizen of London. Cf. Appendix G.

County	Plaintiff	Defendant	Subject	Date	Reference
Southampton	*Conrad Afflen of Almain	John Wetegod, mayor; Thomas Wagg, bailiff	Trespass	E.1356	383
Southampton	*Tidemann of Limberg	John Crulle	Trespass	E.1354	375 m.16
Warwick	Richard de[1] Lynne of Coventry	*Henry Pouchemaker of Brabant	Trespass	M.1357	389 m.52d.
Yorks	*Boniface of Florence	Thomas, son of Robert de Wykeslay	Trespass	E.1363	410 m. 52
Lincoln	John Matheu	*William of Ipre	Account		
Middlesex	‡Rex	*Peter de Lere, Lombard; Bernard de Lere; Nicholas Shordich	Intimading jury and seizing manor in Hackney	H.1350	358 m.7d. Rex
Norfolk	Simon of[2] Almain	*Peter Soot of Seland and others	Violation of[3] Statute of Labourers	M.1375	459 m.36
Norfolk	Rex	*Flemings, Brabanters and others	Receiving felons	H.1365	417 m.5d. Rex
Norfolk & Suffolk	Rex	*Flemings, Brabanters and others	Divers articles	E.1362	406 m.17d. Rex m.11d. Rex

[1] See p. 81 above.

[2] He was citizen of Norwich *C.C.R. 1369–74*, p. 222.

[3] Cf. B. H. Putnam, *Enforcement of the Statute of Labourers* (New York, 1908) Pt. i Chap. ii, Pt. ii Chap. ii.

County	Plaintiff	Defendant	Subject	Date	Reference
Sussex	‡Rex	*Hugh de Ficullys, Lombard; Robert Huweprest de Ficullys	Resisting collectors of 1/10 & 1/15	T.1360	400 m.19 Rex
Yorks	Rex	*Merchants of Almain: Tidkin Spicenagle; Henry Copyn; Constantine Smythous; Hildebrand Beresward; Henry Genepape; Wynard de la Revle; Godshalk	Trespasses and felonies (Customs frauds)	T.1362 E.1364	407 m.36 Rex 414 m.13 Rex

APPENDIX F

THE LOMBARDS *V.* THE MERCERS OF LONDON

Chronology of the Case

1357, 26 June   The affray
                  Complaint to the council
                  Hearing before the council
                  Arrest of some of the mercers
                  City authorities ordered to do justice
    3 August   All Lombards summoned before the council
    1 November   Order for taking of Adam de Wroxham revoked
    1 December   Thomas de Maldon released
1358, 1 February   Nicholas Sharpenham released
    4 March   Order for taking of Thomas Everard revoked
1359,   Petition of the Lombards for protection
    8 July   Writ of subpoena issued summoning mercers before the council
                  Mercers before council and warned
                  Some of the mercers returned to Tower
    7 October   City authorities ordered to make inquisition

8 October	Inquisitions taken
November	Case sent to the King's Bench
	Forster, Maldon and Meleward allowed to make fine.
	Phelip to be taken
	Other mercers mainperned to keep peace and released.
1360, Hil.	Phelip not found
Trin.	Phelip outlawed
	Forster, Maldon and Meleward found new mainpernours
1361	Payment of fines postponed from term to term
1362, Hil.	Fines made and warning given to keep peace

The Lombards *V*. The Mercers of London

London. Alias scilicet termino sancte Trinitatis anno regni Regis nunc Anglie tricesimo tertio rotulo decimo septimo[2] in placita Regis irrotulatur sic—London—Nomina quorundam mercerorum London patenta in subscriptis—Johannes Bernes, vicecomes London, Simon Worsted, Aldermannus, Willelmus Totenham, Johannes Worsted, Alanus Everard, Johannes Stapel, Walterus Berneye, Johannes Wythyngham, Thomas Starcolf, Johannes Redyng, Walterus Bret, Johannes Elesden, Nicholaus Plunket, Henricus Cove, Willelmus Cove. Et sciendum quod coram magno consilio domini Regis munitum fuit omnibus merceris suprascriptis ex parte dicti Regis quod ipsi ceteris merceris et mercatoribus alieniginis in civitate London venientibus et commorantibus molestiam non inferant iniuriam nec gravamen in corporibus nec in rebus eorum sub periculo et forisfactura omnium que erga dominum Regem forisfacere poterunt.

Postea scilicet die martis proximo post Octabis sancti Martini isto eodem termino coram domino Rege apud Westmonasterium venit venerabilis pater Willelmus de Edyngton Episcopus Wyntoniensis cancellarius domini Regis per manus suas proprias liberavit hic in curia quoddam breve domini Regis maiori et vicecomitibus civitatis London directum et duas inquisitiones virtute eiusdem [inquisitionis][3] coram eis captas quod quidem breve sequitur in hec verba: Edwardus dei gratia Rex Anglie et Francie et Dominus Hibernie maiori et vicecomitibus London salutem: cum nuper conceptis

---

[1] PRO Controlment Roll 17, m. 24d.

[2] *Ibid.* m. 20; also PRO Coram Roll 395, m. 17 Rex. These two entries are the same as the above to *Postea scilitet*. They both continue with the following references to the above: 'ad quem diem patet plenius videlicet termino Michaelis anno xxxiii rotulo Kegworth Regis.' i.e. PRO Controlment Roll 17, m. 24d.

[3] *Bris* is obviously meant instead of *inquis* given on roll.

invidiosa grossura et rancore per quosdam merceros de civitate nostra predicta contra mercatores de Lumbardia in eadem civitate morantes quidam dictorum mercerorum ipsos mercatores in vicis et plateis eiusdem civitatis continuis instanciis explorantes et demum Francisco Bothel et quibusdam aliis Lumbardis sub protectione nostra existentibus in eadem civitate obviantes in ipsos vi armata et horribili strepitu irruerunt et ipsos verberaverunt vulneraverunt et enormiter pertractarunt per quod ad querelam nobis inde factam vobis mandaverimus quod super premissis viis et modis oportunis diligencius inquireretis et dampnificatis debitam fieri faceretis correctionem et ut celerius remedium super tam horribili facto fieret quosdam merceros eiusdem civitatis quos fama quasi publica inde reddidit culpabiles arestari et in Turri nostra London fecimus custodiri postmodumque ad rogatum vestrum et quorundam aliorum proborum eiusdem civitatis dictos imprisonatos sub spe reformacionis dicte transgressionis tam dampna passis quam emende nobis pro pace violata celeriter facietis per certam manucaptionem extra dictam custodiam[1] fecerimus deliberari qui a diu est sic deliberati nec nobis aut dictis lesis quicquam huiusque facere in effectu voluerint vel offere nec vos pro correctione huiusmodi facienda partes vestras cum efficacia apponere prout decuit voluistis set vos et ipsi transgressores ut inde non curantes [nec] nos et ipsos lesos absque satisfactione aliqua facienda contemptibiliter protraxistis[2] et ob hoc ipsos sic manucaptos apud dictam Turrim reduci fecimus inibi ad voluntatem nostram moraturos. Nos nolentes tam enorme factum in presencia nostra

---

[1] *C.C.R. 1354–60, pp. 432, 495, 498.* Document C in *Select Cases before the Council (Selden Society,* xxxv, contains a list of mainpernours which probably refers to this first release of the mercers. As the document is printed in that volume, with the heading; '*[Responsio] Johannis Bures et Johannis [de Byerne]s vicecomitum,*' it looks as if it were connected with the preceding writ of 8 July, 1359, (B), addressed to those sheriffs. This may be a misprint, for the heading has no connection with document C, being part of the endorsement of the writ (B). The writ is damaged and all that remains of this part of the endorsement is *Johis Bures and Johiss vic'* but there seems to be no reason for translating *vic* 'sub-sheriffs,' especially when it is stated in note 37 on the same page that they were sheriffs in that year. In the original C has neither heading nor endorsement. It contains the lists of mainpernours for five mercers, four of whom are identical with those given in the Close Rolls for this period. Document D does not seem to agree with any other lists of mainpernours given in the case. The mercers mainperned in D are those accused by the Lombards in their petition (A) and, with the exception of Thomas Everard, for whom John Maldon was substituted, those who were arrested for the second time and released on mainprise after the case had been sent to the King's Bench. The documents printed in *Select Cases before the Council* are found in PRO Parliamentary and Council Proceedings (Chancery) File 8, no. 3.

[2] Between the events described up to this point and those which follow come the petition of the Lombards, the issuing of the writ of *subpoena* and the second hearing before the Council.

perpetratum transcurrere impunitum set desiderantes de veritate dicti negocii plenius certiorari vobis mandamus quod de nominibus omnium et singulorum qui dictos transgressionem et excessum sic temere perpetrarunt et eisdem interfuerunt et qui vim et auxilium aut abbetum ad hoc presti-terunt vel qui causam inde dederunt per inquisiciones si opus fuerit capi-endas viisque modis aliis quibus melius expedire videritis vos diligencius informetis et nos de nominibus eorum quos sic reos inveneritis cum omni celeritate certificari faceretis ut ex hoc cum deliberato consilio nostro fieri faciamus quod iuris fuerit et rationis. Teste me ipso apud Sandwycum vii die Octobris anno regni nostri Anglie tricesimo tercio regni vero nostri Francie vicesimo.[1]

Prima inquisicio talis est.[2] Inquisicio capta coram Johanne Lovekyn maiore civitatis Londoñ Johanne de Chichestre et Simone de Benyngton vicecomitibus eiusdem civitatis octavo die mensis Octobris anno regni Regis Edwardi tertii post conquestum Anglie tricesimo tertio ad inquiren-dum qui malefactores et pacis domini Regis perturbatores quoddam enorme affraimentum invidiosa grossura et rancore de quibusdam merceris de civitate predicta contra mercatores de Lumbardia in eadem citivate com-morantes maliciose perpetrarunt et quendam Franciscum Bothel et alios Lombardos sub protectione domini Regis in dicta civitate existentes vi et armis verberaverunt vulneraverunt et enormiter pertractarunt et de omni-bus aliis articulis et circumstanciis prout in quodam brevi domini Regis prefato maiori et vicecomitibus inde directo et hiis inquisitionibus consuto plenius continetur per sacrum Galfridi Lovekyn, Johannis atte Noke, Willelmi Baldewyn, Johannis Moot, Willelmi de Geestone, Latoner, Ri-cardi de Storteford, Johannis Pepel, Whotemanni atte Broke, Roberti de Roystok, Johannis de Barton, Johannis de Tunwell et Johannis de Londoñ qui dicunt super sacrum suum quod die Lune proximo post festum sancti Johannis Baptiste anno regni Regis Edwardi tertii post conquestum trices-imo primo Henricus Forester mercerus, Thomas de Maldon mercerus, et Johannes Meleward mercerus quoddam enorme affraimentum in veteri Judaismo in Warda de Colmanstrete Londoñ fecerunt et in quosdam Fran-ciscum Bothel et Reymundum Flamy Lumbardos vi et armis ex malicia precogitata insultum fecerunt et ipsos verberaverunt vulneraverunt et male tractaverunt et alia enormia eis contra pacem domini Regis intulerunt. Dicunt eciam quod Ricardus Phelip mercerus abbettavit predictos Henri-cum Forester, Thomam de Maldon et Johannem Meleward ad faciendum

---

[1] See *Cal. Letter Book G*, p. 112.
[2] See *Memorials of London*, pp. 302, 303.

affraimentum et transgressionem predictam. Et dicunt quod predictus Ricardus Phelip fuit presens quando premissa facta fuerunt set idem Ricardus predictos Franciscum et Rymundum non percussit. Quesitum fuit a juroribus predictis si aliqui alii transgressiones et excessus predicta fecerunt aut perpetrarunt aut eisdem interfuerunt aut vim et auxilium aut abettum ad hoc prestiterunt vel causam inde dederunt, dicunt quod ad eorum scientiam quod non. In cuius rei testimonium jurores predicti huic inquisitioni sigilla sua apposuerunt. Datum London viii die mensis Octobris anno regni Regis Edwardi tertii post conquestum tricesimo tertio.

Secunda inquisicio talis est. Inquisicio capta coram Johanne Lovekyn maiore civitatis London Johanne de Chichestre et Simone de Benyngton vicecomitibus eiusdem civitatis octavo die mensis Octobris anno regni Regis Edwardi tertii post conquestum tricesimo tertii ad inquirendum qui malefactores et pacis domini Regis perturbatores quoddam enorme affraimentum invidiosa grossure et rancore de quibusdam merceris de civitate predicta contra mercatores de Lumbardia in eadem civitate commorantes maliciose perpetrarunt et in quendam Franciscum Bothel et in alios Lumbardos sub protectione domini Regis in dicta civitate existentes vi et armis verberaverunt vulneraverunt et enormiter perpetractarunt et de aliis articulis [et] circumstantiis prout in quodam brevi domini Regis prefatis maiori et vicecomitibus inde directo et hiis inquisitionibus [consuto] plenius continetur per sacrum Willelmi de Sancto Albano, Roberti de Whitton, Johannis Beste, Johannis le Pea[er Si]monis de Rasue, Petri de Acton, Salamonis le Coffrer, Philippi de Irlaund Ricardi de Wrotham, Roberti de Beverle, Spicer, Johannis de Hankeshale et Willelmi Algar, Sherman, Qui dicunt super sacrum suum quod die Lune proximo post festum sancti Johannis Baptiste anno regni Edwardi tertii post conquestum tricesimo primo Henricus Forester, mercerus, Thomas de Maldon, mercerus et Johannes Meleward, mercerus, in vetero Judaismo in Warda de Colemanstrete London obviaverunt Francisco Bothel et Reymundo Flamy Lumbardis et in ipsos ibidem vi et armis ex eorum malicia precogitata insultum fecerunt et ipsos verberaverunt vulneraverunt et male tractaverunt contra pacem domini Regis et alia enormia eis intulerunt et dicunt quod de cuius vel quorum abbetto hoc fiebat penitus ignorant. In cuius rei testimonium jurores predicti huic inquisitioni sigilla sua apposuerunt. Datum London viii die mensis Octobris anno regni predicti Regis Edwardi tricesimo tertio.

Et modo coram domino Rege hic tam predicti Henricus Forester, Thomas de Maldon et Johannes Meleward superius indicati quam Henricus Cove, Willelmus Cove, Adam de Wrexham, Willelmus de Wodeford (occasione) predicta arestati etc per custodem Turris London ducti venerunt qui committuntur marescallo etc. Et statim per marescallum ducti predicti Henricus Forester, Thomas de Maldon et Johannes Meleward allocuti sunt separatim qualiter de premissis sibi impositis se velint acquietare dicunt singillatim quod ipsi premissa sibi imposita non possunt dedicere set ponunt se inde ad gratiam domini Regis etc et petunt admitti ad finem cum ipso Rege in hac parte faciendum etc. Et quia curia nondum advisatur de gravitate finium ipsorum etc Ideo dimittuntur per manucaptionem videlicet predictus Henricus Forester per manucaptionem Simonis de Reynham, Alani Everard et Willelmi Somerford mercerorum London qui manuceperunt pro ipso Henrico habendi corpus eius coram domino Rege in Octabis sancta Trinitatis ubicumque etc tam pro fine suo faciende quam de suo bono gestu erga omnes merceros et mercatores alienigenos et indigenos in civitate London venientes et commorantes sub pena trescentarum marcarum de bonis et catallis terris et [tenementis] ipsius Henrici et manucaptorum suorum predictorum ad opus domini Regis levanda si contingat ipsum Henricum ad diem predictam coram domino Rege non venire vel ipsum contra dictos merceros et mercatores in aliquo contra pacem domini Regis amodo delinquere et inde legitime fuerit covictus etc. Et predictus Thomas de Maldon per manucaptionem Johannis Chaumpeneys, Draper, Ricardi Ardern, pelliper et Henrici Lorchon, Armorer qui similiter manuceperunt pro eo habendi eum coram domino Rege ad prefatum terminum sub pena trescentarum marcarum ad opus domini Regis in forma predicta levanda si etc. Et predictus Johannes Meleward per manucaptionem Johannis de Rokwode, clerici, Johannis de Colyngbourne de Comitatu Wiltescirie, et Henrici Lorchen de London, Armorer, qui similiter manuceperunt pro eo habendi eum coram domino Rege ad prefatum terminum sub pena trescentarum librarum ad opus domini Regis in forma predicta levanda si etc. Per quod dictum est marescallo quod deliberet eos etc.[1] Et predicti Henricus Cove, Willelmus Cove, Adam de Wrexham, et Willelmus de Wodeford superius arrestati etc, similiter dimittuntur per manucaptionem de suo bono gestu erga dominum Regem et merceros et mercatores supradictos etc videlicet predicti Henricus Cove et Willelmus Cove per manucaptionem Jacobi de Wychingham, Petri Rake, Thome Hynendon et Petro Elsyngham omnes de London qui manuceperunt pro eis sub pena quattuorcentum marcarum ad opus domini Regis de bonis et catallis, terris et tenementis predictorum Henrici Cove et Willelmi Cove ac manucaptorum suorum predictorum levanda si contingat ipsos Henricum

---

[1] The postponement of the payment from term to term is recorded on PRO Controlment Roll 18, m. 20.

et Willelmum contra merceros et mercatores predictos in aliquo contra pacem domini Regis amodo delinquere et inde legitime fuerint convicti etc. Ideo dictum est marcescallo quod deliberet eos etc. Et predicti Adam de Wroxham et Willelmus de Wodeford per manucaptionem Henrici de Brisele, Willelmi Venour, Willelmi Essex et Simonis de Reynham qui manuceperunt pro eis sub pena trescentarum marcarum de bonis et catallis terris et tenementis predictorum Ade et Willelmi de Wodeford ac manucaptorum suorum predictorum in forma predicta levanda si etc. Ideo dictum est marescallo quod deliberet eos etc. Et preceptum est vicecomitibus quod caperent predictum Ricardum Phelip si etc. Et saluo etc. Ita quod habeant corpus eius coram domino Rege in Octabis sancti Hillarii ubicumque etc. [Ad quem diem vicecomites retornaverunt Philip non inventus . . .].[1]

Ad quem diem vicecomites retornaverunt quod die (lune) in sancte Trinitatis anno xxxiiii predictus Ricardus Philip utlagatur. Et ad eundem diem Henricus Forester, Thomas de Maldon et Johannes Meleward invenerunt novas manucaptores prout patet per Trinitatis xxxiiii rotulo viii inter placita Regis[2] rotulo Friseby xx.[3] Postea scilicet termino Hillarii anno xxxvi fecerunt finem prout patet per rotulum finium de termino predicto et muniti sunt quod se bene gerent erga dominum Regem prout patet per Hillarii xxxvi rotulo inter placita Regis etc.[4]

On the *Coram Rege* Roll for Trinity term, 1360, there are the following entries:

De Henrico Forester mercero de fine pro quibusdam affraiamentis et transgressionibus in civitate London̄ factis et super ipsum presentatis unde per cognitionem suam propriam est convictus, per plegium Ade Staple, Simonis de Reynham, Laurencii Beaumond, Nicholi Marchaunt, Alani Everard, et Rogeri Powe de London̄   xx marcas.

De Thoma de Maldon mercero de fine pro eodem per plegium predictum   xx marcas.

De Johanne Milleward, mercero de fine per eodem per plegium predictum   xx marcas.[5]

Henricus Forester, mercerus, Thomas de Maldon, mercerus et Johannes Mulleward mercerus dimissi fuerunt per manucaptionem usque ad hunc diem scilicet in Octabis Purificationis Beate Marie Virginis isto eodem

---

[1] This line is very faint and practically illegible.

[2] PRO Coram Rege Roll 400, m. 8d. Rex. The new mainpernours were John Staple, Alan Everard, William Maldon and Henry Cove.

[3] PRO Controlment Roll 18, m. 20.

[4] See following page.

[5] PRO Coram Roll Rege 405, Fines d.

termino de diversis affraiamentis et transgressionibus in civitate Londōn
factis. Ad quem diem veniunt predicti Henrici et alii per manucaptionem
predictam et petunt ipsos admitti ad finem cum domino Rege faciendum in
hac parte prout alias petierunt et admittuntur per plegium Ade Stapel,
Simonis de Reynham, Laurencii Beaumont, Nicholi Marchaunt, Alani
Everard et Rogeri Powe de civitate Londōn prout patet per rotulos finium
de isto eodem termino et eciam predicti Adam et omnes alii manuceperunt
pro predictis Henrico, Thoma et Johanne quod amodo se bene geret erga
dominum Regem et populum suum sub pena centum librarum etc.[1]

APPENDIX G

LIST OF ALIEN MERCHANTS WHO WERE FREEMEN OF LONDON AND OTHER CITIES

None of the following lists pretends to be complete. They are illustrative
rather than exhaustive. List A contains the names of those aliens who, as
far as we can tell, were made freemen of London. Since the early freemen's
lists no longer exist, it is impossible to verify this or to say when any alien
merchant received the freedom of the city. The lists have been made from
references to alien merchants as citizens of London in other sources and the
dates indicate the earliest of such references found. They are no guide to
the date when citizenship was granted.

List B includes those who were said to be in scot and lot, or who were
granted the liberties of London by the king, but are not mentioned otherwise
as citizens. It also includes some who were citizens and may have been aliens.

List C is taken from the lists of those who paid the subsidy of 1332,
printed by Unwin in *Finance and Trade under Edward III*.[2] Some on the
list are known to have been citizens and the others may have been.

List D includes aliens who became citizens of places other than London,
and is derived, like List A, from references in various sources. The citizens
of York given here are only those who received grants of denization. The
freemen's lists of York have been printed[3] and contain the names of about
thirty aliens for the years between 1327 and 1377, most of whom seem to
have been cloth workers and moneyers.

[1] PRO Coram Rege Roll, m. 13d Rex.
[2] Pp. 61–92.
[3] *Register of the Freemen of the City of York* i. 1272-1558 (F. Collins, ed., Surtees Society, Durham, 1897). J. L'Estrange, *Calendar of the Freemen of Norwich, 1317–1603* (W. Rye, ed., London, 1888) contains the names of a few aliens for this period.

The names are given as they most commonly occur. Those marked *
received grants of denization from the king.

LIST A

Name	Date	Origin	Trade
*Adam, John[1]	1352	Lucca[2]	Apothecary
Bache, Francis[3]	1333	Genoa	
Bandini, Francis[4]	1354	Lucca	
Bochel, Francis[5]	1354	Lucca	
*Bochel, Simon[6]	1369	Lucca	
Cest, Guido[7]	1333		
Chymel, Bartholomew[8]	1333		
Citeron, Anthony[9]	1332	Spain[10]	
*Citeroun, Nicholas[11]	1329	Spain	
Cowfot, Tidemann[12]	1349	Hansard	
Davaunter, Reginald[13]	1333		
Donat, John[14]	1358		Spicer
Donat, Nicholas[15]	1369		Spicer
*Falcoun, John[16]	1358	Lucca	
Isplyngrode, Wigere de[17]	1333		

[1] *C.P.R. 1350–54*, p. 196. He was dead by Mich. 1359, for there is mention then of the executors of his will. PRO De Banco Roll 400, m. 15.

[2] *Loc. cit.*

[3] PRO K.R. Mem. 109, m. 52.

[4] *Ibid.* 130, Communia Trin. In 1359, however, he was called citizen and merchant of Lucca. PRO De Banco Roll 400, m. 15. He was dead by the spring of 1369. PRO L.T.R. Mem. 141. Brevia retorn. Mich.

[5] PRO K.R. Mem. 130, Communia Trin.

[6] *C.P.R. 1367–70*, p. 244; *ibid. 1361–64*, p. 42. In 1365–68, he was paying customs as an alien on wine and wool. PRO K.R. Customs, 70/18; K.R. Accounts, Various, Butlerage 80/17, 18.

[7] PRO K.R. Mem. 109, m. 52.

[8] *Ibid.*

[9] *C.C.R. 1330–33*, p. 593.

[10] PRO Exch. Plea Roll 57, m. 21.

[11] PRO K.R. Mem. 142, Brevia directa.

[12] *C.C.R. 1349–54*, p. 27.

[13] PRO K.R. Mem. 109, m. 52.

[14] He was said to be enjoying the liberties of London in 1358. *C.P.R. 1358–61*, p. 48. In 1365, he was definitely called citizen. PRO De Banco Roll 419, m. 266. He was the brother of Nicholas Donat.

[15] *Cal. Mayors' Letters, London, 1350–70*, p. 171; *Cal. Letter Book H*, p. 32.

[16] *C.P.R. 1358–61*, p. 99.

[17] PRO K.R. Mem. 109, m. 52.

Name	Date	Origin	Trade
Magoun, Peter Lopice[1]	1331		
Mangeon, Ferandus[2]	1332	Spain[3]	
Mareis, Salamon de la[4]	1336	Lucca	
Maskerell, Bandouche[5]	1354	Lucca	
Michel, Andreu[6]	1373	Pistoia	
*Myne, Bartholomew[7]	1361	Lombard	Spicer
Oddy, Torus[8]	1328	Lucca	
Pallavicini, Pallavicino[9]	1364	Genoa	
Pallavicini, Martin[10]	1364	Genoa	
*Portenare, Ponche de[11]	1327	Florence	
Pyncelegh, John[12]	1340	Genoa	
*Serland, Thomas[13]	1360	Lucca	
*Skipper, Herman le[14]	1330	Almain	
Rombold, Henry[15]	1333		
Spicer, Burnett[16]	1333		
Spicer, Gore[17]	1333		
Spicer, Peter le[18]	1340	Florence	
*Thomasyn, Bartholomew[19]	1340	Lucca	Apothecary

[1] *C.P.R. 1330–34*, p. 87. The name is always written thus, but Magoun may be *magon*, butcher.

[2] *C.C.R 1330–33*, p. 559.

[3] *Ibid. 1330–33*, p. 309.

[4] Guildhall, Recognizance Roll 9.

[5] PRO K.R. Mem. 130, Communia Trin.

[6] *Cal. Letter Book G*, p. 314.

[7] *C.P.R. 1358–61*, p. 550. In 1369, he was regarded as an alien for jury purposes. PRO Coram Rege Roll 433, m. 19 Rex.

[8] *C.P.R. 1327–30*, p. 241.

[9] PRO Chanc. Misc. 30/8 (4); *C.C.R. 1374–77*, p. 438.

[10] PRO Chanc. Misc. 30/8 (4).

[11] *Cal. Plea and Mem. Rolls, London*, I, 27. See p. 69 above.

[12] PRO K.R. Mem. 116, Communia Pasch.

[13] PRO Coram Rege Roll 433, m. 19 Rex. See p. 69 above. After 1366, he was paying customs on wine as an alien. PRO K.R. Accounts, Various, Butlerage 80/18.

[14] PRO K.R. Mem. 106, m. 37d. See p. 69 above.

[15] *Ibid.* 109, m. 52.

[16] *Loc. cit.*

[17] *Loc. cit.* In 1342, he was granted a jury *de medietate lingue. ibid.* 118, Communia Mich.

[18] *Ibid.* 116, Communia Pasch.

[19] *Loc. cit.; C.P.R. 1350–54*, p. 22. He was dead by Mich. 1358. PRO De Banco Roll 383, m. 348.

Name	Date	Origin	Trade
Viele, Nicholas la[1]	1329	Amiens	
Walter, Baroncinus[2]		Lucca	
Waterball, Jacob[3]	1333		
William, John[4]	1355		Apothecary
William, Nicholas[5]	1338	Lucca	Apothecary[6]
Wylot, John[7]	1333		
*Zacharie, Benedict[8]	1365	Lombard	Vintner[9]

[1] *C.P.R. 1327–30*, p. 399.

[2] *C.C.R.1360–64*, p. 431.

[3] PRO K.R. Mem. 109, m. 52.

[4] PRO De Banco Roll 383, m. 335d. He was the son of Nicholas William, of Lucca, citizen of London and he may not have been alien born. *Cal. Letter Book G*, p. 130.

[5] *Cal. Plea and Mem. Rolls, London*, I, 148.

[6] *Cal. Letter Book G*, p. 130.

[7] PRO K.R. Mem. 109, m. 52.

[8] *C.P.R. 1364–67*, p. 103.

[9] *Cal. Plea and Mem. Rolls*, II, 110.

LIST B

Name	Date	Origin	Trade
*Bardi, Walter de[1]	1366	Florence	
Canaceon, Matthew[2]	1339	Asti	
*Gouche, John[3]	1370	Florence	Spicer
Muscarde, Bartholomew[4]	1336		
Naples, William de[5]	1348		
*Suderman, Hildebrand[6]	1335	Hansard	

[1] *C.P.R. 1364–67*, p. 234; *Foedera*, iii, 2, p. 788. He was granted the liberties of London by the king.

[2] *C.C.R. 1339–41*, p. 598. In 1339, Matthew Canaceon and his fellow merchants of the society of the Leopardi were granted the same liberties which citizens of London possessed 'that they might stay in the realm, which would be advantageous to the king.' In 1341, they were called citizens of London and quit of the 40*d.* custom on wool paid by aliens.

[3] *C.P.R. 1370–74*, p. 263. He was granted the liberties of London.

[4] Guildhall, Recognizance Roll 9. It is not stated that he was an alien.

[5] *Ibid.* 10. It is not stated that he was an alien.

[6] *C.P.R. 1334–38*, p. 192. He was said to be in scot and lot with the citizens of London. See pp. 66, 68 above.

LIST C[1]

Name	Ward
Citeroun, Anthony	Bread Street
Cowfot, Tidemann	Dowgate
Gentyl, John	Coleman Street
Gentyl, Philip	Coleman Street
Lombard, Curtius le	Cheap
Lombard, Gore	Cheap
Lombard, John	Castle Baynard
Lombard, Eustachius	Langbourne
Lombard, Ragate	Bishopsgate
Mangeon, Ferandus	Vintry
Oddy, Torus	Walbrook
Portenar, Andres	Bishopsgate
Thomasyn, Bartholomew	Cheap
Urland, John (Lombard)	Cheap
William, Nicholas	Cheap

[1] Cf. List A.

LIST D

Name	Freeman of	Date	Origin
Chamberleyn, Nicholas[1]	Bath	1324	Amiens
Labbe, Walter[2]	Bath	1347	France
Lengelachie, Giles[3]	Bath	1347	France[4]
Monyer, Henry le[5]	Canterbury	1347	Amiens
Camperiano, Vigerosus de[6]	Dover	1332	
Cras, John le[7]	Salisbury	1345	
Boyter, Peter le[8]	Wells	1326	France
Monyer, Peter le[9]	Wells	1342	Amiens

[1] *C.P.R. 1327–30*, p. 310.
[2] *Ibid. 1345–48*, p. 348.
[3] *Loc. cit.*
[4] *Ibid. 1350–54*, p. 294.
[5] *Ibid. 1345–48*, p. 258.
[6] *Ibid. 1330–34*, p. 243. He was accepted by the king as freeman of Dover.
[7] *Ibid. 1345–48*, p. 20.
[8] *Ibid. 1324–27*, p. 311. A John Boyter of France was citizen of Ross in Ireland. *Ibid. 1324–27*, p. 304.
[9] *Ibid. 1340–43*, p. 500.

Name	*Freeman of*	*Date*	*Origin*
Tany, Gaillard[1]	Winchester	1369	Florence
*Wynand, John[2]	York	1352	Zeeland
*Smythousen, Godscalk de[3]	York	1352	Almain
*Hagh, Gocelin de[4]	York	1352	Almain
*Lakensnyder, Arnold[5]	York	1351	Almain
Fromle, Dunagus de[6]	Lenton, Notts.	1338	Almain

[1] *Ibid. 1367–70*, p. 274.

[2] *Ibid. 1350–54*, p. 374. This name and the two following ones do not appear on the free-men's lists printed in the *Surtees Society*, vol. xcvi. The men were called citizens, however, in the letters patent of denization.

[3] *Ibid. 1350–54*, p. 355.

[4] *Loc. cit.*

[5] *Loc. cit.; Surtees Soc.* xcvi, 44.

[6] PRO K.R. Mem. 114, m. 33. See p. 68, n. 3 above.

INDEX

This index does not include names in the lists on pages 182–189, and 197–201.